6/03

Dessert Circus at Home

Fun, Fanciful,

and Easy-to-Make

Desserts

Dessert Circus
at Home

Jacques Torres

with Christina Wright and Kris Kruid

Photography by John Uher

WILLIAM MORROW AND COMPANY, INC.

NEW YORK

Library of Congress Cataloging-in-Publication Data
Torres, Jacques.
    Dessert circus at home : fun, fanciful, and easy-to-make desserts /
Jacques Torres with Christina Wright and Kris Kruid ; photography by
John Uher.
        p.   cm.
    Includes index.
    ISBN 0-688-16607-5
    1. Desserts.   I. Wright, Christina.   II. Kruid, Kris.   III. Title.
TX773.T666   1999
641.8'6—dc21   98-38692
                                                                   CIP

Printed in the United States of America

First Edition

2   3   4   5   6   7   8   9   10

BOOK DESIGN BY RICHARD ORIOLO

www.jacquestorres.com
www.williammorrow.com

Contents

Acknowledgments

My life has been blessed with many wonderful people who have lent their support and encouragement to whatever project I have adopted. No matter what I do, Kris is enthusiastically by my side with love and patience. I am grateful for her commitment to be with me in all that I do.

Tina Wright has been irreplaceable on this project. She is my business partner, but more important, a cherished friend. Without her, this book might still be sitting on my desk.

Sirio Maccioni and his family generously provide an environment that fosters creativity. I am grateful for his never-ending patience and support. He is truly the ringmaster, and I sincerely appreciate all he has taught me. I am lucky to have the best boss in the world!

Thank you to Dorothy Cann Hamilton and Doug Hamilton for guidance and wisdom. Dorothy sets the stage for artistic freedom, and Doug transforms the performance into intelligent business. I am forever grateful for their generosity and for allowing me to use the French Culinary Institute for the television series.

Thank you to our television producer, Charlie Pinsky, for supporting my artistic vision and for having the energy to follow through to the end. I am extremely honored to have had the talented crew of Lewis Rothenberg, Pete McEntyre, Bob Benedetti, Jeff Cirbes, Craig Haft, Bruce Engler, and Benjamin Gerstein enthusiastically return for a second season.

We have been blessed with the most generous sponsors:

- Michel Roux, chairman of the Grand Marnier Foundation, who sets the example for innovation. I am grateful for his insights and his unfaltering generosity. He says, "You are nothing until you have planted a tree." On behalf of all coming generations, I thank Michel for his commitment to making life better.
- Stolichnaya Vodka, the true natural flavor.
- John Helferich and the entire M&M/Mars family. Never before have I experienced such a nurturing group of people. Special thanks to my new friend Bill Bellody for helping me find my way around the delightful world of M&M/Mars. Thank you to Dove Chocolates and especially Leslie Verdi. I appreciate being able to use Dove® Promises® Dark and Milk Chocolates, "M&M's"® Milk Chocolate Mini Baking Bits, and Snickers® Munch® Bars in my American attempts.

We are grateful to the following companies for providing equipment: The Edlund Company (scales); Shep Doniger and Braun Inc. (immersion blenders, hand-held mixers, juicers); Bourgeat (copper pans); Catherine Fischer and All-Clad Metalcrafters Inc. (pans); Kevin Fink and the Hobart Corporation (stand mixer); Amco, a Leggett & Platt Company (measuring cups and spoons); Apollo Mold Company (lollipop molds); and Paige Watson at Broadway Panhandler (general kitchen equipment).

We also thank the following companies for generously providing the use of beautiful china, flatware, tableware, and glassware: Annieglass, Bernardaud North America, Carnavale, Inc., Christofle Silver, Inc., Fossilglass, Hermès, Rosenthal U.S.A., Studio K, Swid Powell, the Foreside Company, Lillian Vernon Group, the Loom Company (including Gilmore Glassworks and Happy Medium), Tuscan Square, and Villeroy & Boch.

To my parents: Papa et Maman, merci d'être venu m'aider pour le tournage de cette seconde serie. Je pense beaucoup à vous et vous me manquez beaucoup.

My very dearest friends, Glenn and Euphrasia Dopf, were a large part of this entire project as they are in everything I do. Thank you to "my big brother." Your friendship means more than I can express. Without your introductions and contacts, *Dessert Circus* might never have happened.

Very special thanks go to Linda and John Kuipers for their love and support. Linda's talents as "satellite editor" were invaluable. We love you more than you can know.

We are grateful to our editor, Pam Hoenig, and the entire William Morrow family for making our project a priority and for guiding us to a successful end.

Our photographer, John Uher, is a creative genius with the camera. Thank you to John, Michelle Edwards, Bob Piazza, and Meredith Uher for the fabulous work and for making it fun.

Fern Berman and Robin Insley of Fern Berman Communications make sure the whole world knows about our book and television show. No one can do it with the style and grace that you two do. Thank you for your talent and your promotional expertise.

Lou Manna is simply the best! Thank you for the beautiful candid shots of the series and for capturing the magic of the moment on film.

Thank you to my colleagues at Le Cirque: Benito Saverin, Keitaro Goto, Hiroko Asada, Sottha Khunn, Francisco Gutierrez, and the pastry crew—Jennifer Lynch, Donna Sardella, Allison Losch, Terry Jones, Erin Puzio, Kaoru Mori, and Angie Opanukij.

Special thanks to Donna Sardella for assistance with food styling and Lynn Orosz for recipe testing.

Thank you to Richard Cotter, Maria Razumich, James Staiano, and the New York Palace family for making me feel at home in their beautiful hotel. Mr. Cotter's generosity knows no bounds. I am grateful for everything you did for me.

Special thanks to Maryland Public Television, John Potthast, Margaret Sullivan, and Tina Waganer. All of your outstanding efforts are truly appreciated, and we're glad to be partners with such kind and giving people.

During the taping of the show, we would have been lost without the support of the entire French Culinary Institute family: Dieter Schorner was always there to lend professional and emotional support. Frederic Von Coppernolle handled all of the details and an endless number of last-minute requests. Warm thanks to Gary Apito for all he made possible and for being there so many nights. Thanks to the president of FCI, Glen Zeitzer. Chris Parma dropped everything to find us what we needed at the last minute.

Thank you to my colleagues and true friends Alain Sailhac, André Soltner, and Jacques Pépin for all of your support. You are legends in this industry and I thank you for paving the path and making it easier for me to follow.

Special thanks to Leah Stewart. Your patience and understanding know no limit.

I would like to extend my most sincere thanks to my crew for the television show: Nancy Stark, Judy Lee Batelli, Stephanie Giman, Anthony Del Tufo, and Cheryl Ledet. Can you believe you lived through it? You are the greatest, and I appreciate how hard you all worked.

To Peter Marengi and Sue Reinius Pacifco: Thank you, thank you, thank you. It is rare to find two such lovely people and such dear friends in one place.

Thank you to our trusted advisers and friends, Marc and Kelly Minker.

We could never begin to thank Gordon Anthony and Scott Cohen of LMG for everything from technical advice to crowd control. No matter what we do, you two are always there, and we are so very grateful for your friendship.

To Ray and Erika Wright and Gigi Wright, thank you for your continued support.

Thank you to Adam Tihany for your outstanding creativity.

Special thanks to Louis Franchain (dit LouLou), my mentor and friend, and Christian Cottard (l'artiste et ami).

Thanks to Hilary and Robert Hoopes for allowing us to take over your kitchen for recipe testing and for your enthusiasm for our project.

Thank you to all of our friends who generously donated their time to appear on our television show. Special thanks to Jack Ford, Lillian Vernon, Burt Wolfe, Elizabeth Allston, Arthur Schwartz, Bill Boggs, Peter Kaminsky, Dan Leader, and Mary Manksch.

To all of our friends: We thank you not only for your support but for your treasured friendship. Thanks especially to Birgitt Stepanow Adams, Patrice Caillot, Jean Pierre Dubray, Claude and Nicole Franques, Laura Fastie Grapshi, Patty Hunstein, Remi Lauvant, Tanya Olenik, Andre Renard, John and Laura Ressner, Laurie Rosatone, Andrew Shotts, Jean Phillippe Maury, Claude Solliard, and Anne Traynor.

Introduction

This year, Kris and I celebrate ten years together. For me, it also means a tenth anniversary of living in this country and the year I hope to attain my American citizenship. There's a lot to celebrate! I have learned a lot about this country.

I am always amazed at the number of home cooks who bake. My sister-in-law Linda is a prime example of someone who always has home-baked goodies on the counter when I visit. One of my priorities in the last ten years has been to try as many American desserts as I can. I haven't found any that I don't like, and I know there are many more to try. This book is my tribute to American desserts.

I learned that many people bake without understanding why things happen, why cookies turn out differently, or what makes recipes different besides the obvious ingredients. I hope to offer the reasons why things happen and explain how you can adjust your baking so your recipe will turn out the way you want it. Armed with this knowledge, you can take your recipes to the next level.

My job as a pastry chef is to wake people up at the end of a meal, when they are full and think they don't want dessert. The pastry chef has to excite them about eating again and surprise them with the desserts so they will be energized when they leave the restaurant. One of my techniques is to send a different dessert to every person at the table. The sharing of the desserts brings them all together. Sometimes people from another table will lean over to ask what they have and if they knew what to order. When you make desserts, you have a unique opportunity for creative expression with food.

My travels have taken me to many places in this country. I am surprised at the number of cookbooks I find produced by church groups and women's organizations. Here are pages of closely guarded family recipes, some merely typed, copied, and stapled together. They seem to represent a way of life where neighbors greet new neighbors with cakes, and county fairs feature foods made by church groups. Kids earn money for 4-H projects by hosting bake sales or sell lemonade on the street with cookies. I love the neighborhood spirit in this country and the way simple foods bring people together. Be a good neighbor. Make something sweet and give it for the sheer pleasure of making the world a better place.

Please read the recipe all the way through before you begin. The notes and variations are there to provide additional insight or ideas. I have found it is always easier if you weigh and measure everything before you start.

I really value your thoughts and hope you will share your discoveries with me. Please feel free to leave me a message on my website at http://www.jacquestorres.com. While you are there, look for sources of specialty tools and hard-to-find ingredients or find out when our television show is airing in your neighborhood. I also post my schedule so you will know when I am going to be in your area or when I will be giving classes or demonstrations. If you prefer, drop me a line in care of Team Torres, P.O. Box 303, New York, New York 10101-0303. I look forward to hearing from you and, as always, Eat Dessert First!

Teaching Philosophy

When I first started my apprenticeship, I was often frustrated because I could not find the answers to technical questions. I wanted to understand how each ingredient would react with another, how they would be affected by temperature, and why things worked the way they did. I thought that if I knew what made dough tough, I could make it that way when I wanted to or I could be sure it would be soft for another recipe. The boss of the pastry shop did not have the answers, so I went to school to earn the equivalent of a master's degree in food technology.

In France, the government decides on the program content of a school but leaves it to the teacher to choose a teaching method. Since teachers know what is required for the graduation exam, they can decide to teach only that information. When Dorothy Cann Hamilton, president and founder of the French Culinary Institute, came to me about building a pastry program in New York, I realized that I would have two wonderful opportunities: First, I would have the chance to give back to an industry that has been quite good to me. Second, I would be able to influence how my craft would be taught in the future.

One of my main goals was to develop a pastry program that would teach why we do the things we do. I hoped to have future students avoid the frustration that I felt. I wanted them to start with more information than I did, with the hope that they would be able to go further in their pastry careers than I have.

Dorothy said, "Build the best pastry school," and sent me on my way. I thought about the curriculum but knew that the physical setting would also have to be conducive to giving each student the best opportunity for practical experience. I wanted the program to expose a student to as many aspects as possible of being a real-life chef. I included tarts, all the doughs, the cakes, petits fours, weddings, buffets, chocolate techniques, working with sugar, ice cream, and a host of other subjects to comprise a six-month program. I designed a basic tool kit and designed each station so every student would have space to work. The goal was to replicate all the stages of a European apprenticeship and to give each student the best possible skills for success in a culinary career. When students leave the school, they still need time to practice what they have learned, but I am confident that anyone with a lot of drive will be able to make it.

I really believe we have to share our knowledge and encourage one another to achieve our goals. I still want to learn, to be challenged, and to contribute to my field. When I think of all the things I have accomplished so far in my career, I have to admit that it is of teaching that I am the most proud.

Getting Started:
Equipment,
Ingredients,
and Terms

'**ve said it** before and I'll say it again: always use the best ingredients you can find when preparing desserts. If you start with good products, you will have a much better chance of ending up with something good. Use the freshest, ripest fruit. Take advantage of the season and select your recipe with produce availability in mind. Select the right flour for the recipe. Always be sure it is unbleached and unbromated. I almost always use bittersweet chocolate and I buy the best chocolate I can afford. Go ahead and use real butter, unsalted of course; after all, life is short and we should eat dessert first!

Pastry making is an exact science, so use an electronic scale if at all possible. I weigh everything with my Edlund scale. The measures in this book were converted as closely as possible to cups and teaspoons, but the volume measure of cups is very inaccurate. A cup of flour can vary as much as 2 ounces, depending on how it was packed in the cup. If you use the dry cup measures, scoop the ingredient and then level the top with an offset spatula. When an ingredient is sifted, weigh it before you sift it.

I don't know how I ever lived without my hand-held immersion blender. I never go anywhere without it or my scale. I try to use basic equipment you are likely to have in your kitchen, though some recipes call for unusual tools. When you see the result, you will probably agree that using these tools was worth the time.

Equipment

Acetate: This is a clear plastic found in most art stores or florist shops. I use a medium weight (.003). If you buy it in a roll, cut the sheets to 12 × 18 inches.

Baking sheet: I use professional baking sheets that are 12 × 18 inches. They are similar in size and shape to jelly roll pans.

Candy thermometer: These usually measure temperatures that range from 176°F to 320°F (80°C to 160°C). My thermometer is encased in a metal cage, which makes it sturdier. Always keep the thermometer upright as it cools, or the mercury will separate and the thermometer will be useless. It is a good idea to hang it to store. When you get a new thermometer, always place it in boiling water for about 5 minutes to test that it reads 212°F (100°C) at the boiling point. This way you will know your exact thermometer reading and can make adjustments if necessary.

Chef's knife: The three knives I use the most are an 8- or 10-inch chef's knife, a paring knife, and a 10- or 12-inch serrated knife.

Cutting board: I usually use white plastic cutting boards. Wooden boards can hold oils and odors that fruit or sugar will absorb.

Decorating tips: I use the Inox stainless-steel tips that have thirteen to a set. They are very strong and will hold up over time.

Double boiler: This is used to heat ingredients without exposing them to the direct heat of the burner. In this book, a double boiler is most often used to melt chocolate. To make a double boiler if you don't own one, place a saucepan half filled with water over medium heat and cover it with a mixing bowl large enough to rest snugly on the rim of the saucepan. The water in the saucepan and the bottom of the bowl should never come in contact with each other. If steam escapes from the seal between the pan and the bowl, either the bowl does not fit the pan properly or the water is too hot and you should lower the heat slightly.

Ice bath: I use ice baths often to quickly cool down mixtures, which helps save time. To prepare an ice bath, pour ice cubes into a 4-quart bowl. Generously sprinkle salt over the ice and add water to cover the ice. Place a clean, dry 2-quart bowl over the ice bath and add the mixture/ingredient you need to cool.

Immersion blender: I can't live without my Braun immersion blender. I use it for everything.

Measures: For all of the dry measures, I used the Amco stainless-steel set of cups and measuring spoons.

Mixer: I always use a stand mixer, but these recipes were also tested with a hand-held electric mixer unless otherwise specified. My stand mixer has three attachments: paddle, whip, and dough hook.

Offset spatula: I like one that is fairly firm, not very flexible. They are available in different sizes and are very strong.

Ovens: The recipes were tested in conventional ovens. It is a good idea to test your oven with an oven thermometer to ensure the accuracy of the temperature. A convection oven cuts the baking time by allowing air to circulate, which makes the baking much more even. No matter which oven you have, always rotate your baking sheets onto the different racks to avoid any hot spots.

Parchment paper: Also called *baking paper*. I use parchment paper in almost every recipe because it is very clean, never sticks, and eliminates the need to add fat to a recipe. It is very fast, convenient, and inexpensive.

Pastry bag: I use plastic disposable bags so I don't have to worry about bacteria (cloth bags hold bacteria). You can also buy cloth bags in specific sizes in most baking supply stores.

Plastic scraper: This is one of the most useful tools in my kitchen. I always have several in the pocket of my chef's coat.

Rubber spatulas: I use the white heavy-duty spatulas.

Cake pan

Tube pan

Muffin pan

Loaf pan

Baking sheet

Tartlet pan

Silicon mat (silpat)

Revolving cake stand

Springform cake pan

Assorted cutters, plain and fluted

Cake ring

Porcupine dome mold

Plastic dome mold

Fluted tart pan with removable bottom

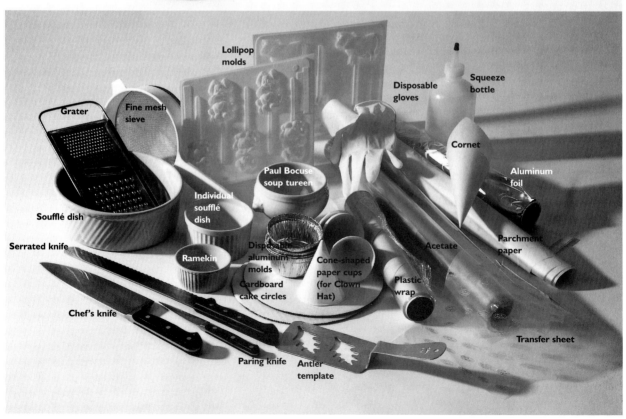

Lollipop molds

Disposable gloves

Squeeze bottle

Grater

Fine mesh sieve

Cornet

Aluminum foil

Paul Bocuse soup tureen

Individual soufflé dish

Soufflé dish

Acetate

Parchment paper

Serrated knife

Ramekin

Disposable aluminum molds

Cone-shaped paper cups (for Clown Hat)

Plastic wrap

Cardboard cake circles

Chef's knife

Transfer sheet

Paring knife

Antler template

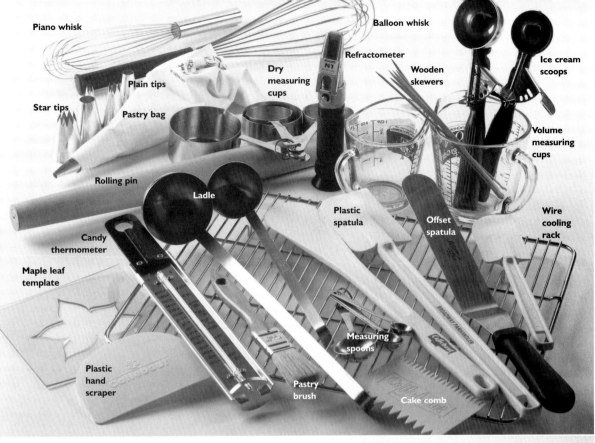

Piano whisk

Balloon whisk

Plain tips

Dry measuring cups

Refractometer

Wooden skewers

Ice cream scoops

Star tips

Pastry bag

Volume measuring cups

Rolling pin

Ladle

Plastic spatula

Offset spatula

Wire cooling rack

Candy thermometer

Maple leaf template

Plastic hand scraper

Pastry brush

Measuring spoons

Cake comb

Large heavy-bottomed saucepan

Stand mixer with paddle attachment

Frying pan

Immersion blender

Hand-held electric mixer

HOBART

Small heavy-bottomed saucepan

Electronic scale

Dough hook attachment

Whip attachment

Saucepans: I always use heavy-bottomed saucepans. They allow the food to cook evenly and help keep milk products from burning. I use All-Clad pans in my kitchen.

Scale: I use an Edlund digital scale, DS-10, that weighs measures from 0.1 ounce to 10 pounds or 2 to 5,000 grams.

Silicon mats: These are known professionally as *silpat*. They are flexible mats made of silicon used for baking and cooking and eliminate the need for parchment paper or nonstick bake ware. They may be transferred from the refrigerator to the freezer. These mats come in a variety of sizes and are very popular in professional kitchens.

Transfer sheet: This is a sheet of acetate covered with designs made from food coloring. It is used to transfer a design to another surface like chocolate.

Whisks: I prefer to use the black-handled balloon whisks by Matfer.

Ingredients

All-purpose flour: See Flour.

Almond flour: A mixture of finely ground almonds and sugar, available in specialty gourmet stores and health food stores.

Almonds: You can buy them skins on, blanched (skins off), whole, halved, slivered, or granulated. Slivered and granulated almonds are generally sold blanched. I use them all!

Baking powder: A chemical leavener; a mixture of baking soda and an acid (salt crystals). A little cornstarch is also added as a stabilizer. Double-acting baking powder is the easiest to find and the most popular. *Double-acting* means it has two reactions—the first, when the powder comes in contact with the wet ingredients (it forms small gas cells or air pockets) and the second, when it comes in contact with the heat of the oven (the gas cells or air pockets expand, which causes the product to rise). Single-acting baking powder reacts only with liquid. Store baking powder in a cool dry place and replace it every six months. Check the expiration date on the package or add 1 teaspoon to about ½ cup of hot water. If it bubbles a lot, it is still good.

Baking soda: Also known as *bicarbonate of soda*, it is a chemical leavener used in baked goods. It reacts when it comes in contact with a wet ingredient. Baking soda needs the presence of an acid to cause the reaction.

Baking spray: I often use a vegetable cooking spray like PAM.

Bittersweet chocolate: See Chocolate.

Bread flour: See Flour.

Butter: I always use unsalted butter in bars. Whipped butter contains air, and if you use it, your butter measurements will not be accurate. In the United States, butter must contain at least 80 percent butterfat. In French butters, the butterfat content is often higher. Keep unsalted butter in the refrigerator well wrapped in plastic wrap because it will absorb other odors. Keep it in the freezer if you need to store it for more than a week or two.

Cake flour: See Flour.

Candied ginger: Also known as *crystallized ginger*, candied ginger is fresh ginger that has been cooked in a sugar syrup and rolled in granulated sugar. Store it in an airtight container in a cool place. It will last indefinitely.

Cardamom: A spice produced mainly in Sri Lanka and India, cardamom is a member of the ginger family. It grows in pods that contain seeds that are ground into powder.

Chestnut flour: A flour made from milled dried chestnuts, usually found in specialty gourmet or health food stores. Store it in the refrigerator.

Chocolate

Unsweetened chocolate is pure cocoa paste (chocolate liquor) consisting of 53 percent cocoa butter and 47 percent cocoa solids. It contains no sugar and is generally used in products having other sources of sweetness.

Bittersweet chocolate consists of 27 percent cocoa butter and 35 percent cocoa paste. It has a strong pronounced flavor and is slightly less sweet than other chocolates. It should not be confused with unsweetened chocolate.

Semisweet chocolate consists of 27 percent cocoa butter and 15 percent cocoa paste. It is slightly sweeter than bittersweet chocolate but can be used interchangeably, according to taste.

Milk chocolate contains milk solids that create a milder, sweeter chocolate. Best used in recipes requiring minimal heat, because the milk makes it heat sensitive.

White chocolate is not considered chocolate because it does not contain cocoa solids. The cocoa butter gives it an ivory or cream color. It is sensitive to heat and should be used where its taste and texture can be fully enjoyed. Always use a white chocolate containing cocoa butter, not vegetable fats.

I almost always use bittersweet chocolate for recipes that call for dark chocolate because I prefer its taste. Most specialty gourmet shops carry it. Always buy the best quality of chocolate available, no matter the type. Taste a few different chocolates to find the one that pleases your palate. The taste will not change when baked, heated, or tempered.

Melting Chocolate: Chocolate melts best at temperatures between 104°F and 113°F (40°C and 45°C). *Never melt chocolate directly over a heat source.* Use an indirect heat source like a hot water bath.

Tempering Chocolate: Tempering determines the final gloss, hardness, and contraction of the chocolate. When you melt chocolate, the molecules of fat separate. To put them back together, you temper it. There are a variety of ways to do it.

One of the easiest ways is to place it in the microwave for 30 seconds at a time on high power until the chocolate is melted. Be very careful not to overheat it. The chocolate will not look as if it has melted because it retains its shape. It should be only slightly warmer than your bottom lip. You may still see lumps in it, but don't worry; the residual heat of the chocolate will melt them. You can also use an immersion blender to break up the lumps and start the recrystallization process.

Usually, the chocolate begins to set (recrystallize) along the side of the bowl. As it begins to crystallize, mix those crystals into the melted chocolate and they will begin the recrystallization process. I like to use a glass bowl because it retains the heat and keeps the chocolate tempered for a long time.

Another way to temper chocolate is called *seeding*. In this method, tempering is achieved by adding small pieces of unmelted chocolate to melted chocolate. The amount of unmelted chocolate to be added depends on the temperature of the melted chocolate but is usually one fourth of the total amount. I usually use an immersion blender to mix the two together.

The classic way to temper chocolate is call *tabliering*. Chocolate is melted over a hot water bath to a temperature between 88°F and 90°F (31°C and 32°C). (White and milk chocolate are melted to a temperature approximately 2°F less, depending on the amount of milk fat they contain.) Two thirds of the melted chocolate is poured on a cold table or marble surface. The chocolate is spread out and worked with a spatula until the temperature of the chocolate is approximately 81°F (27°C). At this stage, it is thick and begins to set. This tempered chocolate is then added to the remaining one third of nontempered chocolate and mixed thoroughly until the mass in the bowl has a completely uniform temperature. If the temperature is still too high, part of the chocolate is further worked on the cold table until the correct temperature is reached. This is a lot of work, requires a lot of room, and makes a big mess.

A simple method to check tempering is to apply a small quantity of chocolate to a piece of paper or to the point of a knife. If the chocolate has been tempered correctly, it will harden evenly and show a good gloss within 5 minutes.

Storing Chocolate: Chocolate is susceptible to moisture and absorbs external odors. It is also important to protect it from light and air. Store it in a cool, dry place in closed packaging. The ideal temperature for storing chocolate is between 54°F and 68°F (12°C and 20°C). Do not store chocolate in the refrigerator, where the humidity (moisture) will affect it.

Cinnamon: A spice made from the dried interior bark of trees in the laurel family. It is commonly found in most grocery stores in stick or powder form. There are two types: true cinnamon, which is tan in color, and cassia, which is reddish brown.

Cinnamon sugar: A mixture of cinnamon and sugar. You can buy this at most grocery stores or make your own. Mix it to your preferred taste.

Cocoa butter: A natural fat found in cocoa beans. It is very difficult to find. You can try a gourmet store, but you may have to inquire through a major food distributor.

Cocoa powder: When cocoa butter has been extracted from chocolate, the remaining "cake" is finely ground into cocoa powder. If it is treated with an alkaline solution (potassium carbonate), it is called *Dutch-processed*. The alkaline solution raises the pH level of the chocolate, which darkens the color, makes the flavor milder, and makes it easier to dissolve. When it is untreated, it has a slightly acidic taste. I always use Dutch-processed unsweetened cocoa powder.

Coconut, shredded: Comes sweetened and unsweetened. I usually use sweetened.

Coffee extract: A concentrated coffee flavoring. The brand I use is Trablit.

Cornstarch: A thickening agent derived from corn. I usually dissolve it in a liquid before adding it to a mixture to prevent lumps from forming.

Cream: A form of milk with a higher concentration of fat. The fat allows it to hold its shape when whipped. Cream comes in three grades: light cream is 18 to 30 percent butterfat, light whipping cream is 30 to 36 percent butterfat, and heavy whipping cream is 36 to 40 percent butterfat. I usually use heavy whipping cream.

Cream, clotted: Also known as *Devonshire cream*, it is traditionally served with scones at teatime. It is a rich, thick cream with a consistency between cream cheese and sour cream. It comes from the same family as sour cream and crème fraîche.

Cream of tartar: Also known as *tartaric acid*, it is present in baking powder. When used in candy making, it helps prevent sugar from crystallizing. It also helps egg whites whip higher and lighter.

Eggs: The egg white is mostly comprised of water and some protein. The yolks contain vitamins, minerals, cholesterol, fat, and protein. Eggs are a natural emulsifier, which is why they are often used to make a sauce smooth and thick.

Grade AA eggs have a thicker white and a stronger yolk. Grade A eggs have thinner albumen (not as strong) and a weaker yolk membrane (it breaks more easily). I usually use large eggs. I don't have a preference between brown and white eggs.

Flour: It is *really* important to use the right flour in a recipe to achieve the desired results. Some commercially processed flours contain toxic chemicals that are legal to use to whiten and oxidize it. I have found that these chemicals significantly affect the outcome of certain recipes, and I prefer to use a pure flour that does not contain any unnecessary additives. I hope the following information helps you choose the right flour for the recipe you would like to make.

What Is Gluten, and What Does It Do?
Flour contains two proteins, glutenin and gliadin, that produce a substance called *gluten* when mixed with a liquid. Gluten stretches but eventually stops trying to snap back to its original shape and will maintain a new shape. These two characteristics cause bread dough to catch, expand, and contain the carbon dioxide bubbles produced by yeast as it grows and divides. (It is also what allows you to roll out pastry into thin sheets that don't shrink back or fall apart.) Wheat is the only grain that contains significant amounts of these proteins, meaning that doughs made from wheat flours are the only ones that can truly be leavened.

What Is Enriched Flour?
Enriched flour is flour that has added to it small amounts of iron, niacin, thiamin, and riboflavin. Some enriched flours may also contain folic acid, a member of the vitamin B complex.

What Else Is Added to Flour?
Malted barley flour is usually added to all-purpose flours to increase the level of enzyme activity in the flour. Malted barley flour is made from dried ground sprouted barley. The

sprouting stimulates the production of enzymes that break starch into sugars, on which yeast feeds.

What Does It Mean When Flour Is Bleached?

Some companies add bleaching and oxidizing chemicals. It is legal to add a number of chemicals, many of which are toxic, to whiten a flour and to instantly oxidize it rather than to allow it to "age" naturally. (Flour that is oxidized, or aged, has better baking qualities.) Potassium bromate, a potentially carcinogenic chemical, has been used extensively as both an oxidizer and a conditioner. In California, any food containing potassium bromate must carry a warning label.

There are other permissible chemical additives used to whiten and oxidize flour, like chlorine dioxide, benzoyl peroxide, and chlorine gas. People with especially sensitive palates can detect a bitter aftertaste in flours treated with these chemicals, which leave a residue of benzoic acid and hydrochloric acid after baking.

Which Flours Are Used Most Often in This Book?

Unbleached all-purpose flour is used for recipes that do not require much strength in the flour.

Bread flour is designed for yeast baking. It contains a high amount of protein, which gives strength to a dough.

Cake flour is used to make tender pastry. I also use it in conjunction with all-purpose flour to make French-style breads.

Whole wheat flour is flour milled from the entire kernel. It produces heavier baked goods than regular flour and gives a richer, fuller flavor. Baked goods made with wheat flour should be refrigerated or frozen when stored so the oil in the wheat germ does not turn rancid.

How Should Flour Be Stored?

All-purpose, bread, pastry, cake, white, or medium rye flours can all be stored in a cool, dry place for an indefinite period of time. Whole grain flours (containing the oil-rich germ) will slowly turn rancid. They will keep for about three months if stored where it is cool and dry. Place them in the refrigerator in an airtight container to store them for up to six months. Freezing the flour will allow it to last even longer. Tuck a bay leaf into any flour stored at room temperature to discourage buggy "visitors."

Food coloring, powdered: This is usually found in specialty baking or gourmet stores.

Gelatin: A gelling agent that can be found in the form of sheets or powder (envelopes). Most brands weigh 2 to 3 grams per sheet or 7 grams per envelope. In the United States, the grocery stores mostly sell the powder form. I prefer the sheets because they are easier to measure. They can be found in gourmet food stores and specialty baking stores. One envelope equals three sheets or 1 teaspoon of powdered gelatin equals one sheet.

Grand Marnier: Orange liqueur used as a flavoring.

Half-and-half: Half cream and half milk. It is found in the dairy sections of grocery stores.

Hazelnuts: Also known as filberts.

Mascarpone cheese: A soft sweet Italian cheese similar to cream cheese. It is made from cow's milk and has a very high butterfat content.

Meringue powder: A powder that contains dried egg whites, sugar, vanillin, and salt. It adds strength to egg whites, adding dried albumin. It helps a meringue hold.

Milk: I always use Grade A whole milk (about 4 percent milkfat), homogenized and pasteurized.

Milk chocolate: See Chocolate.

Mint: An aromatic herb available fresh, dried, or as an extract or oil. Most commonly used and found as peppermint (the most pungent) and spearmint. Store fresh mint in the refrigerator, loosely wrapped in a damp towel.

Muscato d'Asti: An Italian sparkling wine. You can substitute an American or French sparkling wine in its place.

Nutmeg: An Indonesian spice derived from a kernel enclosed in a hard shell whose membrane is the spice known as *mace*. It can be found ground or in whole kernels. It is best to buy the kernels and grate as needed using a nutmeg grater.

Oil: Unless specified, I always use a neutral-flavored oil like canola or vegetable oil.

Oil, flavored: Also known as *essence*. Liquid flavoring derived from natural sources. These oils are very concentrated and should be used sparingly. Store tightly sealed in a cool place. They are found in baking supply stores and gourmet supermarkets.

Oil, olive: Many grades are available on the market. It is graded according to method of extraction and acid content. I used cold-pressed extra virgin olive oil. This oil comes from the first pressing of the harvested olives and is low in acidity.

Peanuts: Technically not a nut but a seed that grows beneath the ground. The nuts are enclosed in a thin brown shell. It can be found with or without the shell. Store unused peanuts in the refrigerator or freezer to prevent the oil in the nuts from becoming rancid.

Phyllo dough: Paper-thin sheets of dough made from flour and water, originally from Greece. Phyllo dough must be baked. It is often used as a wrapping because it bakes to a crunchy texture and keeps the contents moist. Be sure to keep unused phyllo dough covered, or it will dry and be unusable. It can be found in the freezer section of most grocery stores. Always thaw before using.

Pignoli nuts: Also known as *pine nuts*, they come from the seed of a pinecone. Usually they are bought shelled and skinned. They are extremely expensive, so store them in the refrigerator or freezer to prevent the oil in the nuts from becoming rancid. Look for them in health food stores, nut shops, or gourmet food stores.

Pistachio paste: Contains sugar, almonds, pistachios, vegetable oil, an emulsifier, and lecithin. Available in some gourmet food stores.

Powdered pectin: This is fruit pectin for homemade jams and jellies. It contains dextrose (corn syrup), fruit pectin, and fumaric acid (this assists in making the gel). Most grocery stores carry the Sure-Jell brand. I use the regular Sure-Jell, but it is also available as Sure-Jell Light or Slim-Set. If you can't find Sure-Jell in your grocery store, call 1-800-437-3284.

Ricotta cheese: Made from cow's milk or the whey of sheep's milk. Available full-fat regular, low-fat, and part-skim. I always use full-fat, but they are completely interchangeable.

Rum: I always use dark rum from the Caribbean, and I prefer Myers's rum from Jamaica.

Sour cream: Cream to which an acid (e.g., lactic acid, lemon juice, or vinegar) has been added. The mixture is allowed to stand for several hours until the cream curdles. You can buy fat-free or low-fat versions, but I always use the regular sour cream. It can be universally substituted for crème fraîche.

Sugar and other sweeteners: The sugars I use in this book are granulated sugar, light brown sugar, powdered sugar, corn syrup, and honey. Corn syrup and honey are what are known as *invert sugars*; when regular sugar is called for, you substitute half as much corn syrup or honey for the entire amount of sugar and retain the same sweetness.

Brown sugar: Brown sugar is a mixture of granulated sugar and molasses and is available either light or dark. I usually use light brown sugar. You can substitute brown sugar for granulated sugar anytime the flavor of the recipe will not be altered by a slight taste of molasses. Measure brown sugar firmly packed.

Granulated sugar: This is available in about five categories of "fineness," but I always use "regular," which is fine or extrafine.

Powdered sugar: Also known as *confectioners' sugar* or *10X*, it is just granulated sugar ground to a powder. You can't make it at home because no home processor will grind it to the powdery texture. It is used for its texture to sweeten and thicken because it dissolves more easily than granulated sugar. It usually contains cornstarch to keep it from clumping.

Rock sugar: Also known as *crystal sugar.* It is white sugar that has been processed into small pellets. Used for garnishing.

Vanilla sugar: This is granulated sugar to which a dried vanilla bean has been added. It can be stored indefinitely in an airtight container at room temperature.

Corn syrup: This is a starch extracted from corn kernels that is treated with an acid or enzyme to develop a sweet syrup. It prevents sugars from crystallizing. Corn syrup is an invert sugar. It helps baked goods retain their moisture and increases shelf life. I always use light corn syrup. Corn syrup lasts indefinitely if you keep it in an airtight container in the refrigerator.

Honey: Honey is an invert sugar. It is used to add sweetness and moistness to baked goods. It also helps to extend the shelf life because it releases its water slowly and absorbs humidity. The darker the color, the stronger the flavor.

Cooking sugar: In some of the recipes in this book, cooked sugar is added to eggs to make a *pâte à bombe* (egg yolks) or an Italian meringue (egg whites). I usually suggest that you start the sugar and then go on to another step. As the sugar cooks, the water evaporates. If you are not ready to use the sugar, simply add a few tablespoons of water and allow it to continue to cook. This way you can hold the sugar until you are ready.

When sugar is cooked to 250°F (121°C), it has reached the soft ball stage. Sugar cooked to the soft ball stage is used when making a *pâte à bombe* or an Italian meringue.

When sugar is cooked to 300°F to 311°F (148°C to 155°C), it is cooked to the hard crack stage. Sugar cooked to this stage is used to make the Caramel Grid (page 57).

STAGES OF SUGAR	TEMPERATURE RANGE
Thread	230–235°F/110–112°C
Soft ball	240–250°F/115–121°C
Hard ball	255–265°F/124–129°C
Soft crack	270–290°F/132–143°C
Hard crack	300–311°F/148–155°C
Caramel	320–350°F/160–176°C

Vanilla bean: A pod fruit from a climbing vine in the orchid family. It usually comes from Tahiti (larger and more aromatic) or Madagascar (called *Bourbon vanilla*). The pods contain vanillin, which is the source of the fragrant flavor and aroma. The seeds from the vanilla bean are stronger than vanilla extract. I strongly recommend using vanilla beans over extract as often as possible. Store vanilla beans in a sealed bag in the refrigerator for up to a week or in the freezer for longer.

Vanilla extract: Produced from the vanilla bean, it is very concentrated in flavor and should be used sparingly. Store in a cool, dry place. By law, anything labeled *vanilla extract* must be made from true vanilla.

Walnuts: Fruit of the walnut tree enclosed in a hard shell. The most popular varieties are English and black walnuts. The English variety is the easiest to shell. Walnuts can be found shelled and unshelled and are readily available in most supermarkets and health food stores. Store them in the refrigerator or freezer to prevent the oil in the nuts from becoming rancid.

White chocolate: See Chocolate.

Wine, Marsala: An Italian wine that ranges from dry to sweet. The sweet version is most commonly used in desserts.

Yeast: Compressed and dry yeast are the two most common forms of yeast found in baking. They have different traits but are from the same species. Compressed yeast is partly dried, then pressed into solid cakes. It should be slightly moist and cakey and should crumble easily. Compressed yeast shows little activity when dissolved in water (or liquid) before being added to flour (unlike dry yeast) because it needs sugar on which to feed. It will lose less activity if stored in the freezer than if stored in the refrigerator. If it is too old, it will have a strong smell.

Dry yeast has almost ten times less moisture than compressed yeast. It needs to be hydrated in very warm water (105°F to 110°F; 40°C to 43°C). If you hydrate it in lower or higher temperatures, you will lose most of its fermentation power. Most often, you see it bubbling in water when it hydrates. It is best to store dry yeast in the freezer.

In general, yeast activity (fermentation) is dependent on temperature. The ideal temperature is 95°F (35°C). Sugar is needed for fermentation to occur. Salt inhibits yeast activity and, if too much is added, can actually kill the yeast. If you can't find compressed yeast, you can use half the amount required of dry yeast.

Substitutions

INGREDIENT	SUBSTITUTE
1 teaspoon coffee extract	2 teaspoons espresso powder
1 cup firmly packed light brown sugar	1 cup granulated sugar + ¼ cup molasses
1 cup firmly packed dark brown sugar	1 cup granulated sugar + ½ cup molasses
3 gelatin sheets	1 envelope powdered gelatin
1 gelatin sheet	1 teaspoon powdered gelatin
1 package (.25 ounce) dry yeast	1 full tablespoon (.75 ounce) fresh compressed yeast
1 teaspoon baking powder	¼ teaspoon baking soda + ½ teaspoon cream of tartar
1 cup cake flour	Place 1½ tablespoons cornstarch in a 1-cup measure and fill the rest of the cup with all-purpose flour
All-purpose flour	Half bread flour, half cake flour
Half-and-half	Half milk, half cream
Bittersweet chocolate	Semisweet chocolate
Meringue powder	Dried egg whites

Terms

Albumen: The white of an egg.

Bavarian: A creamy mixture that can be either fruit based or crème anglaise based. It always contains whipped cream.

Bloom: Refers to hydrating powdered gelatin. Can also refer to the white coating that appears on chocolate that is not tempered properly.

Cornet: Every chef makes his/her cornet differently. This is how I make mine. Cut an 8 × 12 × 14½-inch triangle from a piece of parchment paper. Hold the middle of the long side of the triangle between two fingers of one hand. Take the tip of the triangle on the short, wide end and roll it toward the other tip of that same wide end while simultaneously pulling it in an upward motion. The tip of a cone will form where your thumb and finger hold it on the long side. Release your grip from the long side so you are now holding the

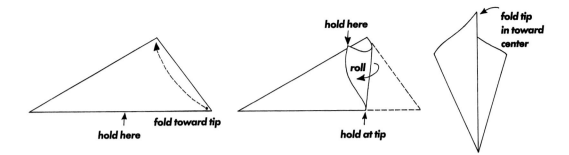

two corners where they meet. The paper will already resemble a partially formed cone. Then just roll the remaining tail until it is completely rolled into a cone. There will be one point sticking up from the open end. Fold it inside toward the center and crease the fold. Now you should have a cornet. When you fold a filled cornet closed, fold it away from the seam. This will keep the seam from opening. Use a pair of scissors or a sharp paring knife to cut an opening in the tip of the cornet to the desired size.

Dock: Pierce lightly with a fork (or docker) to make small holes in the dough that let steam escape during baking. This helps the dough to remain flat and even. A docker looks like a spiked paint roller.

Emulsion: A mixture of two liquids, such as oil and water, that don't naturally combine smoothly. This is formed by the suspension of one liquid in the other. Butter is an emulsion.

Fermentation: Fermentation takes place in any dough containing yeast. The process begins as soon as the ingredients are mixed together and continues until the dough reaches an internal temperature of 138°F to 140°F (58°C to 60°C) during baking, at which point the yeast dies. The ideal proofing environment is 80°F to 98°F (27°C to 36°C) and 80 to 85 percent humidity. The temperature of the added water determines the rate of fermentation (hot=fast, cold=slow). As the yeast eats the added sugar and the sugar already contained in the flour, carbon dioxide is released. Salt controls the rate of fermentation (too little and the yeast is overactivated; too much and the yeast is killed).

French meringue: Egg whites whipped until foamy to which sugar (granulated or powdered) is added. The egg whites are then whipped to stiff peaks and triple in volume. They are stiff and glossy. It is important to add the sugar slowly and at the beginning so it has time to dissolve into the egg whites; otherwise the meringue will be grainy. Adding the sugar slowly gives strength to the egg whites, which helps them hold as they are whipped.

Ganache: A mixture of hot heavy cream and melted chocolate. The cream melts the chocolate and an emulsion is formed as they are whisked together. In this book, ganache is generally used as a filling, but by altering the amount of chocolate and heavy cream, it can also be used as a glaze.

Gluten: See page 10.

Italian meringue: Whipped egg whites to which cooked sugar (at the soft ball stage) is added. The mixture is then whipped until cool and stiff. It becomes thick and glossy and doubles in volume. This is the most stable meringue.

Macerate: Generally used to describe marinating fruit in liquid (alcohol, juice, syrup, etc.) to enhance the flavor of the fruit.

Nonreactive: A pan that is not lined with aluminum, which can react with certain ingredients. I always use All-Clad pans.

Oxidation: The union of a substance and oxygen. Fruit exposed to oxygen will often turn brown.

Parfait: A whipped, cooked sugar–and–egg yolk mixture (called a *pâte à bombe*) folded together with whipped cream and flavored. Can also be served frozen.

Pâte à bombe: Whipped yolks to which cooked sugar (at the soft ball stage) is added. The mixture is then whipped until lukewarm, thick, and doubled in volume. Used as a base for parfait.

Paton: Term used when making puff pastry. A paton is dough to which butter has been added.

Proofing: A term used to describe dough as it ferments and rises.

Quenelle: An oval-shaped scoop of any mixture (mousse, Bavarian, meringue, etc.) generally formed between two spoons.

Seize: Used in reference to chocolate to describe when liquid chocolate suddenly contracts and hardens upon contact with water or when mixed with another ingredient that is too cold.

Soft peaks: In this book, used in reference to whipped cream. When the beaters are lifted from the whipped cream, peaks are briefly formed, but they do not hold their shape. Also describes the stage when whipped cream has the most volume.

Stiff peaks: In this book, used in reference to egg whites. When the beaters are lifted from the egg whites, peaks are formed that hold their shape. When egg whites have reached the stiff peak stage, they are opaque, thick, and shiny or glossy.

Temper: To bring the temperature of one mixture closer to that of another until the desired temperature is reached.

Back to Basics

This chapter represents all of the things I always have on hand in the kitchen. I don't change these recipes too much because they work well. I call them my staples. If you have my first book, *Dessert Circus,* you may already have tried some of them—I've been using them for years.

Pastry Cream

Yield: About 2¼ cups (20 ounces; 570 grams)

Pastry cream is one of the basic recipes in any pastry chef's repertoire. I have a few different pastry cream recipes. Over the years I have made slight changes to my pastry creams to alter the taste and texture. I guess it's like perfume; sometimes you just need a change.

Cornstarch	2 tablespoons	I ounce	25 grams
Granulated sugar	Scant ½ cup	3.5 ounces	100 grams
4 large egg yolks			
Whole milk	Generous 2 cups	17 ounces	485 grams
I vanilla bean			
Unsalted butter (optional)	I tablespoon	0.6 ounce	15 grams

Sift together the cornstarch and half of the sugar in a medium-size mixing bowl, add the egg yolks, and whisk until well combined. The egg mixture should be thick, smooth, and homogenous.

Pour the milk and the remaining sugar into a nonreactive 2-quart heavy-bottomed saucepan and place the saucepan over medium-high heat. I use a large saucepan because the pastry cream gains volume as it cooks and room is needed to vigorously whisk without spilling. While the milk is heating, use a sharp knife to slice the vanilla bean in half lengthwise. Separate the seeds from the skin by scraping the blade of the knife along the inside of the bean. Add the seeds and the skin to the heating milk and bring to a boil.

Temper the egg mixture with the hot milk by carefully pouring about half of the milk into the egg mixture. Immediately whisk to prevent the eggs from scrambling. Pour the tempered egg mixture into the saucepan and continue to whisk, remembering to whisk into the edge of the saucepan where the pastry cream can stick and burn. As the temperature rises, the mixture will slowly start to thicken. The pastry cream will become very thick very quickly just before it boils. (The eggs and starch cause it to thicken.) Continuously whisk to ensure that the mixture cooks evenly. Once the pastry cream has come to a boil, continue to whisk and cook for another 2 minutes to fully develop the flavor of the pastry cream and to cook out the flavor of the starch. Remove the pan from the heat. Strain the pastry cream through a fine-mesh sieve to remove any pieces of cooked egg and the vanilla bean. Be sure to save the vanilla bean skin to make vanilla sugar.

If you would like to add butter, and I always do, this is the time to add it. I just cut the butter into small chunks and stir it in until it is well incorporated. Pour the pastry cream into a clean, airtight container and place a piece of plastic wrap directly on top of the pastry cream to prevent a skin from forming. Let cool at room temperature, then store in the refrigerator for up to 3 days, until ready to use.

Variations: It is very easy to flavor pastry cream to complement the dessert you are making. With a whisk or spatula, fold about 1 tablespoon of any flavored liqueur into the pastry cream at any point in the recipe. I usually add it right before I use the pastry cream; that way I can flavor only the amount I need for a specific dessert. Be sure to add the liqueur slowly and to taste often. If you add too much, the pastry cream will become runny and lose its ability to hold its shape. If you prefer to add flavor without alcohol, you will need to do so at the beginning of the recipe. Place the grated zest of 2 oranges in the heating milk to infuse it with the flavor of the orange.

Crème Anglaise

Yield: 3 cups (25 ounces; 700 grams)

The trick to making crème anglaise is how long you cook it. There is a fine line between done and overcooked. If overcooked, you end up with pieces of scrambled eggs. With practice, you will learn to tell when the crème anglaise is finished by the way it moves in the pan and how it coats a spoon. For your first attempt, you might want to use a candy thermometer and cook the mixture to 182°F (83°C).

You will need to prepare an ice bath before you begin. When the crème anglaise has finished cooking, it is important to cool it as quickly as possible. Otherwise, the mixture will retain heat and continue to cook.

Granulated sugar	Generous ½ cup	4.5 ounces	125 grams
7 large egg yolks			
Whole milk	Generous 2 cups	18 ounces	500 grams
Heavy cream	½ cup	3.9 ounces	115 grams
Honey	1½ tablespoons	1.2 ounces	30 grams
1 vanilla bean			

continued

Pour half of the sugar into a large mixing bowl and set the remaining sugar aside. Add the egg yolks and whisk until well combined. The mixture should be thick, smooth, and homogenous.

Pour the milk, heavy cream, honey, and remaining sugar into a nonreactive 3-quart heavy-bottomed saucepan over medium-high heat. Use a sharp knife to slice the vanilla bean in half lengthwise. Separate the seeds from the outside skin by scraping the blade of the knife along the inside of the bean. Add the seeds and the skin to the mixture and bring to a boil. Remove the saucepan from the heat.

Temper the egg mixture with the hot milk mixture by carefully pouring about one third of it into the egg mixture. Whisk immediately to keep the eggs from scrambling. Pour the tempered egg mixture into the saucepan, place over medium heat, and cook, stirring constantly with a heatproof rubber spatula. The liquid will begin to thicken. When it reaches 182°F (83°C) and is thick enough to coat the back of a spoon, it is finished and should be removed from the heat. If you do not have a thermometer, you can tell that it is finished by using the following method: In one quick motion, dip the spatula into the crème anglaise and hold it horizontally in front of you. Use the tip of your finger to wipe a clean line down the center of the spatula. If the trail keeps its shape, the crème anglaise is ready. If the trail fills with liquid, cook it for another minute and repeat the test. The objective is to remove the crème anglaise from the heat just *before* it boils.

If the crème anglaise boils, the egg yolks will scramble. If this happens, you can still use it as an ice cream base if you blend it with an immersion blender, a food processor, or a blender; you need a blade to liquefy the scrambled egg pieces. You will not be able to use it as a sauce, because once the eggs are scrambled they lose their ability to hold a sauce together.

Strain the crème anglaise through a fine-mesh sieve into a bowl placed in an ice bath to remove the vanilla bean and any cooked egg. Stir occasionally to allow the crème anglaise to cool evenly. Once it has cooled completely, pour it into a clean container. Place plastic wrap directly on top of the crème anglaise to prevent a skin from forming, and store in the refrigerator for up to 3 days.

Variation: It is very easy to flavor crème anglaise. Just add a tablespoon (more or less to taste) of any flavored liqueur or nut paste at any stage in the recipe. I recommend that you add your flavor when the crème anglaise has finished cooking. You can divide it into smaller portions and flavor each differently.

Almond Cream

Yield: 1¾ cups (16 ounces; 425 grams)

Almond cream is always baked to a spongy, cakelike texture and can be used by itself or in combination with nuts or fruits. The addition of starch to this recipe ensures that it will not run out of a pastry shell during the cooking process. Its moist and flavorful qualities make it perfect for use as a filling in cookies, tarts, and puff pastries.

The recipe is easy to remember: 1 part butter, 1 part almond flour, 1 part sugar, ⅕ part eggs, ⅐ part all-purpose flour. With that in mind, you can make as much or as little of it as you like.

Unsalted butter, softened	**½ cup + 1 tablespoon**	**4.5 ounces**	**125 grams**
Granulated sugar	**Generous ½ cup**	**4.5 ounces**	**125 grams**
Almond flour (page 6)	**Generous 1 cup**	**4.5 ounces**	**125 grams**
1 large egg			
All-purpose flour	**Scant ¼ cup**	**0.75 ounce**	**20 grams**

Place the butter, sugar, and almond flour in a medium-size mixing bowl and beat with an electric mixer set on medium speed until light and fluffy, about 5 minutes. The mixture will be dry and sandy until the butter begins to incorporate. Add the egg and mix well. Use a rubber spatula to scrape down the side of the bowl as needed. The egg is well incorporated when the mixture is light and creamy, about 3 minutes. The batter lightens in color and increases in volume due to the incorporation of air by the mixer. It is important to allow time to beat in air; otherwise the almond cream will be too heavy and will not have as great a rise when baked, causing the texture to be dense.

Add the all-purpose flour and beat on low speed just until it is no longer visible, about 30 seconds. If you overmix, gluten (page 10) will overdevelop and the almond cream will lose its delicate texture when baked.

Pour the almond cream into an airtight container and store in the refrigerator for up to 5 days until ready to use. While in the refrigerator, the almond cream will darken in color and lose some of its volume. This happens because the butter hardens and the incorporated air escapes. You can also freeze the almond cream for several weeks. In either case, allow it to come to room temperature before using and beat it lightly with an electric mixer set on medium speed until it returns to its initial volume and is once again light in texture and color.

Raspberry or Mango Sauce

Yield: 1¼ cups (10.2 ounces; 285 grams)

To make this sauce, it is best to use a blender, food processor, or immersion blender. You will also need a fine-mesh sieve. Use ripe, flavorful fruit or your sauce will have no taste. Fruits that make especially good sauces are the berries and really colorful fruits like mango and papaya. Use this recipe as a guideline to create your own fruit sauce.

Prepared fresh fruit	About 3 cups	10.5 ounces	300 grams
Powdered sugar	Scant ½ cup	1.8 ounces	50 grams
A few drops fresh lemon juice (if using raspberries)			

Peel, core, seed, or pit the fruit as appropriate and chop into medium-size pieces. Puree the fruit until completely smooth. Add the sugar 2 tablespoons at a time, incorporating it well after each addition and making sure any lumps are dissolved. When using raspberries, add the lemon juice to prevent oxidation (browning) and to enhance the flavor. Watch the consistency and frequently taste for sweetness. The desired sauce is equally sweet and tangy, and smooth. You may not use all of the sugar, or you may need to add a little bit more. If too little sugar is added, the sauce will be runny and tart. To fix this, add more sugar. If too much sugar is added, the sauce will be overly thick, sweet, and it will taste starchy. To fix this, add more fruit puree. The sauce is the ideal consistency when it holds its shape when dribbled onto a plate.

Strain the sweetened puree through a fine-mesh sieve into a clean bowl. This will separate the pulp from the fruit puree and remove any small seeds. Stir the puree until completely smooth. It will keep in the refrigerator in a small airtight container or zippered-top plastic bag for up to 3 days or in the freezer for up to 2 months.

Chocolate Sauce

Yield: 2⅔ cups (23.5 ounces; 675 grams)

Taste is the most important aspect of this sauce, so use the best-quality chocolate you can find. A lesser-quality chocolate will produce a sauce with inferior flavor.

Whole milk	Generous 1 cup	9 ounces	250 grams
Bittersweet chocolate, chopped		10.5 ounces	300 grams
Heavy cream	Generous ½ cup	4.5 ounces	125 grams
Unsalted butter	2 tablespoons	1.2 ounces	30 grams
Granulated sugar	Generous ⅓ cup	2.6 ounces	75 grams

Pour the milk into a 2-quart heavy-bottomed saucepan, place over medium-high heat, and bring to a boil. When the milk boils, remove it from the heat and make a ganache by adding the chopped chocolate. Whisk well, stirring into the edge of the saucepan to combine. The ganache should be homogenous and smooth. Set the ganache aside.

In a 1-quart heavy-bottomed saucepan, combine the heavy cream, butter, and sugar. Place the saucepan over medium-high heat and bring to a boil, stirring occasionally. The butter should be completely melted and the sugar completely dissolved. Once the mixture has come to a boil, pour it into the warm ganache.

Place the sauce over medium-high heat and bring to a boil, stirring constantly with a whisk. As the chocolate sauce cooks, it will begin to thicken slightly. When it reaches a boil, remove it from the heat and pour it into a clean, dry bowl. Cover by placing plastic wrap directly on top of the sauce to prevent a skin from forming. Let the chocolate sauce cool to room temperature before storing in the refrigerator. When cold, the chocolate sauce will become thick enough to be scooped with a spoon.

One of the wonderful qualities of this chocolate sauce is that it can be reheated whenever needed. If using a microwave, simply place the chocolate sauce in a microwaveable bowl and heat it at medium-high power in 30-second intervals until it becomes liquid. On the stovetop, place in a heavy-bottomed saucepan over medium heat and stir occasionally until it becomes liquid. If you store it in a squeeze bottle, you can easily drizzle it over a dessert or decorate a plate. It will keep in the refrigerator for up to 3 weeks. It can also be frozen for up to 2 months if stored in an airtight container, to be kept on hand for a last-minute dinner party. Thaw in the refrigerator and reheat as described above until liquid.

Linda's Red Raspberry Jam

Yield: Seven 8-ounce jars

This is simply my very favorite recipe for raspberry jam. It was handed down by Kris's Gram and taught to me by her sister, Linda. I love everything Linda makes and won't let the family go out for dinner when Kris and I visit her.

Since the days of Gram, the canning instructions have been greatly simplified. It is no longer necessary to use a hot water bath. Use the best berries you can find. Make sure they are ripe and try to choose the ones with the nicest color. Linda usually picks her own!

Fresh raspberries	5 cups	25.6 ounces	684 grams
Powdered pectin	1 box	1.75 ounces	49 grams
Granulated sugar	6¾ cups	47.8 ounces	1,350 grams
Unsalted butter	1½ tablespoons	0.75 ounce	21 grams

Carefully wash the berries and pat dry. Set aside. Wash and rinse seven 8-ounce glass canning jars. Keep the jars warm until ready to fill by leaving them in a sink filled with clean hot water. Fill a small saucepan with water and place over medium heat. Place the washed and rinsed canning lids and metal bands in the pan and bring to a simmer. Remove the pan from the heat and set aside, leaving the lids and bands in the hot water until ready to use.

Place enough of the berries in an 8- to 10-quart heavy-bottomed enamel or stainless-steel pan or kettle to fill the bottom. It is important to use a large pan because the jam splatters and rises when it boils. Use a potato masher to gently crush the berries, one layer at a time. Add another layer of berries, crush, and repeat until all of the berries are in the pan. Add the powdered pectin and bring to a full boil over high heat, stirring constantly with a wooden spoon. Add the sugar and butter and stir thoroughly. Bring the mixture to a full, rolling boil. A rolling boil is one that cannot be stirred down. At this stage, boil hard for 1 full minute, stirring constantly. Remove from the heat. Use a large spoon to skim and discard the foam that has formed on the surface.

Remove a hot jar, lid, and band from the hot water. Use a jar funnel to fill the jar with the hot jam to ¼ inch from the top. Carefully clean the rim of the jar with a clean damp cloth. Place the lid and band on the jar and twist the band just until the lid is firmly secured, but do not twist tightly at this stage. Fill each of the remaining jars. Set aside.

Modern techniques instruct you to simply invert the jars for 10 minutes, then turn upright and allow them to cool. As the jars cool, a tight vacuum seal is formed. You will hear the lids make a dull "ping" and see that each lid has indented slightly. If you have a jar that was not filled at least ¼ inch from the top or if the rim of a jar was not completely clean, it may not seal. Store it in the refrigerator and use within 1 month. The canned jam can be stored at room temperature in a cool, dark place for 1 year. Refrigerate after opening.

Apricot Glaze

Yield: About ¼ cup (2.6 ounces; 75 grams)

use glaze to give a professional finish to a tart or cake. You can make almost any kind of fruit glaze you like using any flavor of jam. I use apricot because it is clear and has a neutral flavor. You may have to adjust the amount of water based on the consistency of the jam. Heat the glaze until it is liquid enough to apply with a pastry brush.

| Apricot jam | ¼ cup | 2.6 ounces | 75 grams |
| Water | About 1 tablespoon | 0.6 ounce | 15 grams |

Mix the apricot jam with the water in a small microwaveable bowl and heat in the microwave on high power or in a nonreactive 1-quart heavy-bottomed saucepan over medium heat until liquid. Brush it on with a pastry brush. The glaze can be stored in the refrigerator in an airtight container for up to 3 days.

Hydrated Raisins

Yield: I cup

like to use hydrated raisins in a lot of recipes. I always keep a jar of them in the refrigerator. The proportion I use for adding the liquor is 10 to 20 percent of the weight of the water. If you do not dilute the liquor with water, be prepared for a very strong burst of flavor!

Raisins	I cup	4 ounces	120 grams
Water as needed			
Dark rum or flavored liquor	½ cup	3.5 ounces	100 grams

Place the raisins in a mixing bowl or glass jar and add water so that it covers the raisins by at least ½ inch. Stir in the rum or flavored alcohol. Cover with plastic wrap and place in the refrigerator for 24 hours. It is even better to allow the raisins to hydrate for 2 to 3 days; they will become very plump as they absorb the liquid. You can keep them in the refrigerator for a few weeks. When you are ready to use them, strain the amount that you need through a fine-mesh sieve before adding them to the recipe.

Tantalizing Tarts

Tarts are at the beginning of every pastry chef's career. There is an infinite variety of filling combinations. You can make a very simple tart with just dough and fruit, or you can build a more elaborate tart by adding pastry cream, almond cream, or nut fillings. I like to suggest that kitchen novices start with tarts to build confidence. The results of the effort are seen in a short amount of time. You can learn a lot of fundamental techniques when making tarts: using a knife, working with dough, presenting your dish, and determining flavor combinations, to name a few.

My colleague Francisco Gutierrez has been making the tarts at Le Cirque for the last eighteen years. I am always amazed at the new combinations he creates.

I prefer to use a nonstick tart pan with a removable bottom when making tarts. This pan makes it really easy to unmold your creation. If you live near a good baking school, you can probably find the long rectangular tart pans. Remember not to overwork the dough, or it will be tough, hard to roll, and it will shrink when you bake it. Use the freshest ripe fruit available. Remember, any tart recipe can be made as smaller individual tarts instead. In this chapter, I've included free-form tarts to add variety and demonstrate that you don't even need a tart pan to make one of these yummy desserts.

Pâte Brisée

Yield: 15 ounces (415 grams); enough for one 10- or 12-inch tart

Pâte brisée is one of the three classic recipes that form the basis for most tarts. It is similar to a shortbread dough. It is very important to use a good-quality butter, since the taste is very prominent in this recipe.

I learned how to make pâte brisée from my mentor, Louis Franchain. He explains that while the components of the recipe are quite simple, the results depend on the technique for making the dough and understanding how the ingredients interact. Mastery of this very simple recipe is a key to making good tarts.

Cake flour	1⅔ cups	9 ounces	250 grams
Pinch of salt			
Pinch of granulated sugar			
Cold unsalted butter, diced	½ cup+ 2 tablespoons	4.5 ounces	125 grams
Cold water	Scant ⅓ cup	2.3 ounces	65 grams

Combine the flour, salt, and sugar in a large mixing bowl. Add the butter all at once and coat evenly with the flour mixture. Work in the butter with your hands until the mixture resembles coarse meal. The easiest way to do this is to grab a handful of flour mixture and butter, then gently rub the two between your hands to combine them. As you rub, the mixture drops back into the bowl. Keep doing this until most of the butter is combined. If your hands are too warm, the butter will melt. If necessary, wash your hands in ice-cold water every few minutes. Make sure your hands are dry when you return to the mixture. Stop working the mixture while you can still see small chunks of butter. This will make the dough softer and more crumbly.

Add the water all at once and work it in with your hands until the dough holds together. Be careful not to overmix or you risk overdeveloping the gluten, which will cause the dough to be tough and chewy rather than delicate and crumbly. When the dough holds together in a ball, place it on the work surface and knead gently until smooth, about 30 seconds. If the dough is sticky when you begin, very lightly flour the work surface before you knead the dough. If the dough is dry and ropey, just keep kneading it until it becomes smooth and moist. Pat the dough into a disk and place on a parchment paper–covered baking sheet. Cover with plastic wrap and let rest in the refrigerator for at least 30 minutes before using. This will give any gluten strands that have developed a chance to relax. Then proceed with the dough as directed in your particular recipe. The dough will keep well wrapped in the refrigerator for 1 week or in the freezer for 1 month.

Pâte Sablée

Yield: 19.5 ounces (560 grams); enough for two 10-inch tart shells

I like a tart dough with lots of butter because it is flakier. The fat in the butter coats the protein in the flour. This helps make the dough tender. I love the taste of the butter, too!

Here is a trick I use when I bake this tart shell without a filling: immediately after baking, brush the shell with a little bit of corn syrup and dry it in the oven for about 5 minutes. This keeps the shell from becoming soggy.

Cold unsalted butter	Generous ½ cup	5.5 ounces	150 grams
Pinch of salt			
Powdered sugar	¾ cup	3.2 ounces	90 grams
1 large egg			
Almond flour (page 6)	¼ cup	1.2 ounces	30 grams
Cake flour	Scant 2 cups	10 ounces	280 grams

Place the butter, salt, sugar, egg, and almond flour in a medium-size mixing bowl. The almond flour will add flavor to the dough. Use an electric mixer set on medium speed to beat the mixture just until combined.

Add the cake flour and mix just until the dough is smooth and holds together, about 30 seconds. Remove the dough from the bowl and pat into a disk. Wrap the dough in plastic wrap and place it in the refrigerator for at least 1 hour before using. This will give any gluten that may have developed a chance to relax. If you use the dough immediately after making it, it may be tough and elastic.

When you are ready to use the dough, remove it from the refrigerator and give it four or five quick raps with a rolling pin. This softens the cold butter. Roll the dough to the desired size on a lightly floured work surface.

Baking instructions vary and will be specified in any recipe using this dough. The dough will keep, well wrapped in plastic wrap, in the refrigerator for 1 week or in the freezer for 1 month. Thaw the dough in the refrigerator until ready to use. If you want to store the dough already rolled into a tart pan, wrap it in plastic wrap.

Classic Puff Pastry

Yield: 40 ounces (1,130 grams)

P uff pastry is a remarkable dough. It can rise eight to ten times its original height when baked even though it has no leavening agents. The layers are created when the fat is incorporated into the dough as it is rolled and folded. The leavening action happens in three ways: The moisture in both the dough and butter layers turns into steam when heated. The steam pushes apart these layers, separating the fat layers from the dough, which causes the puff pastry to rise. Second, each time the dough is folded, air is trapped between each layer. The air expands during baking and pushes apart the layers. Last, when the fats are heated, air bubbles form and the fat boils, which raises the layers of the dough.

There are a few things to keep in mind when making puff pastry. All-purpose flour will yield the best result. Bread flour would create an elastic dough, and cake flour would create a weak dough. Using both melted and cold butter ensures it will be evenly distributed throughout the dough. If you are consistent when rolling and folding the dough, it will build a well-defined structure. Forgetting to give the dough even one fold will cause it to lose hundreds of layers.

This recipe is time consuming but relatively easy to make. It will be easier after you make it a few times. Remember, you can always choose to buy ready-made puff pastry if you prefer. It is usually found in the freezer section of the supermarket. I never use a hand-held electric mixer to make this recipe because the motor will not hold up to the strength of the dough.

Unbleached all-purpose flour	4 cups	18 ounces	500 grams
Salt	1 ¼ teaspoons	0.5 ounce	12 grams
Unsalted butter, melted and cooled	¼ cup	1.8 ounces	50 grams
Water	About 1 ¼ cups	About 9.5 ounces	About 270 grams
Cold unsalted butter	Generous 1 ¼ cups	10.5 ounces	300 grams

Place the flour, salt, melted butter, and most of the water in the bowl of a stand mixer fitted with the paddle attachment and mix on medium speed for about 1 minute. Stop the mixer as soon as the ingredients begin to form a dough and pull away from the side of the bowl. If the dough appears too dry and does not come together, add the remaining water and mix just until combined. When certain proteins in flour mix with water, they form gluten, which makes dough elastic and tough. The more the dough is worked, the more

Roll each corner away from the center of the dough until it is ¼ inch thick.

Pull the rolled-out corners of the dough up and over the butter.

gluten develops. Do not overmix, or you will overdevelop the gluten. It is very important to keep gluten development to a minimum in this recipe, or the finished puff pastry will be tough and chewy instead of delicate and crispy. Remove the dough from the mixer and pat it into a 5-inch square about 2 inches thick. Wrap the dough completely in plastic wrap and let it rest in the refrigerator for 2 hours. Resting the dough allows gluten strands that have developed to relax.

Remove the cold butter from the refrigerator and work it into a square that is about a third smaller than the dough square and about 1 inch thick. Place the butter on a lightly floured work surface and use a rolling pin to give it a few quick raps. This will soften the butter. It should be about the same consistency as that of the puff pastry dough. Keep the butter shaped in a square. Lightly flour the butter and rolling pin as needed to keep it from sticking to the rolling pin and the work surface.

Remove the dough from the refrigerator and place on a lightly floured work surface. Use the rolling pin to make a mark about 1 inch from each corner of the dough. Roll only this part of each corner away from the center of the dough until it is ¼ inch thick. The center of the dough should be about 1 inch thick. Place the butter square in the center of the dough square. Pull the rolled-out corners up and over the butter, completely enclosing it in a dough package. When the butter has been added, the dough is referred to as a *paton.*

The paton is now ready to be folded. You will need to give the dough six single folds, allowing the dough to rest in the refrigerator for at least 2 hours after every two folds. Use a rolling pin to roll the paton into a 10×23-inch rectangle. Try to keep it an even thickness. Place the dough horizontally in front of you so it will be easier to fold. Fold the dough in thirds by first folding the left end over the middle and then folding the right third over it. Rotate the dough to make sure the seam is on your right. This is known as a *single fold.* It is also called a *letter fold* because it resembles the way a letter is folded. Repeat the single fold starting with a 10 × 23-inch rectangle placed horizontally in front of you. To remind myself that I have folded the dough two times, I make two indentations in the dough with my fingertips. At this stage, the puff pastry must be kept well wrapped in the refrigerator for at least 2 hours or up to 1 day.

Remove the dough from the refrigerator and give it two more single folds, starting each time with a 10 × 23-inch rectangle. To remind myself that I have folded the dough four times, I make four indentations in the dough with my fingertips. At this stage, the puff pastry must be kept well wrapped in the refrigerator for at least 2 hours or up to 1 day.

Remove the dough from the refrigerator and give it the final two folds, starting each time with a 10 × 23-inch rectangle. Let the dough rest in the refrigerator for at least 1 hour before using. Then it will be ready to be rolled and formed into the shape required in the specific recipe. The finished puff pastry will keep, well wrapped in plastic wrap, in the refrigerator for 1 day or in the freezer for up to 2 months.

Roll the paton into a 10 × 23-inch rectangle.

Fold the dough into thirds by first folding the left end over the middle.

Then fold the right third over it. This is known as a single fold.

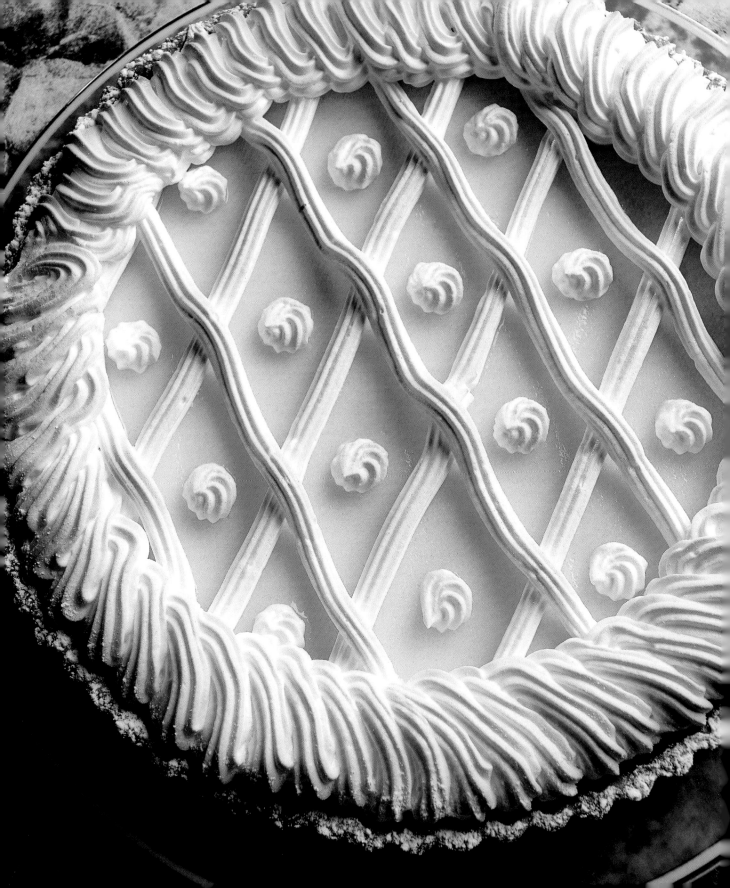

Lemon Tart

Yield: One 10-inch tart; 8 to 10 servings

Lemon curd is one of my mom's favorite things to eat. When I go home in the summer, she always asks me to make it for her. Please use fresh lemons for this. Freshly squeezed juice will give the lemon curd so much more flavor than store-bought juice.

I like to use a tart pan with a removable bottom. It is easier to fill the tart shell while it is still in the tart mold. You can easily unmold it by removing the side of the pan and sliding the tart off the bottom.

For the crust

Pâte Brisée (page 30) or ½ recipe Pâte Sablée (page 32)

For the lemon curd

1 gelatin sheet or ⅓ envelope powdered gelatin			
Juice of 4 large fresh lemons, strained			
Grated zest of 1 lemon			
Unsalted butter	Generous 3 tablespoons	1.8 ounces	50 grams
Granulated sugar	Generous ¾ cup	6 ounces	170 grams
3 large eggs			
3 large egg yolks			

For the French meringue

4 large egg whites			
Granulated sugar	Generous ½ cup	4 ounces	120 grams

Prepare the crust: Make the dough as directed in the recipe. Pat the dough into a disk and wrap in plastic wrap. Let it rest for a few hours in the refrigerator. This will allow any gluten that may have developed to relax.

Preheat the oven to 375°F (190°C). Remove the dough from the refrigerator. Lightly give the dough a few quick raps with the rolling pin to soften it slightly. This will make it easier to roll. Lightly flour the work surface and each side of the dough. Roll the dough into a 12-inch circle about ¼ inch thick. Transfer the dough to a 10-inch tart pan by rolling it around the rolling pin. Unroll the dough over the tart pan. Gently press the dough into the pan, especially where the bottom and side of the pan meet. Don't forget to press the dough up the side of the pan; this will help the dough hold its shape as it bakes. Remove any excess dough by rolling the rolling pin over the top of the pan to make a nice clean cut. Dock the bottom of the tart shell with a fork. Place the tart shell in the oven and bake until evenly golden brown, about 25 minutes. If the dough begins to rise unevenly as it bakes, release the air by gently piercing the dough with the tip of a paring knife. Cool the tart shell on a wire rack until ready to use.

Prepare the lemon curd: If you are using a gelatin sheet, place it in a medium-size mixing bowl with enough cold water (about 2 cups) to cover. Let stand for about 5 minutes to allow the gelatin to soften and hydrate. Cold water hydrates the gelatin without letting it absorb too much liquid. Remove the gelatin from the bowl and squeeze out the excess water with your hands. If you are using powdered gelatin, sprinkle it over 2 tablespoons (1 ounce; 25 grams) of cold water. Let the gelatin bloom until it has absorbed all the water, about 1 minute.

Pour the lemon juice, zest, butter, and about half of the sugar into a nonreactive 3-quart heavy-bottomed saucepan and place over medium-high heat. While the mixture is heating, pour the remaining sugar, the whole eggs, and the yolks into a medium-size mixing bowl and whisk well to combine. The egg mixture should be thick and smooth. When the juice mixture comes to a boil, temper the egg mixture by carefully pouring about half of the hot juice mixture into the eggs. Whisk immediately to prevent the eggs from scrambling. Use a rubber spatula to scrape all of the tempered mixture into the saucepan and continue to whisk. Remember to whisk into the edge of the saucepan where the lemon curd can stick and burn. Whisk constantly until the lemon curd thickens and comes to a boil. At this point, remove it from the heat and add the hydrated gelatin. Whisk well until all the gelatin is completely dissolved and dispersed. Immediately pour the lemon curd into the prebaked tart shell. Use a large offset spatula to spread the lemon curd evenly into the tart shell. I pour the hot lemon curd directly into the tart shell to keep it from becoming too loose, which is what will happen if you cool the lemon curd and then spread it into the tart shell. Place the lemon tart in the refrigerator for a couple of hours until the curd cools and sets.

When you are ready to serve the tart, prepare the French meringue: Preheat the broiler. Place the egg whites in a large mixing bowl and whip with an electric mixer set on medium speed until foamy. Make the meringue by adding the granulated sugar 1 tablespoon at a time. When you whip egg whites, add the sugar slowly to allow the whites to gain some volume. When you have volume, add the rest of the sugar. Increase the mixer speed to medium-high and whip to stiff but not dry peaks, about 5 minutes. When the whites are slightly stiff, I usually reduce the mixer speed to low to allow even more air to incorporate without overwhipping the egg whites. Continue to whip for about another 2 minutes. Stop whipping if the egg whites look dry or separated. I use the same amount (by weight) of sugar and egg whites for this meringue. If you want a stronger meringue, you can use twice the amount of sugar to the egg whites, but I think that will be too sweet for this tart.

Place the meringue in a pastry bag fitted with a ½-inch star tip. Pipe the desired decoration on top of the tart. You can also use a spatula to simply cover the top of the tart with the meringue.

Place the decorated tart under the broiler for about 5 minutes until the meringue takes on color. Watch it closely; once it starts, it browns very quickly. Remove it from the oven.

Unmold the tart: Simply push up on the bottom of the tart to release the side. Then slide the tart from the bottom of the tart pan onto a flat plate. If the tart sticks to the bottom of the pan, loosen it with a long offset spatula. I think raspberries and lemon are a great combination, so sometimes I decorate the finished tart with fresh raspberries if I have them in the house.

> **If the sides of the tart shell begin to collapse as it bakes, remove it from the oven. Carefully pinch the dough back into place. At this stage, you could also use pie weights to hold the tart shell. Be sure to line the shell with parchment paper before adding the pie weights. Return the tart shell to the oven and finish baking.**

Scintillating Strawberry Tart

Yield: One 12-inch tart; 10 to 12 servings

This is one of the first tarts I learned to make during my apprenticeship. It looks so yummy and is as pleasing to the eye as it is to the palate. Try to use the best strawberries you can find. I order mine directly from Driscoll in Watsonville, California. The berries are always ripe and flavorful and the texture nearly perfect.

Our friends at Driscoll sent us the most fabulous strawberries to use as set decoration on the television show. When we broke for the weekend, we knew the strawberries would not be at their best by Monday, so we took them home. Kris, her sister, Linda, and her friend Birgitt spent the entire Saturday making the most incredible strawberry jam I have ever tasted. Everyone on the crew was happy to get a jar, too!

Pâte Brisée (page 30) or ⅔ recipe Pâte Sablée (page 32)			
½ recipe Pastry Cream flavored with Stoli Strasberi vodka (page 20)			
Fresh strawberries, cleaned	About 5½ cups	25 ounces	700 grams
Apricot Glaze (page 27)			

Prepare the dough as directed in the recipe and let the it rest in the refrigerator for at least 30 minutes before using.

Prepare the pastry cream as directed in the recipe. For this tart, I like to flavor the cold pastry cream with the strawberry vodka because I think it enhances the flavor of the tart. You may omit the liquor if you prefer. Store the pastry cream in the refrigerator, tightly covered in plastic wrap, until ready to use.

Preheat the oven to 350°F (176°C). Remove the dough from the refrigerator. Lightly give the dough a few quick raps with the rolling pin to soften it slightly. This will make it easier to roll. Lightly flour the work surface and each side of the dough. Roll the dough into a 14-inch circle about ⅛ inch thick. Transfer the dough to a parchment paper–covered baking sheet by rolling it around the rolling pin. Unroll the dough onto the baking sheet. Lightly place a 12-inch cardboard cake circle or a cake pan or plate on top of the dough. Let this guide you as you use a sharp paring knife to cut a circle of dough slightly larger than the guide. Remove the guide and the excess scraps of dough. Fold the edge of the circle back onto itself by about ¼ inch and pinch the dough together with your fingers. The edge should be higher than the rest of the dough circle. Now pinch this edge between the thumb and forefinger of both hands to create a V-shaped pattern all the way around the edge of the tart. This edge allows the dough to act as its own tart pan. If the dough becomes too soft, return it to the refrigerator for 20 minutes, then continue. Dock the dough with a fork. Place the tart shell on the baking sheet in the oven and bake until evenly light golden brown, about 25 minutes.

Fold the edge of the circle back onto itself by about ¼ inch.

Pinch the dough together with your fingers to create a high edge around the circle.

Pinch the raised edge between the thumb and forefinger of both hands to create a V-shaped pattern all the way around the tart.

continued

Remove the tart shell from the oven and cool on a wire rack. When completely cooled, slide the tart shell onto a flat platter or cake circle. Use an offset spatula to spread a ¼-inch-thick layer of the flavored pastry cream all the way to the fluted sides of the tart shell.

Set one strawberry aside and hull and halve the rest. Hull the whole berry and set it tip up at the center of the tart. Place the berry halves by leaning them tip up against the whole berry. Continue placing the berry halves in this concentric circle pattern to the edge of the tart.

Prepare the apricot glaze as directed in the recipe and use a pastry brush to apply it to the tart. This will keep the fruit from oxidizing (browning), and it adds a shine to the tart. I use apricot glaze because it does not flavor the tart.

Serve within a few hours, or the tart will get soggy.

Blueberry Peasant Tart

Yield: One 10-inch tart; 8 to 10 servings

This is one of the "lost recipes" from our profession. My dear friend Andre Renard showed me this classic technique that features a sugar, flour, and almond flour mixture under the fruit. It is something that was done by the previous generation of pastry chefs but has been overlooked by my generation. I am grateful for the opportunity to give some of these lost recipes a new audience.

I decided to let Tina try this recipe. We were all on vacation in Bandol one summer. She lost a bet and had to make dessert. I had already made the dough and sent her into the kitchen to finish the tart. When she started to bang on the tart dough, my dad thought she was taking out a wall and went running to stop her. Rap the dough lightly. You're just trying to break up the cold butter.

Pâte Brisée (page 30) or ½ recipe Pâte Sablée (page 32)

Granulated sugar	Scant 2 tablespoons	1 ounce	25 grams
Cake flour	3 tablespoons	1 ounce	25 grams
Almond flour (page 6)	Scant ¼ cup	1 ounce	25 grams
Fresh blueberries, cleaned	2 U.S. dry pints	39 ounces	1,100 grams
Apricot Glaze (page 27)			

Prepare the dough as directed in the recipe. I usually make it in advance to give it time to rest in the refrigerator. This allows any gluten that may have developed time to relax.

Preheat the oven to 375°F (190°C). Remove the dough from the refrigerator. Give the dough a few quick raps with the rolling pin to soften it slightly. This will make it easier to roll. Lightly flour the work surface and each side of the dough. Roll the dough into a 12-inch circle about ¼ inch thick. Transfer the dough to a 10-inch tart pan by rolling it up and around the rolling pin. Unroll the dough over the tart pan. Gently press the dough into the pan, especially where the bottom and the side of the pan meet. Don't forget to press the dough up the side of the pan; this will help the dough hold its shape as it bakes. Remove any excess dough by rolling the rolling pin over the top of the pan to make a nice clean cut. Lightly dock the bottom of the tart shell with a fork.

continued

Combine the sugar and both flours in a small mixing bowl. Spread this mixture evenly over the bottom of the tart shell. Cover with the fresh blueberries. The blueberries should fill the tart shell completely. Remember, they will shrink as they bake and release their juice. The sugar/flour mixture will hold all of the juice. This keeps the tart from becoming soggy and creates a tasty filling. Place the tart on a baking sheet in the oven. Bake until the dough around the edge of the tart is evenly golden brown, about 35 minutes. The blueberries will look wet and some may burst during baking. Remove from the oven and cool the tart on a wire rack.

To unmold, simply push up the bottom of the tart pan and remove the side. Use a flat metal spatula to slide the tart onto a flat plate or platter. (If you use a plate with a slightly raised edge, the tart will break.) If your tart pan does not have a removable bottom, you will need to invert the tart to remove the pan. To do this, invert a flat plate over the cooled tart. Place one hand on each side, grasping both plate and tart pan, and flip both over so the tart pan is now on top. Gently lift off the tart pan. Invert a second flat plate over the bottom of the tart. Once again, flip both plates so that the tart is upright. Remove the top plate.

Prepare the apricot glaze as directed in the recipe and use a pastry brush to apply it to the tart. This will add shine to the tart and keep it looking fresh.

I like to serve this tart slightly warm, with a scoop of vanilla ice cream.

Apple Blossom Tart

Yield: One 12-inch tart; 10 servings

When I first heard the phrase "as American as apple pie," I was very intrigued to taste that dessert. I have to admit, sometimes I really crave the double-crust cinnamon flavor of what I have come to know as American apple pie. My twist on the recipe is a little more technical and lighter. Rarely do you find a tart in this country made with puff pastry, and I like the flower pattern, too. This is my salute to American pie.

½ recipe **Classic Puff Pastry (page 33)**			
¼ recipe **Pastry Cream (page 20)**			
5 Granny Smith apples			
Light corn syrup	3 tablespoons	2 ounces	60 grams
Water	1 teaspoon	0.2 ounce	8 grams
Apricot Glaze (page 27)			

Prepare the puff pastry as directed in the recipe but do not bake it. You can also use store-bought puff pastry. Divide the puff pastry in half and store both halves in the refrigerator until ready to use.

Prepare the pastry cream as directed in the recipe and let it cool. Store in the refrigerator, covered with plastic wrap, until ready to use.

Preheat the oven to 400°F (204°C). Remove one of the puff pastry pieces from the refrigerator. Lightly flour the work surface and each side of the puff pastry. Roll the dough into a 12-inch square about ¼ inch thick. Transfer the puff pastry to a parchment paper–covered baking sheet by rolling it up and around the rolling pin. Unroll the puff pastry onto the baking sheet. Place a 10-inch plate lightly on top of the dough. Use a sharp knife to cut a fluted edge around the plate, keeping in mind the size of the cutter you will use in the next step. The design should resemble a flower when finished. Gently lift off the plate and discard the puff pastry scraps.

Remove the second piece of puff pastry from the refrigerator and lightly flour each side. Roll the dough into a rectangle about ¼ inch thick. Use a 3-inch fluted cutter to cut half circles from the dough, which will become the petals of the flower: Start at the bottom left-hand corner of the rectangle and press the top half of the round cutter into the dough, making sure to cut all the way through the dough while creating a half-circle shape. Lift the cutter, move it up one inch, and repeat the cut. Cut out as many as you need.

Use a pastry brush to lightly brush the fluted edge of the tart with water and adhere the half circles to the tart. This decorative touch is also functional. The half circles give the tart a raised edge when baked.

Use an offset spatula to spread a ¼-inch-thick layer of pastry cream over the center of the tart.

Peel, halve, and core the apples. Use a sharp paring knife to cut each into ⅛-inch-thick slices. Arrange the slices in a concentric circle around the tart, starting at the edge and working toward the center. Place the tart in the oven and bake for about 15 minutes. Remove the tart from the oven. Combine the corn syrup and water in a small bowl and brush the entire tart with this mixture. This will make the tart shiny and sweeter. Return the tart to the oven and finish baking, about another 15 minutes. The finished tart should be evenly light golden brown. The fluted sides should be well risen, and the bottom of the tart should be evenly baked. Place the baked tart on a wire rack and let cool completely.

Prepare the apricot glaze as directed in the recipe and use a pastry brush to apply it to the tart. This will keep the fruit from oxidizing (browning) and add shine to the tart.

Variation: If you would like to make a healthier alternative, substitute applesauce for the pastry cream. You can buy it or make it.

Francisco's Banana Walnut Tart

Yield: One 10-inch tart; 8 to 10 servings

This recipe was developed by my colleague Francisco Gutierrez. He has worked at Le Cirque for the last eighteen years, making tarts with the best ingredients available during the season. As far as I'm concerned, he makes the best tarts in town. One day we had a lot of extra walnut mix from the soufflé recipes. Francisco added some bananas and some almond cream and created this tart. We feature it at the restaurant and it is always one of the most popular tart specials on the menu.

I like to use a tart pan with a removable bottom for this tart.

For the crust

Pâte Brisée (page 30) or ½ recipe Pâte Sablée (page 32)

For the caramel-walnut base

Granulated sugar	**Scant 1 cup**	**7 ounces**	**200 grams**
Heavy cream	**Scant ½ cup**	**3.5 ounces**	**100 grams**
Whole milk	**Scant ½ cup**	**3.5 ounces**	**100 grams**
Walnuts, chopped	**About 1¾ cups**	**7 ounces**	**200 grams**

For the filling

½ recipe Almond Cream (page 23)

4 to 5 large ripe bananas

To finish the tart

Powdered sugar for dusting or Apricot Glaze (page 27)

Prepare the crust: Make the dough as directed in the recipe. I like to make this well in advance to give it time to rest in the refrigerator. This will allow any gluten that may have developed time to relax.

Prepare the caramel-walnut base: Pour the granulated sugar into a 2-quart heavy-bottomed saucepan and place over medium-high heat. Cook, stirring occasionally with a wooden spoon, until the sugar melts and turns a light caramel color. Watch it carefully; once the sugar begins to caramelize, it can burn very quickly. When the sugar has melted and has turned a light golden brown color, slowly and carefully add the heavy cream. The addition

of the cold cream to the hot caramel will cause the mixture to hiss and possibly splatter, so do not lean over the saucepan while you are adding it. When all of the cream has been added, mix thoroughly with a wooden spoon. Remember to mix into the edge of the saucepan where the caramel can stick. Add the milk and mix thoroughly. Add the chopped walnuts and mix until well combined and the walnuts are evenly dispersed. Insert a candy thermometer and cook over medium-high heat until the mixture reaches 225°F (110°C). At this point, the caramel will have thickened and darkened slightly. Remove the saucepan from the heat and pour the filling into a heatproof bowl. Let cool. (This recipe amount yields more than needed for one tart and can be stored in the refrigerator, tightly covered with plastic wrap, for several weeks. I like to eat it on toast for breakfast!)

Prepare the filling: Make the almond cream as directed in the recipe. Sometimes I like to add a splash of dark rum for extra flavor. You will use the almond cream right away, so there is no need to refrigerate it. If using refrigerated almond cream, allow it to return to room temperature. Beat it with an electric mixer set on medium-high speed until it returns to its original volume and is once again light in color.

Preheat the oven to 375°F (190°C).

Assemble the tart: Remove the dough from the refrigerator. Lightly give the dough a few quick raps with the rolling pin to soften it slightly. This will make it easier to roll. Lightly flour the work surface and each side of the dough. Roll the dough into a 12-inch circle about ¼ inch thick. Transfer the dough to a 10-inch tart pan by rolling it around the rolling pin. Unroll the dough over the tart pan. Gently press the dough into the pan, especially where the bottom and the side of the pan meet. Don't forget to press the dough up the side of the pan; this will help the dough hold its shape as it bakes. Remove any excess dough by rolling the rolling pin over the top of the pan to make a nice clean cut. Dock the bottom of the tart shell with a fork.

Spread about a ¼-inch-thick layer of almond cream in the bottom of the tart shell. Peel the bananas and cut them into ¼-inch-thick slices. Arrange the banana slices in concentric circles, starting at the edge of the tart shell and working your way toward the center. Leave about a 2-inch-diameter circle in the center of the tart. Fill this circle with the caramel-walnut mixture. Sometimes I like to sprinkle granulated sugar over the tart just before baking; this gives the bananas a nice crust.

Bake the tart until light golden brown and the filling forms a light crust, about 45 minutes. Remove from the oven and place on a wire rack until the tart has completely cooled.

Unmold the tart: Simply push up on the bottom of the tart pan and remove the side. Use a flat metal spatula to slide the tart onto a flat plate or platter. (If you use a plate with slightly raised edges, the tart will break.) If you did not use a tart pan with a removable bottom, you will need to invert the tart to remove the pan. To do this, invert a flat plate over the cooled tart. Place one hand on each side, grasping both plate and tart pan, and flip them both over so that the tart pan is now on top. Gently lift off the tart pan. Invert a second flat plate over the bottom of the tart. Once again, flip both plates so that the tart is upright. Remove the first plate.

You can lightly dust the tart with powdered sugar before serving or top with apricot glaze. If you use apricot glaze, prepare it as directed in the recipe and brush it onto the tart with a pastry brush.

Variations: This tart can also be made with peaches, apples, apricots, or figs. (Peel and core the apples. Pit the peaches or apricots. Slice the apples, peaches, apricots, or figs.) When I have a little more time, I poach some pears (peeled and cored) in 1 quart (32 ounces; 1 liter) of water with 1 cup (7 ounces; 200 grams) of granulated sugar, 2 scraped vanilla beans, the juice of 1 lemon, and the grated zest of 1 lemon. I bring them to a gentle simmer over medium-low heat until tender. Before adding the cooled poached pears to the tart, I drain them on a wire rack placed over a parchment paper–covered baking sheet. Then I slice them and arrange them on the tart.

Linzer Tart

Yield: One 10-inch tart; 8 to 10 servings

I find the Linzer tart dough to be similar to the English shortbread dough. We don't make this tart very often in the South of France. It is made more often in places where fruit is canned. The technique in this recipe is interesting because of the use of hard-boiled egg yolks. The fat is not liquid and does not combine with the flour in the same way as when you use raw eggs. This makes the dough more crumbly.

Linda's Red Raspberry Jam (page 26)	1 cup	14 ounces	400 grams
For the dough			
6 large hard-boiled egg yolks			
Cake flour	2 cups	10.5 ounces	300 grams

Almond flour (page 6)	½ cup	1.8 ounces	50 grams
Powdered sugar	Scant ½ cup	1.8 ounces	50 grams
Ground cinnamon	2 teaspoons	0.175 ounce	5 grams
Dark rum	1½ tablespoons	0.6 ounce	15 grams
Cold unsalted butter	1¼ cups	10 ounces	280 grams

Prepare the jam as directed in the recipe. You can set aside the amount needed for this recipe and let cool. Can the rest.

Prepare the dough: Pass the yolks through a fine-mesh sieve into a medium-size mixing bowl. Add the cake flour, almond flour, sugar, cinnamon, rum, and butter to the bowl. Beat with an electric mixer set on medium speed just until the ingredients hold together in a dough, about 1 minute. You can also do this by hand by simply kneading everything together. In either case, do not overmix, or the dough will be too stiff. You want the dough

to look and feel like wet sand. Turn the dough out onto a lightly floured work surface and knead gently by hand until smooth, about 15 seconds. Pat the dough into a disk and place it in the refrigerator for a few hours to let it rest. This will allow any gluten that may have developed to relax.

Preheat the oven to 375°F (190°C). Remove the dough from the refrigerator and divide it into two pieces, one twice the size of the other. Keep the smaller piece in the refrigerator until ready to use. Give the larger piece a few quick raps with the rolling pin to soften the dough slightly. This will make it easier to roll. Lightly flour the work surface and each side of the dough. Roll the dough into a 12-inch circle about ¼ inch thick. Transfer the dough to a 10-inch tart pan by rolling it around the rolling pin. Unroll the dough over the tart pan. Gently press the dough into the pan, especially where the bottom and the side of the pan meet. Don't forget to press the dough up the side of the pan. This will help the dough hold its shape as it bakes. Remove any excess dough by rolling the rolling pin over the top of the pan to make a nice clean cut. Use a fork to dock the bottom of the tart shell. Spread the raspberry jam in a ¼-inch-thick layer over the bottom of the tart shell. Set aside while you roll and cut the top.

Remove the smaller piece of dough from the refrigerator and pat it into a rectangle. Give the dough a few quick raps with the rolling pin. Roll this piece into a 7½ × 11-inch rectangle. Use a sharp paring knife to cut 10 equal strips from the dough. Your finished tart will look nicer if all of the strips are the same width. Lay five evenly spaced strips diagonally across the filled tart. Next lay another five strips in the opposite direction across the filled tart. The top of the tart should have a criss-cross pattern. Remove any excess dough by rolling the rolling pin over the top of the pan to make nice clean cuts. Pat the scraps into a small disk and let rest. I like to use the scraps to make small tarts. Place the tart in the oven and bake until evenly golden brown, about 40 minutes. It can be hard to determine the finished color on the tart because the dough is quite dark. You will be able to smell the baked tart when it is ready. Cool on a wire rack before serving.

To unmold the tart, simply push up on the bottom of the pan and release the sides. Use an offset spatula to slide the tart off the tart pan bottom onto a flat plate or platter. If you did not use a tart pan with a removable bottom, you will need to invert the tart to remove the pan. To do this, invert a flat plate over the cooled tart. Place one hand on each side, grasping both plate and tart pan, and flip them both over so that the tart pan is on top. Gently lift off the tart pan. Invert a second flat plate over the bottom of the tart. Once again, flip both plates so that the tart is upright. Remove the first plate. This tart is great when served slightly warm, dusted with powdered sugar.

Practically Good
for You

This chapter is for anyone who needs to rationalize eating dessert. If you want something light or you are watching your weight, you don't have to eat something flavorless. There are many different options for dessert. This chapter includes everything from simple fruit soups to more elaborate presentations like the Paul Bocuse Papillote. If someone in your family is allergic to nuts, or can't eat dairy, there is probably an alternative in this group. When customers at the restaurant ask for fruit plates, it inspires me to be more imaginative in my offerings. There are opportunities to practice techniques in this chapter, but for the most part, all the desserts are easy to make. Look here when you have to entertain a crowd.

Exotic Mint Soup

Yield: 6 to 8 servings

There's a place outside Traverse City, Michigan, where Kris and I love to go camping. It is a beautiful spot with a gorgeous stream that runs under the trees. One day we were watching hummingbirds dart over the wetland when I thought I smelled mint. I looked down at my feet and saw mint growing all along the edge of the wetland. My nature guru, Gary O'Connell, explained that the plant was native to the area. That night we drank mint tea around the campfire, and I decided to try this recipe when I returned to the restaurant.

This is a very refreshing course that can be served as a dessert or as a predessert. It is good to serve as a predessert with a light meal or as a full dessert after a very heavy meal. This is also a healthy dessert for anyone who is trying to cut down on fat.

For the soup base

Cold water	3½ cups	28 ounces	800 grams
Granulated sugar	¾ cup + 1 tablespoon	6.2 ounces	175 grams
Juice of 2 limes, strained			
Juice of 1 orange, strained			
Grated zest of 2 limes			
Grated zest of 1 orange			
½ vanilla bean			
Handful of fresh mint leaves, cleaned			

To finish the soup

1 ripe papaya, peeled and seeded

1 ripe kiwifruit, peeled

1 ripe pineapple, peeled and cored

1 ripe mango, peeled and pitted

1 ripe banana, peeled

Combine the water, sugar, fruit juices, and zests in a nonreactive 2-quart heavy-bottomed saucepan and place over medium-high heat. Use a sharp knife to slice the vanilla bean in half again, this time lengthwise. Separate the seeds from the skin by scraping the blade of the knife along the inside of the bean. Add the seeds and skin to the mixture and bring it to a boil. Remove the saucepan from the heat and add the fresh mint. Cover with a lid or plastic wrap and let the mixture stand for about 5 minutes to allow the flavor of the mint to infuse into the soup base. If you allow the mint to remain in the soup longer than 5 minutes, the flavor will be too strong and could become bitter.

Strain the mixture through a fine-mesh sieve into a bowl placed over a larger bowl filled with ice cubes. Cool, stirring occasionally. Place the mixture in the refrigerator, covered with plastic wrap, until ready to use. (At this point, the soup base can be stored in the refrigerator for up to 1 week.)

Shortly before serving the soup, dice the fresh fruit into ½-inch cubes. If you try to keep the pieces all the same size, your finished dish will look nicer. I like to use kiwifruit for the beautiful color it adds to the soup.

When ready to serve, evenly distribute the soup base among the soup bowls. (To serve a larger number of people, use espresso or cappuccino cups instead of soup bowls.) Sprinkle in the diced fruit. Sometimes I garnish the soup with a scoop of sorbet or a Caramel Grid (page 57).

A ripe mango should be slightly soft when gently squeezed and usually has some nice red color in the peel. Here's an easy way to pit and peel a mango. Find the flat side of the fruit and insert a knife near the stem so the blade is parallel to the pit. The mango pit is oblong and flat with a slight rise through the middle. Use the pit to guide the knife as you slice the mango in half. Set aside the pitted half. Use the same method to cut around the pit in the other half. Place the mango halves cut side down. Use a very sharp paring knife to remove the peel. You will be able to anchor the mango half with your fingers while you are shaving off the peel.

Exotic Mint Soup (page 54) with Caramel Grid (page 57) and Strawberry Rhubarb Soup (page 59)

Caramel Grid

Yield: 16 to 20 grids

This is an old technique used by pastry chefs to make decorations for desserts. It looks impressive but is actually quite easy to do at home. It is edible, but you are more likely to use it as a decoration. Be sure the sugar you use is very clean. If there are any foreign particles (like dust) in it, the sugar will crystallize. To be safe, start with a brand-new bag of sugar. Sugar does not like humidity, so you usually make this within a few hours of the time you will use it. Try to work with sugar on a dry day. If it is rainy or humid, the sugar will be very sticky and will actually melt.

Water	Scant ½ cup	3.5 ounces	100 grams
Granulated sugar	Generous 2¼ cups	18 ounces	500 grams
Light corn syrup	Scant ⅔ cup	7 ounces	200 grams

Place the water, sugar, and corn syrup in a 2-quart heavy-bottomed saucepan over medium-high heat. The corn syrup will make the cooked sugar harder and crunchier. It will also help prevent the cooked sugar from melting as quickly due to the humidity in the air. Insert a candy thermometer and cook the sugar mixture to 311°F (155°C), what is known as the hard crack stage (page 14). Stir the sugar gently and slowly as it cooks to ensure that it cooks evenly. If you do not stir it, the mixture will have hot spots where the sugar will cook faster than in the rest of the mixture. Use a pastry brush to keep the inside of the saucepan clean as the sugar cooks, or the sugar may recrystallize. To do this, dip a clean brush in cold water and brush the inside of the pan clean.

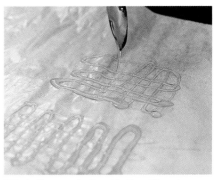

Drizzle the sugar back and forth until you have created the desired pattern.

Remove the cooked sugar from the heat and pour into a medium-size heatproof glass bowl. The glass bowl will hold the temperature and stop the cooking process. It will also allow you to reheat the sugar in the microwave, if necessary. If you leave the sugar in the saucepan, the sugar will continue to cook and turn dark brown. Stir the hot sugar occasionally to keep it from becoming too dark as it cools. Scrape the sides into the middle to keep the temperature even, as the sides cool down more quickly than the center. I put a towel under the bowl to keep it from tipping over and to protect my hands from the heat of the glass.

Spray a sheet of parchment paper or a marble surface lightly with vegetable cooking spray. Dip a stainless-steel spoon into the bowl of hot sugar and make a grid on the work surface by allowing the sugar to drip off the spoon. You can use this technique to make any design or trace any pattern. Continue to dip the spoon and drizzle the sugar back and forth until you have created the desired pattern. Be careful that you do not make your grid lines too thick. You should be able to see the paper between the lines. Let the grid cool for a few minutes before you attempt to lift it. Gently peel off the paper or, if you are working on marble, just lift the grid. Place the grid over your dessert.

It is easy to make other designs like butterflies. If you are not comfortable drawing them freehand, place a drawing under a piece of acetate (page 2) and trace the design with the sugar.

When cooking the sugar, it is very important to keep the side of the pan clean. We start with sugar in the crystallized form. When heated, it melts. If the melted sugar comes in contact with crystallized sugar, it can cause the melted sugar to recrystallize.

Strawberry Rhubarb Soup

Yield: 8 to 10 servings

discovered rhubarb during my apprenticeship. My boss brought in beautiful stalks of something I thought looked like red celery. I took a big bite and learned that rhubarb needs a little help to be really good. We placed the chopped fresh rhubarb in large pails and liberally sprinkled them with sugar. Overnight, the rhubarb pieces absorbed the sugar. The next day, we made the most fabulous rhubarb tarts.

This is an easy dessert to make on Sunday afternoon. It does not take a lot of time or any fancy ingredients. The end result is very light, which also makes it a great dessert to serve in the summer. This soup is best when served very cold. Use more or less rhubarb depending on your taste.

5 to 8 fresh rhubarb stalks			
Water	**3½ cups**	**28 ounces**	**800 grams**
Granulated sugar	**1 cup + 2 tablespoons**	**9 ounces**	**250 grams**
Juice of 2 limes, strained			
2 vanilla beans			
Fresh strawberries, cleaned	**About 4 cups**	**18 ounces**	**500 grams**

Prepare the rhubarb. Clean the stems well to remove some of the fiber so the rhubarb will not be tough and stringy. I like to clean the rhubarb by using a clean scrubbing sponge to "scrub" off some of the fiber. If you use a sharp paring knife to peel off the outer skin, you will remove all of the color from the rhubarb. Use a sharp paring knife to cut the rhubarb into ½-inch-thick slices. This will ensure that the fruit cooks evenly.

Pour the water into a nonreactive 4-quart heavy-bottomed saucepan and place over medium-high heat. Add the sugar and lime juice and stir. Use a sharp knife to slice the vanilla beans in half lengthwise. Separate the seeds from the skins by scraping the blade of the knife along the inside of the beans. Add the seeds and skins to the mixture. If you can't find vanilla beans, you can use 1 tablespoon of vanilla extract, but the beans will give the soup more flavor. Add the rhubarb pieces to the soup base and stir with a rubber spatula. I don't use a wooden spoon because it will smash the fruit when it begins to soften. Let the mixture continue to cook until it reaches a boil, about 5 minutes. You want to allow the rhubarb time to cook slightly and soften before you add the strawberries. While you are waiting for the mixture to boil, hull and halve the strawberries. When the mixture comes to a boil, drop in the berries and gently shake the saucepan to stir. Remove the saucepan from the heat and let the soup cool. As the soup cools, the fruit will continue to cook. (At this point, you can pour the soup into an airtight container and store it in the refrigerator for up to 3 days.) I usually refrigerate the soup overnight to allow the fruit time to give its color to the soup. I also prefer to serve it cold and, sometimes, with a scoop of vanilla ice cream.

Rhubarb is actually a vegetable that has medicinal properties. When cooking with it, do not use the leaves. The greens contain injurious amounts of oxalic acid.

Here's a trick for safe slicing: Curve your fingers until your fingertips are perpendicular with your knuckles. Then use your fingertips to hold the rhubarb. Hold the knife so that the flat side of the blade slightly rests against your fingers between the first and second knuckles. Allow your knuckles to guide the knife as you make the slices. Do not lift the knife up above your knuckles. Remember to keep the flat side of the blade of the knife straight so you do not cut your knuckles.

Wine-Poached Pears

Yield: 4 servings

Fruit poached in wine is something we do a lot of in France for a buffet like Sunday brunch. It is usually served cold, but you can also serve it warm. My friend Dorothy Cann Hamilton is very knowledgeable about wine and suggests that I use Rhône Valley wine for this recipe. This is a strong wine with a lot of flavor. I like to use Bosc pears because the firm texture makes them a good poaching fruit. These pears don't fall apart when poached.

Strong, dry red wine	6⅔ cups	53 ounces	1,500 grams
Granulated sugar	Generous 1¼ cups	10.5 ounces	300 grams
Pinch of ground cinnamon			
Grated zest of 1½ lemons			
1½ vanilla beans			
4 ripe Bosc pears			
For the wine jelly glaze			
Powdered pectin or Sure-Jell	4 teaspoons	0.75 ounce	20 grams
Granulated sugar	4 teaspoons	0.75 ounce	20 grams
Wine poaching liquid, strained	1¼ cups	10.5 ounces	300 grams

Pour the wine, sugar, cinnamon, and lemon zest into a nonreactive 4-quart heavy-bottomed saucepan and place over medium-high heat. Use a sharp knife to slice the vanilla beans in half lengthwise. Separate the seeds from the skins by scraping the blade of the knife along the inside of the beans. Add the seeds and skins to the mixture and continue heating.

Peel and core the pears, but do not halve them. Coring the pears from the bottom will encourage the poaching liquid to seep inside the pears. This way, they cook evenly inside and out when poached. Add the pears to the heating wine mixture and bring to a boil. When it reaches a boil, reduce the heat to a simmer and let cook for about 1 hour. As the wine boils and simmers, the alcohol will evaporate but the flavor will penetrate the fruit. I usually make a parchment paper lid to cover the poaching pears. This keeps the pears immersed in the liquid and helps them poach evenly. To make the lid, cut a round disk that is slightly smaller than the diameter of your pan from a sheet of parchment paper.

continued

Place the paper lid directly on top of the pears and poaching liquid. Do not overcook the pears; they should be soft enough to pierce easily with a wooden skewer or toothpick.

When the pears are fully poached, pour them and the poaching liquid into a clean container. The pears can stay in the poaching liquid in the refrigerator for up to 3 days. Each day they will become more flavorful and colorful.

A few hours before serving, remove the pears from the poaching liquid and drain them on a wire rack placed over a parchment paper–covered baking sheet. You will need one whole pear for each serving.

Prepare the wine jelly glaze: Combine the powdered pectin or Sure-Jell and sugar in a small bowl. Pour the poaching liquid into a nonreactive 1-quart heavy-bottomed saucepan and place over medium-high heat. Add the sugar mixture and stir gently. Allow the mixture to come to a boil, whisking occasionally. At the boil, reduce the heat to a simmer and cook for a couple of minutes, until it thickens slightly. Pour the glaze into a clean bowl. The glaze should be warm when you use it. I like to store my glaze in a squeeze bottle in the refrigerator. It will keep for up to 2 weeks. When I need it, I put it in the microwave on high power for 20 seconds, until it liquefies.

To finish the dessert, halve each pear and cut each half into slices that are about ½ inch thick. Fan the slices on a plate and coat them with wine jelly glaze. If your glaze is in a squeeze bottle, just drizzle it onto the slices; you can also use a pastry brush. To add some color to the plate, sometimes I sprinkle it with some diced fresh fruit like kiwifruit and mango. You could also present the pears whole on a platter.

Strawberries on a Cloud

Yield: One 10-inch tube cake; 8 servings

I imagine the cake used in this recipe is called angel food because it is as light as the cloud on which an angel might rest. Angel food cake is an especially great alternative for anyone who is trying to cut down on fat, and with desserts that is often hard to do. This cake recipe contains no egg yolks or butter, so it has no fat.

It is very important that you use a tube pan for this cake. The center tube keeps the cake from collapsing while it cools.

For the angel food cake

Cake flour	I cup	5.5 ounces	150 grams
Powdered sugar	⅔ cup	2.6 ounces	75 grams
Granulated sugar	¾ cup	5.5 ounces	150 grams
Salt	I teaspoon	0.175 ounce	5 grams
Cream of tartar	I teaspoon	0.175 ounce	5 grams
10 large egg whites			
Splash of vanilla extract			
Grated zest of I lemon or lime			

For the pan-roasted strawberries

Unsalted butter	About ½ cup	4 ounces	113 grams
24 large fresh strawberries, cleaned but not hulled			
Granulated sugar	¼ cup	1.9 ounces	55 grams
I vanilla bean, scraped			
Stoli Strasberi vodka	¼ cup	1.75 ounces	50 grams
Juice of ½ lemon, strained			

Prepare the angel food cake: Preheat the oven to 350°F (176°C). Sift the flour and powdered sugar together onto a sheet of parchment paper and set aside.

Combine the granulated sugar, salt, and cream of tartar in a small mixing bowl. Place the egg whites in a medium-size mixing bowl and begin to whip with an electric mixer set on medium speed. Slowly add the sugar mixture to the whipping whites. Add the vanilla and

zest and continue to whip until the egg whites have reached stiff but not dry peaks, about 5 minutes. They should look smooth and creamy, not separated. Use a rubber spatula to fold in the sifted flour mixture, being careful not to deflate the egg whites. Remember to fold all the way to the bottom of the bowl. Use the rubber spatula to scoop the mixture into the tube pan. Try not to trap any air bubbles in the bottom of the pan as you fill it. Place the cake in the oven and bake until evenly risen and golden brown on top, about 25 minutes.

As soon as you take it out of the oven, invert the pan over the neck of a wine bottle (filled with water to make it more stable) and let cool. When completely cool, remove the cake pan from the wine bottle. Run the blade of a knife around the inside of the pan to loosen the cake from the side. Invert the cake pan onto a platter and allow the cake to drop out of the pan. Gently lift off the pan.

Prepare the strawberries: Immediately before serving the cake, place a medium-size frying pan over medium-high heat. Add the butter and let it begin to melt. Add the strawberries, stir gently, and sauté until all of the butter has melted and completely coated the strawberries. It is okay if the butter begins to boil; just don't let it burn. As the strawberries cook, they begin to soften and release their juice. Add the sugar, vanilla bean seeds, and flavored vodka and continue to cook. I add the lemon juice to enhance the flavor of the strawberries. If you want your sauce to be a little creamier, add a little more butter, sauté for 30 seconds, and serve immediately. When they are soft and while there is still some liquid in the pan, remove the strawberries from the heat. I don't hull the strawberries because I like the color the hulls add to the dessert. Leaving on the hulls also causes the berries to release a little less juice and hold their shape.

Assemble the dessert: Use a serrated knife to slice the angel food cake. Serve each slice with some pan-roasted strawberries. When I am feeling decadent, I like to eat this with pistachio or vanilla ice cream.

Peach Sauté

Yield: 8 servings

This summer I visited my friend Michel Roux. He invited me to his beautiful home in Provence. He took me to the market to show me the local produce and we found some beautiful Provençal peaches. We created this dessert in less than 10 minutes. When peaches are in season, use fresh ripe peaches, peeled and pitted. If you use them when they are still warm from the sun, the flavor will be more intense.

24 canned peeled peach halves, drained, or fresh			
Stoli Persik vodka	⅔ cup	5.5 ounces	150 grams
2 vanilla beans			
Granulated sugar	2 cups	15.5 ounces	440 grams
Unsalted butter	Generous ¼ cup	2.8 ounces	80 grams

continued

Use a sharp paring knife to cut the peaches into quarters. Place the quarters in a small mixing bowl and cover with the vodka. Set aside while you caramelize the sugar.

Use a sharp knife to slice the vanilla beans in half lengthwise. Separate the seeds from the skin by scraping the blade of the knife along the inside of the bean. Add the seeds to the sugar in a small mixing bowl.

Heat a medium-size heavy-bottomed frying pan over medium-high heat. If it starts to smoke, the pan is too hot and you need to run it under cool water, dry it, and start again. When warm, sprinkle the vanilla sugar into the pan. Try to keep the sugar in an even layer to allow it to caramelize at the same time. As soon as you see the sugar begin to melt, start moving the pan over the burner to keep the sugar from burning. Tilt the pan from side to side so that the melted sugar runs over the unmelted sugar. Cook until all of the sugar is a light golden brown. I usually add a tablespoon of butter at this stage because it makes the caramel smoother. Add the peach slices and vodka and spread them evenly in the pan. Sauté over medium-high heat until most of the liquid has evaporated and the peaches are soft.

Spoon the sautéed peaches and any juice into bowls and serve. This dessert is also great topped with vanilla ice cream.

Peaches in Phyllo Pockets

Yield: 8 servings

My friend Drissia inspired me to make this dessert. She owns a restaurant in New York called Café Fès, where she specializes in Moroccan food. My favorite item on her menu is Couscous Royale because it reminds me of a dish my mom makes. The desserts from the desert usually do not contain cream or other ingredients that would spoil in the heat. Drissia knows I am a pastry chef, so I always have to save room for her desserts. For this dessert I use the same technique she uses for her appetizers wrapped in phyllo pockets.

8 sheets phyllo dough (page 13)

Unsalted butter, melted	**1 cup**	**8 ounces**	**226 grams**
Powdered sugar, plus extra for sprinkling	**Scant 2 cups**	**7 ounces**	**200 grams**
Granulated sugar	**Scant ½ cup**	**3.5 ounces**	**100 grams**
Unbleached all-purpose flour	**Scant ¾ cup**	**3.5 ounces**	**100 grams**

20 canned peeled peach halves, drained, or fresh

Preheat the oven to 400°F (204°C).

Lay one sheet of phyllo on your work surface. Keep the remaining phyllo sheets covered with a clean dishcloth to keep them from drying. Use a pastry brush to spread about 2 tablespoons of the melted butter over the entire surface of the phyllo sheet. It will be easier if you start by brushing one line of butter lengthwise down the center and then fill in by brushing top to bottom from the center toward each edge. Remember to brush all the way to the edges, where the phyllo is the driest. Place the powdered sugar in a fine-mesh sieve and liberally sprinkle the buttered phyllo sheet with it. Cover with a second sheet of phyllo and repeat with the butter and powdered sugar. Make three more sets of doubled phyllo sheets in the same way.

Use a sharp paring knife to cut each of the doubled phyllo sheets in half from top to bottom to make eight squares. Cut the corners off each square to shape each more like a circle. Use a pastry brush to spread butter over each circle.

Combine the granulated sugar and flour in a small mixing bowl. Sprinkle the center of each circle with an ⅛-inch-thick layer of the sugar mixture. As it bakes, the sugar mixture will absorb the flavor and moisture of the juice released by the peaches.

Cut each peach half into ¼-inch-thick slices. Lay them in a circle over the sugar mixture. You should be left with about a 2-inch phyllo border all around the slices. Fold the phyllo border into the center, over the peach slices. This should form a round package. Turn the package over and place seam side down on a parchment paper–covered baking sheet. Repeat for the remaining servings. When all of the phyllo packages are assembled and placed on the baking sheet, use a pastry brush to brush the tops with some butter and sprinkle each with a light layer of powdered sugar. Place in the oven and bake until golden brown and crispy, about 15 minutes. Remove from the oven and serve warm.

Fruit in Papillote

Yield: 8 servings

A papillote is like a pocket, and cooking in one is a trick used by cooks. I have adapted it for pastry. The flavor of the fruit is trapped inside the papillote. When you open it, the steam escapes and with it comes the wonderful aroma of the cooked fruit. That is part of the experience with this dessert.

You can use any kind of fruit you like and feel free to make combinations of your favorites. Just remember to use fruit that is about the same texture and ripeness so that it cooks evenly. If you slice the fruit in about the same size pieces, it will cook in about the same time.

4 ripe peaches			
4 ripe nectarines			
4 ripe mangoes			
4 red apples			
2 vanilla beans			
Juice of 2 oranges, strained			
Granulated sugar	1 cup	7.7 ounces	220 grams
Honey	½ cup	4 ounces	120 grams
Unsalted butter	½ cup	4 ounces	120 grams

continued

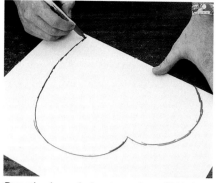

Draw the shape of a heart on a piece of folded parchment. The heart should be tilted to the right slightly, so the bottom half of the heart's left side is on the fold.

Fold in 1-inch increments, folding each subsequent inch over the last third of the preceding inch.

Fold almost all the way around, leaving about a 5-inch opening on the long side of the heart.

Preheat the oven to 400°F (204°C).

Prepare the parchment paper papillote: Fold eight 12×16-inch sheets of parchment paper in half. Place each folded parchment in front of you on a table with the folded side on your left. Use a pen to draw the shape of a heart onto each piece of folded parchment. The heart should be tilted to the right slightly so the bottom half of the left side of the heart is on the fold. Use a pair of scissors to cut the heart from the parchment paper. Starting just above the fold on the left side of the heart, fold the edges together to form a seal. Fold in 1-inch increments, folding each subsequent inch over the last third of the preceding inch. Fold almost all the way around, leaving about a 5-inch opening on the long side of the heart. This is where you will fill the bag. Set the bag on a baking sheet and set aside. Repeat with the remaining sheets of parchment.

Prepare the filling: Peel and pit the peaches, nectarines, and mangoes, and peel and core the apples. Cut each in half. Use a sharp paring knife to slice each half into ¼-inch-thick by 1-inch-long pieces. Place these pieces in a large mixing bowl.

Use a sharp knife to slice the vanilla beans in half lengthwise. Separate the seeds from the skin by scraping the blade of the knife along the inside of the bean. Add the seeds and skins to the fruit mixture and combine. Add the orange juice, sugar, and honey and toss to coat. Gently place some of the mixture inside each parchment papillote, being careful not to tear it. Use all of the fruit mixture. Divide the butter into eight equal pieces and place one piece inside each papillote. Finish folding each papillote closed as described above and check to be sure all the folded edges are well sealed. Place in the oven and bake until the papillotes have puffed up to about twice their original size. Remove the papillotes from the oven and serve them immediately. Cut them open with scissors or a sharp paring knife. The aroma is amazing. Remove the vanilla skins before serving.

When I have extra cake in the refrigerator, I like to serve it with the papillote. Ice cream is also a great addition. You decide.

Variation: If you do not have parchment paper, you can use aluminum foil. Cut a large square of foil and fold it in half. The size does not matter. Just remember, the bigger it is, the more you will feed. Fold two of the open edges about one inch to seal the foil. I also fold the folded edge to give it more strength. Fill the foil package with the fruit, seal the opening, and bake as described.

Paul Bocuse Papillote

Yield: 6 to 8 servings

Paul Bocuse is a culinary icon. He is to the world of professional chefs what Julia Child is to the American public. I had the opportunity to work with him at a special party. He created a fantastic soup that was covered with puff pastry and baked in the oven. The result was magnificent. The soup terrines were topped with beautifully baked puff pastry, and when it was cut open the aroma was heavenly. I've borrowed his idea and created an exotic fruit soup. Be sure to use ripe fresh fruit.

⅓ recipe Classic Puff Pastry (page 33)			
Simple Syrup (page 86)			
1 ripe pineapple			
1 ripe mango			
1 ripe banana			
2 star fruit			
1 passion fruit			
1 ripe kiwifruit			
Juice of 1 lemon, strained			
Grand Marnier	½ cup	4 ounces	120 grams
For the egg wash			
2 large egg yolks			
1 large egg			
Whole milk	¼ cup	1.8 ounces	50 grams

continued

Prepare the puff pastry as described in the recipe. When it is ready to roll, place it on a lightly floured work surface. Use a rolling pin to roll the puff pastry into an 11-inch square. Use an 11-inch plate as a guide to cut a circle from the puff pastry. Remove the scraps and plate and store the puff pastry circle in the refrigerator on a lightly floured baking sheet until ready to use.

Prepare the simple syrup as directed in the recipe and set aside to cool until ready to use.

Preheat the oven to 400°F (204°C).

Use a serrated knife to cut a ¾-inch-thick slice from the top and bottom of the pineapple. Stand the pineapple upright on a cutting board and place the blade of the knife at the top of the pineapple about ¼ inch in from the skin. Use the blade of the knife at a 45-degree angle to cut along the natural curve of the pineapple from top to bottom, slicing off the skin. Repeat until all of the skin is removed. Cut off as many of the eyes as possible. Slice the pineapple in half down the center. You will only need one half. Store the other half in the refrigerator well wrapped in plastic wrap for up to 3 days. Cut the pineapple half in half again down the center and remove the core. Cut the pineapple into ½-inch-thick slices. Place the slices in a large oven-safe soup tureen.

Find the flat side of the mango and insert a knife near the stem so the blade is parallel to the pit. The mango pit is oblong and flat with a slight rise through the middle. Use the pit to guide the knife as you slice the mango in half. Set aside the pitted half. Use the same method to cut around the pit in the other half. Place the mango halves cut side down. Use a very sharp paring knife to remove the peel. You will be able to anchor the mango half with your fingers while you are shaving off the peel. Dice the mango into 1-inch pieces and place them in the soup tureen.

Peel the banana and cut it into ½-inch-thick slices. Add these to the tureen.

You can peel the star fruit but it is not necessary. The hardest thing about peeling this fruit is keeping the star shape. Whatever you decide, cut the star fruit into ½-inch-thick slices and add them to the tureen.

Slice the passion fruit in half and squeeze each half into the tureen. The seeds will drop in, but don't worry; they are very small and full of flavor. The passion fruit juice will add acidity to the soup.

Peel the kiwifruit and cut it into ½-inch-thick slices. Add these to the tureen.

Pour the lemon juice, simple syrup, and Grand Marnier over the fruit. Combine the egg yolks, whole egg, and milk in a small mixing bowl and whisk until smooth. Use a pastry brush to brush the egg wash around the rim of the tureen. This will help the puff pastry adhere to the tureen. Remove the puff pastry circle from the refrigerator and place it over the tureen, covering the top completely. The circle should overlap down the side of the tureen by a couple of inches. Press it tightly against the side of the tureen with the palms of your hands. The puff pastry circle should be tight across the top and down the side of the tureen so that it stays in place while it bakes and rises. Use a pastry brush to brush the egg wash over the top and sides of the puff pastry. This will add shine to the baked puff pastry. Remove the top rack from the oven. Place the tureen in the center of the oven. The puff pastry needs room to rise. Bake until the puff pastry has risen about 4 inches from the rim of the tureen and is golden brown all around, about 20 minutes. Remove from the oven and serve immediately.

To serve, cut the top open using a sharp paring knife and peel apart the puff pastry. Be careful of the steam that is released as soon as you cut into the puff pastry. The puff pastry retains the flavor and aroma of the cooked fruit but is not usually eaten because it does not fully bake. Use a ladle to serve the soup. It tastes great on its own or you can serve it with ice cream or sorbet.

Pâte de Fruit

Yield: About 5 dozen pieces

Pâte de fruit is a very big seller in France at Christmas and throughout the winter. It was originally created at a time when fruit was not available year-round. People made this so they could have a taste of the season whenever they had the urge. This classic treat is found in almost every French pastry shop today. It is good to serve after a heavy meal.

This is an easy recipe to remember: the combined weight of the compote and the apricots must equal the weight of the sugar. The fruit flavor intensifies after a few days.

Chunky applesauce	1 cup	9 ounces	250 grams
Apricots, fresh or canned (and drained), peeled and pitted	1½ cups	9 ounces	250 grams
Granulated sugar, plus extra for dusting	Generous 2¼ cups	18 ounces	500 grams
Fresh raspberries (optional)	About 1 cup	5.5 ounces	150 grams

Pâte de Fruit and Fruit Leather (page 79)

Place the applesauce, apricots, and sugar in a nonreactive 2-quart heavy-bottomed saucepan over medium-high heat. Mix together, then add the raspberries. The raspberries will dominate the flavor. If you want apricot-flavored *pâte de fruit,* omit the raspberries. Use a hand-held immersion blender or whisk to combine all of the ingredients until smooth and homogenous. As the mixture cooks, the natural pectin in the fruit will cause the mixture to thicken. Continue to cook the mixture until it is thick, mixing constantly. To test it for the correct consistency, dip a whisk in the mixture and hold it horizontally in front of you. Watch as the mixture drips off the whisk and back into the pan. If the mixture stays on the whisk and beads up into small balls, like pearls, it is ready. If it drips back into the pan in thin strands, it needs to be cooked a little longer.

When the mixture is ready, pour it into a 10-inch bottomless tart mold or cake ring placed on a parchment paper–covered baking sheet. Let the *pâte de fruit* cool and set, about 3 hours at room temperature. If the *pâte de fruit* appears slightly soft after cooling, return it to the saucepan and boil another few minutes, then cool as directed.

continued

To unmold, run a sharp paring knife between the pâte de fruit and the side of the mold. Lift off the mold. (At this point the *pâte de fruit* can be stored, well wrapped in plastic wrap and in an airtight container, for up to 4 weeks.) Sprinkle the top of the *pâte de fruit* with a thin layer of granulated sugar and flip it over onto another sheet of parchment paper. Remove the parchment that is now on top. Sprinkle this side with more sugar. Use a wet chef's knife to cut the disk into strips and then into squares. Cut these as large or as small as you like. Traditionally, it is served in 1-inch squares. You will probably need to stop cutting and clean the knife after every few cuts. The *pâte de fruit* is very sticky and will be easier to cut with a clean knife. Roll each square completely in sugar and serve.

Do not store it in the refrigerator where the humidity will make the sugar melt.

Variation: Substitute an equal amount of hulled and sliced strawberries, or the juice of 1 large lemon, instead of the raspberries to flavor.

Fruit Leather and Ravioli

Yield: 4 fruit roll-ups or 20 ravioli

When I first met Kris, she used to buy Fruit Roll-Ups all the time. I didn't really know what she was eating because I didn't recognize it by color or texture. When we finally talked about it, she was very excited to learn that I could make these treats using all of her favorite fresh fruits. She was also happy to know that the thickness could be adjusted because the ones she was buying were paper thin!

    I took the recipe one step further by creating the ravioli. Either way, it is a great treat to share with the fruit lovers in your family.

For the fruit leather

Strawberry puree	I cup	9 ounces	250 grams
Juice of ½ lemon, strained			
Granulated sugar	I cup + 2 tablespoons	9 ounces	250 grams
Powdered pectin or Sure-Jell	¼ cup	1.5 ounces	35 grams

For the ravioli filling

Mascarpone cheese	I cup	9 ounces	250 grams
Grated zest of ½ lemon			
Granulated sugar	3 tablespoons	1.6 ounces	40 grams

To garnish the ravioli

Raspberry Sauce (page 24)

Mango Sauce (page 24)

Prepare the fruit leather: Combine the strawberry puree and lemon juice in a nonreactive 2-quart heavy-bottomed saucepan and place over medium-high heat. Combine the sugar and pectin and add to the puree. Whisk well to combine. Allow the mixture to come to a boil while whisking constantly and continue to boil for 3 minutes. Remove the mixture from the heat and pour it onto a 16 × 24-inch sheet of parchment paper that has been lightly sprayed with vegetable cooking spray. Use a large offset spatula to spread the mixture evenly over the sheet of parchment paper. When spread, it will be quite thin. You should almost be able to see through the fruit leather. Set aside to cool. It cools very

Fruit Leather Ravioli (page 79)

quickly and develops a skin. If you just want fruit roll-ups, cut the leather into the size you prefer and simply roll one end into the other, peeling off the parchment paper as you roll.

Prepare the ravioli and filling: Combine the mascarpone, lemon zest, and sugar in a medium-size mixing bowl. Use a spoon to mix until softened and combined.

Use a 3-inch fluted cutter to cut circles from the cooled fruit leather. You will need one circle for each ravioli, so cut as many circles as you would like. Remove the circles from the parchment paper and set on a clean plate or parchment paper–covered baking sheet. Fill the center of each fruit circle with about a teaspoon of the mascarpone mixture. Fold the circle in half and seal by pressing the edges together with your fingers. Place three to five on a plate and serve the ravioli garnished with raspberry and mango sauce or some diced fresh fruit if you prefer.

Meringue Treats

Yield: About 175 assorted treats or 6 large scoops

France is certainly known for having a bakery on every street corner, and baked meringues are a favorite. The bakers prepare the meringues and place them in the ovens right before they go home. The ovens are off, but because they are so big and have been in use all night, they hold their heat. When the bakers return the next evening, the meringues are baked from the ovens' residual heat. The process of baking meringue is really to dry it.

If you want the meringue to dry and be very crispy when you bake it, use twice as much sugar as egg whites. Traditionally, all the granulated sugar is added to the whipping egg whites. When that happens, the meringue is heavier because the more dry elements it contains, the heavier it will be. I only add half the amount of sugar to the whipping whites, and at the end I gently fold in the powdered sugar. This helps keep the meringue light.

4 large egg whites			
Granulated sugar	Generous ½ cup	4 ounces	120 grams
Powdered sugar, sifted, plus extra for dusting	1 cup	4 ounces	120 grams

continued

Meringue Treats filled with Lemon Curd and topped with maraschino cherries

Preheat the oven to 220°F (104°C).

Place the egg whites in a large mixing bowl and whip with an electric mixer set on medium speed until foamy. Make a French meringue by adding the granulated sugar 1 tablespoon at a time. Adding the sugar slowly allows the whites to gain some volume and the sugar to dissolve into the whites. When you have volume, add the rest of the granulated sugar. Increase the mixer speed to medium-high and whip to stiff but not dry peaks, about 5 minutes. When the whites are stiff, reduce the mixer speed to low to allow more air to incorporate without overwhipping the egg whites. Continue to whip for about another 2 minutes. Stop whipping if the egg whites look dry or separated. Fold in the powdered sugar all at once. Fold gently so you don't lose too much volume.

Pipe the meringue: Now you can get creative with your piping skills. You will need a parchment paper–covered baking sheet. Here are some of my favorite designs. Place the meringue in a pastry bag fitted with a ¼-inch star tip. If you do not own a pastry bag, use a large resealable plastic bag. Cut off one of the bottom corners. Fill the bag, seal it, and you are ready to pipe from your homemade bag. Hold the pastry bag at a slight angle with the tip almost touching the parchment paper–covered baking sheet. Pipe ¾-inch-diameter hollow circles, spaced 1 inch apart, onto the baking sheet. As you pipe the rings, give each a second layer of meringue to give them some height.

Small mounds are another easy design to make. Simply pipe 1-inch mounds by holding the pastry bag at a slight angle while allowing the tip to touch the parchment. Squeeze to form the mound. Stop squeezing and lift the tip straight up, leaving a small tail on the top of each mound. These will look nicer when displayed if you try to keep them all the same size.

Another classical design is a backward S. You may have to practice to master the technique of making an even S shape. Try not to make them longer than 2 inches. If this is too bothersome, pipe straight lines that are about 3 inches long.

To pipe shells, place the tip of the pastry bag on the parchment. Hold the pastry bag at a slight angle and squeeze gently. Once you have a small dollop of meringue on the parchment, gently but quickly pull the bag back toward you while squeezing slightly to form a tail. Stop squeezing and lift the tip straight up. The shell should be round at the top and narrow down to a point at the end of the tail.

Sprinkle the tops of all of the piped meringues with powdered sugar and, if you like, chopped nuts or "M&M's,"® before baking. Bake for at least 60 minutes. If the meringue begins to take on color, the oven is too hot; reduce the oven temperature by 50°F (10°C) and continue to bake. It is best to leave the oven door slightly open to allow the moisture to escape while the meringues are baking. Remove the meringues from the oven and cool on a wire rack. If you have time, turn off the oven and cool the meringues on the baking sheet in the oven. This will take about 1 hour and will allow the meringues to dry completely.

When completely cool, you are ready to finish the meringues using a variety of options. I like to fill the hollow circles with lemon curd or flavored pastry cream. Sandwich the mounds together with ganache or raspberry jam. The lengths and backward S's can be dusted with powdered sugar or unsweetened cocoa powder and served.

If you do not want to pipe the meringue, use a hand scraper and make large meringues. If you do not own a scraper, you can make one by cutting one from the side of a plastic bucket. Dip the scraper into the bowl of meringue and gather up a big scoop. Hold the scraper flat in your hand and use an offset spatula to smooth the sides of the meringue mound to resemble a mountain ridge with a rounded top and sloping sides. Use the offset spatula to slide the meringue off the scraper onto a parchment paper–covered baking sheet. Top the meringue with toasted chopped nuts or colorful candies. These larger meringues will take 2 to 3 hours to bake (dry) at 200°F (93°C). When the meringues are almost fully baked, increase the oven temperature 40°F (4°C). The added heat allows the sugar in the meringue to caramelize slightly, which gives the meringue more flavor. You will actually see the caramelized sugar oozing out of the baked meringue. Cool the meringues on a wire rack before serving.

All of the baked meringues will keep at room temperature for 1 week, well wrapped in plastic wrap or in an airtight container to keep out the humidity. If they do get a bit soggy from the humidity, just pop them back in the oven for about 30 minutes.

Variation: To make chocolate meringues, simply substitute 20 percent—or, in this case, about 3 tablespoons (24 grams)—of the powdered sugar with unsweetened cocoa powder.

Piece of Cake

In Europe, it is very common to buy cakes from the bakery for an afternoon snack. Cakes are more for celebrations in this country. The cakes in this chapter are meant for any occasion. I think it's a good idea to always have a cake in the house. You never know when someone might stop by for a visit.

Everyone seems to have a favorite cake recipe. I've found most cakes in this country are very dry. I almost always use Simple Syrup (flavored or unflavored) to keep the cake moist. Once you think you've added enough syrup, add more. It's amazing how much syrup a cake will absorb. To help a cake layer absorb syrup, dock it with a fork, knife, or docker to create pockets where the syrup can soak.

It is very important to preheat the oven. The oven is just a big box. When it preheats, it heats from the bottom. If you put something in the oven while it is preheating, the bottom of it will probably overbake.

Simple Syrup

Yield: About 1 cup (9.1 ounces; 260 grams)

almost always use simple syrup to soak cake layers and usually flavor it with some type of liqueur. Grand Marnier really brings out the flavor of chocolate, and anytime I use fresh fruit I find the naturally flavored Stolichnaya vodkas give the fruit taste an extra boost.

Water	Scant 1¼ cups	4.7 ounces	130 grams
Granulated sugar	⅔ cup	4.7 ounces	130 grams
Liqueur	2½ tablespoons	1.2 ounces	30 grams

Place the water and sugar in a 2-quart heavy-bottomed saucepan over medium-high heat and bring to a boil, stirring occasionally. The sugar should completely dissolve. Remove from the heat and pour the syrup into a medium-size mixing bowl. Set aside to cool before adding the liqueur. If you add the liqueur while the syrup is hot, the alcohol will evaporate.

When the liqueur has been added, cover the bowl with plastic wrap to keep the alcohol from evaporating and set aside until ready to use. I usually store the simple syrup in a squeeze bottle because it is the easiest way to apply it and you will not always need all of the simple syrup. You can also use a pastry brush, but be careful not to tear the cake layer. The cake layers should be soaked so they are wet enough to give them flavor and moisture, but not so much that the cake layers fall apart. Simple syrup will keep in the refrigerator indefinitely.

Variation: If you do not want to use alcohol, add 1 to 2 cups fresh raspberries with the water and sugar and allow the mixture to come to a boil. As the mixture boils, whisk thoroughly to break up the raspberries and allow them to release their juices. This will cause the syrup to turn red. Remove from the heat. Strain the syrup through a fine-mesh sieve into a medium-size mixing bowl and let cool. You can hasten the cooling process by placing the simple syrup over an ice bath, a larger bowl filled with ice cubes.

Basic Pound Cake

Yield: One baking sheet or two 9-inch cakes or two 10½-inch loaf pans

Pound cake traditionally means a pound of each ingredient (butter, sugar, eggs, flour), but, as you have come to expect from me, I needed to make a few changes. First, I replaced some of the weight of the eggs with extra egg yolks. This makes the cake softer and gives it more moisture. I removed some of the sugar and added honey, which gives the cake a nice color and crust, and helps it retain moisture. The vanilla bean and lemon zest add flavor. The baking powder helps keep the cake as light as possible.

Unsalted butter	2 cups	16 ounces	454 grams
Granulated sugar	Generous 1¾ cups	14 ounces	400 grams
Honey	Generous 2 tablespoons	1.8 ounces	50 grams
Grated zest of 1 lemon			
1 vanilla bean			
10 large egg yolks			
5 large eggs			
Cake flour, sifted	3 cups	16 ounces	450 grams
Baking powder	1 tablespoon + 1 teaspoon	0.75 ounce	20 grams

Preheat the oven to 350°F (176°C). Place the butter, sugar, and honey in a large mixing bowl. Use an electric mixer set on medium-high speed to cream the mixture until it is light in color and has gained volume, about 10 minutes. Add the lemon zest and combine. Use a sharp knife to slice the vanilla bean in half lengthwise. Separate the seeds from the skin by scraping the blade of the knife along the inside of the bean. Add the seeds to the mixture and beat until fully incorporated.

Combine the yolks and whole eggs in a small bowl. Combine the flour and baking powder in a bowl. Reduce the mixer speed to medium and add the eggs in three additions, alternating with the flour mixture. Mix just until the ingredients are combined and the batter is smooth. Too much mixing will cause gluten to develop, which will make the cake chewy—you want it to be soft and light. Pour the batter into the desired pans lightly sprayed with vegetable cooking spray or onto a parchment paper–covered baking sheet. If you are using this cake within another recipe, be sure to read that recipe for specific instructions on the type of pan to use.

When baked in loaf or cake pans, baking time is about 1 hour. When baked on a baking sheet, baking time is about 25 minutes. In all cases, the cake should be well risen, light golden brown, and spring back when pressed lightly with your fingertips. Always unmold and cool on a wire rack before using the cake.

The baked cake can be stored, well wrapped in plastic wrap, for up to 3 days in the refrigerator or 3 weeks in the freezer.

Rhône Valley Cake

Yield: One 10-inch cake; 8 to 10 servings

In 1983, I participated in my first national competition held in Paris. The theme was "the streets of Paris." To me, Paris means outdoor cafés, friends, elegance, beautiful architecture, and the city of arts. Almost everyone agrees food and wine are art in Paris. I decided to make a wine cake to celebrate the symbols of the city. This cake won first prize. If you want to take a shortcut, you can buy the pound cake instead of making it. By using an Italian meringue, you will kill any bacteria in the raw egg whites.

For the baked pear chips

2 pears			
Light corn syrup	¼ **cup**	**3.5 ounces**	**85 grams**
Water	**1 tablespoon**	**1 ounce**	**25 grams**

For the mold

½ **recipe Basic Pound Cake (page 87)**

2 Wine-Poached Pears (page 61), drained (reserve the liquid) and halved

For the mousse

Cold heavy cream	**1 cup + 1½ tablespoons**	**9 ounces**	**250 grams**
4 gelatin sheets or 1⅓ envelopes powdered gelatin			

3 large egg whites			
Water	1 tablespoon	1 ounce	25 grams
Granulated sugar	Scant ½ cup	3.5 ounces	100 grams
Light corn syrup	Generous 2 tablespoons	1.8 ounces	50 grams
Very cold dry red wine	1 cup + 2 tablespoons	9 ounces	250 grams

To soak the cake

Cold pear-poaching liquid, strained	⅔ cup	5.5 ounces	150 grams

To finish the cake

Warm Wine Jelly Glaze (page 61)

continued

Prepare the baked pear chips: Preheat the oven to 200°F (93°C). Use a sharp chef's knife to peel the pears and slice them lengthwise into very thin slices. Combine the corn syrup with the water and gently brush this mixture on both sides of each pear slice. Place the slices on a parchment paper–covered baking sheet and bake until the pears are dry and crispy and very slightly browned, 2 to 3 hours. The corn syrup will keep the pears sweet and crunchy as they dry in the oven. Let cool on a wire rack.

Prepare the cake: Make the pound cake batter as directed in the recipe, baking it in a 9 × 2-inch cake pan. Cool on a wire rack and unmold onto your work surface. Remove the parchment paper from the back of the cake. You will need to slice the cake horizontally into ½-inch-thick layers. To do this easily, use a knife to mark the layers into the side of the cake. Place the cake on a revolving cake stand. Use a long, serrated knife to begin to slice the cake as you turn the stand. This will help keep the layer even as you cut it. Do not try to cut all the way through on the first rotation. When you finish the first turn, keep turning while gradually cutting deeper into the layer until you are all the way through it. Separate the layers by sliding each one onto a flat plate or cake circle. You only use two cake layers for this recipe. Store the others in the freezer, well wrapped in plastic wrap, for up to 4 weeks.

Prepare the mold: I like to use a 10-inch ring mold instead of a traditional cake pan to make this because it is easier to unmold. Set the ring mold on a baking sheet or flat platter. Trim the top of each poached pear half so it is level with the height of the mold. Then cut each half lengthwise into ¼-inch-thick slices. Arrange the slices upright around the inside of the ring mold, allowing them to overlap slightly. The finished cake will look nicer if there are no gaps between the pears. Place a layer of pound cake inside the ring mold. If necessary, trim the cake layer to fit. Set aside.

Prepare the mousse: Pour the heavy cream into a medium-size mixing bowl and whip with an electric mixer set on medium-high speed to soft peaks. Store in the refrigerator until ready to use.

If you use gelatin sheets, place them in a medium-size mixing bowl with enough cold water (about 1 quart) to cover. Let stand for about 5 minutes to allow the gelatin to soften and hydrate. Cold water hydrates the gelatin without letting it absorb too much liquid. Remove the gelatin from the bowl and squeeze out the excess water with your hands. If you use powdered gelatin, sprinkle the gelatin over ¼ cup (2 ounces; 60 grams) cold water. Let the gelatin bloom until it has absorbed all the water, about 1 minute. Set aside.

Place the egg whites in a medium-size mixing bowl. Pour the water, sugar, and corn syrup into a 1-quart heavy-bottomed saucepan and place over medium-high heat. Insert a candy thermometer and cook the mixture until it reaches 250°F (121°C), what is known as the soft ball stage (page 14). Remove the mixture from the heat. Use an electric mixer set on medium speed to whip the egg whites for about 5 seconds. Increase the mixer speed to medium-high and make an Italian meringue by pouring the hot sugar down the side of the mixing bowl into the whipping whites. Be careful not to pour the hot sugar directly onto the beaters, or it will splatter. Add the hydrated gelatin and continue to whip the meringue until stiff and glossy, about 5 minutes. Gelatin is a natural emulsifier; adding it to the egg whites will help give them volume.

Remove the whipped cream from the refrigerator. Pour half of the cold wine into the whipped cream and gently fold them together. Using cold wine will keep the cream from collapsing. Warmth would cause the fat molecules in the cream to separate. You can even put the wine in the freezer briefly just before you add it to the whipped cream.

Pour the remaining wine into the meringue and fold until combined. Then fold the meringue into the whipped cream until homogenous. The wine mousse is a very light pink color. If you have leftovers, the color will deepen if stored overnight. Don't be surprised if your cake looks different the next day!

Assemble the cake: Soak the pound cake in the mold with about one half of the poaching liquid. Fill the ring mold with enough mousse to come halfway up the side of the mold. Use the back of a spoon to gently spread the mousse over the cake and up the side of the mold. Top with another layer of pound cake and soak with the remaining poaching liquid. Cover with enough mousse to completely fill the mold. Pull a large offset spatula across the top to create a smooth surface. This will be the top of the cake, so you want it as even as possible. Place the cake in the refrigerator for about 4 hours or in the freezer for about 2 hours to allow it to set.

If the wine jelly glaze is not warm and liquid, gently heat it in a nonreactive 1-quart heavy-bottomed saucepan over medium heat until liquid. It should be lukewarm and smooth, without lumps. Remove the cake from the refrigerator or freezer. Do not unmold it until after it has been glazed. Carefully pour the glaze onto the top of the cake. Use a large offset spatula to spread the glaze evenly over the top of the cake. Do this quickly because the glaze will begin to set as it comes in contact with the cold cake.

Unmold the cake: Place the cake on a flat platter. Run a hot paring knife between the ring mold and the cake. Be careful not to cut into the pears on the side of the cake. Gently and carefully lift off the ring mold. I like to decorate the top of the cake with the pear chips. A small bunch of beautiful champagne grapes would also be nice.

Chocolate Decadence

Yield: One 6 × 9-inch cake; 6 to 8 servings

If you need to make a birthday cake for a real chocolate lover like my friend Euphrasia Dopf, make this cake. One day I asked Euphrasia to describe her fantasy birthday cake, and she said, "Chocolate cake with chocolate filling and chocolate frosting." This is the recipe I developed for her, and it has become one of my classic birthday cakes at the restaurant.

This is basically a flourless cake layer with chocolate cream. It does contain almond flour but that is technically not considered flour. You may choose to mix this by hand but I like to use an electric mixer. Use a good bittersweet chocolate. It is important to use a chocolate with strong flavor, since every time you add an ingredient (eggs, almond flour, etc.) the flavor is diluted. If you don't want to make the ganache, the cake is very tasty by itself.

For the filling and frosting

⅔ recipe Truffle Ganache (page 242)

For the cake layers

Bittersweet chocolate, melted and still warm		18 ounces	500 grams
Light corn syrup	2 tablespoons	1.6 ounces	40 grams
10 large egg yolks			
Unsalted butter, softened	½ cup + 2 tablespoons	5 ounces	140 grams
Almond flour (page 6)	¾ cup	2.8 ounces	80 grams
Dark rum (optional)	Scant ¼ cup	1.6 ounces	40 grams
10 large egg whites			
Granulated sugar	¾ cup	5.6 ounces	160 grams

Prepare the truffle ganache: Make the ganache as directed in the recipe and set it aside on a parchment paper–covered baking sheet to cool. When the ganache has cooled to the consistency of toothpaste but is still easily spreadable, it is ready to be used. If the ganache has cooled and set too much, you can soften it by heating a small amount in a saucepan placed over medium heat until melted. Then, quickly but gently, stir the melted ganache into the harder, cooler ganache. If the ganache is still too hard, repeat the procedure until the desired consistency is reached.

continued

Preheat the oven to 320°F to 330°F (160°C to 165°C).

Prepare the cake layers: The chocolate for the cake layers needs to be melted and warm. If necessary, hold it over a double boiler to maintain its warmth.

Combine the corn syrup, egg yolks, butter, and almond flour in a medium-size mixing bowl and beat with an electric mixer set on medium-high speed until well incorporated, light, and fluffy. I prefer to give the batter an emulsion by creaming the butter rather than using melted butter. This gives the batter more volume and makes the cake lighter due to the incorporation of air during the creaming process. When you use corn syrup in a cake, you can remove an equal quantity of granulated sugar (for example, 2 cups granulated sugar can be replaced with 1½ cups granulated sugar plus ½ cup corn syrup). The overall balance of the cake will not change, but the cake will be a little less sweet. If you prefer a sweeter cake, replace the corn syrup with an equal amount of honey. I also like the flavor that a good-quality dark rum gives to the cake. If you prefer not to use alcohol, you could use the seeds of 1 vanilla bean or the grated zest of 1 orange instead.

Place the egg whites in a large mixing bowl and whip until foamy with an electric mixer set on medium speed. Make a French meringue by adding the granulated sugar 1 tablespoon at a time. Increase the mixer speed to medium-high and whip to stiff but not dry peaks, about 7 minutes. The French meringue should be stiff but not overwhipped and separated, or it will collapse when combined with the warm chocolate. Fold the meringue into the creamed butter mixture all at once. Fold up from the bottom of the bowl and fold carefully so you do not deflate the meringue. When the two mixtures are almost fully combined, add the warm chocolate. Use a rubber spatula and be sure to fold up from the bottom of the bowl. If you have some meringue that does not want to incorporate, carefully and gently break it apart by folding, not whisking, with a whisk. This can happen if you add the chocolate too quickly.

Pour the batter onto a parchment paper–covered baking sheet and spread it evenly with a rubber spatula. Carefully push the batter. Do not smash it, or you will lose the incorporated air and the cake will be flat and chewy. Place the cake in the oven and bake until the cake springs back when gently pressed, about 35 minutes. You can also test the cake with a wooden toothpick: insert it in the center of the cake; if it comes out clean, the cake is done. Remove from the oven and place the baking sheet on a wire rack to allow the cake to cool. The cake will rise in the oven and collapse slightly as it cools. This is normal because the recipe lacks flour, which gives structure to a cake.

When completely cooled, remove the cake from the baking sheet by running a sharp paring knife around the sides of the cake. Invert the cake onto a clean work surface or sheet of parchment paper. Remove the parchment paper that is on the back of the cake. Use a sharp chef's knife to cut the cake into four equal-sized squares. You will only use three squares for this cake. Store the fourth square in the freezer or give it to your helpers to eat. Trim each square to make clean edges. If the cake is too delicate to move, cut the cake into four pieces while it is still on the baking sheet. Place the baking sheet in the freezer until the cake layers are cold enough to move without breaking.

Assemble the cake: This cake is very fragile because it does not contain flour, so work carefully and gently. Slide one square onto a cardboard cake circle or flat platter. I like to anchor the cake layer by first placing a small dab of ganache in the center of the cake circle. This way the cake won't slide as you fill and frost it. Use an offset spatula to spread about a ½-inch-thick layer of ganache onto the cake square. Be sure to spread the ganache all the way to the edges. Top with a second cake layer, making sure the second layer rests evenly on the first. Repeat with the ganache. Top with the last cake layer and press down slightly to adhere. Use a large offset spatula to spread an even layer of ganache over the top and sides of the cake. If the cake is uneven, use the ganache frosting to make it as flat and even as possible. At this point you can place the cake in the refrigerator until the ganache has hardened, about 20 minutes. Then use the offset spatula to make the edges as clean and straight as possible. Place the frosted cake in the refrigerator for about 1 hour to set before decorating.

Remove the cake from the refrigerator and place it on a cake platter. Scrape the remaining ganache into a pastry bag fitted with a ¼- or ⅓-inch star tip. Using a spoon or spatula to transfer the ganache will help to ensure you don't have lumps in the ganache. Lumps will clog the pastry tip and make it difficult to use. Pipe decorations around the side and top of the cake. The decorations can be as simple or as complex as you desire. To improve your decorating skills, practice piping ganache onto an inverted cake pan. You can reuse the ganache by scraping it off the pan and placing it back in the pastry bag. When you are comfortable with your design, decorate the cake. Piping decorations is only a matter of pressure applied to the pastry bag and speed. Once you master the concept, your decorations are only limited by your imagination.

Sometimes I sprinkle the cake with shredded sweetened coconut or chopped toasted nuts. If you do not plan to serve the cake within a few hours of assembling it, store it in the refrigerator until ready to eat. If the cake has been stored in the refrigerator, allow it to come to room temperature for at least 30 minutes before serving. It is easiest to cut the cake with a hot chef's knife. To heat the knife, dip it in a tall container filled with hot water before each cut and wipe off the excess water.

continued

I usually do not serve this cake with anything because it is very rich. If you like, you can serve it with some fresh berries.

Variation: To eliminate the need for a pastry bag, finish the cake by using the back of a fork to add texture to the ganache frosting. Dust the textured cake with powdered sugar and serve. Sometimes I sprinkle chopped toasted nuts over each layer of ganache for added texture and flavor.

If you cannot find almond flour, use an equal amount of finely ground walnuts or pecans instead.

Strawberry Ladyfinger Cake

Yield: One 8-inch cake; 8 to 10 servings

My dad has a beautiful garden in which he grows all of our favorite fruits and vegetables. In the morning before coffee, the first thing we do is go to the garden and pick a few fresh strawberries. He has the regular kind and the special *fraises des bois*, which are the tiny, super-flavorful berries. We transplanted them from our farm up in the Ardèche mountains, and every day we check the progress of the plants. The fruit is usually warm from the morning sun, which intensifies the flavor. Every time I make this recipe, I am transported home by the smell of the berries.

Be sure to use fresh cream for the whipped cream. Old cream sometimes gets a yogurt flavor. If you want to take a shortcut, use store-bought ladyfingers.

continued

To line the pan

Chocolate Ladyfingers (page 245)

For the soaking syrup

Simple Syrup flavored with Stoli Strasberi vodka (page 86)

For the strawberry Bavarian

Fresh large strawberries	**About 2½ cups**	**10.5 ounces**	**300 grams**
Heavy cream	**Scant 1½ cups**	**10.5 ounces**	**300 grams**
Granulated sugar	**½ cup**	**3.8 ounces**	**110 grams**
3 gelatin sheets or 1 envelope powdered gelatin			
Stoli Strasberi vodka or water	**½ cup**	**3.5 ounces**	**100 grams**

For the garnish

Fresh strawberries as needed

Chocolate Ladyfingers

Prepare the cake pan: Make the chocolate ladyfingers batter as directed in the recipe and pipe them 2½ inches long. Bake as directed and set aside to cool until ready to use. When cool, unstick the ladyfingers from the parchment paper.

Place an 8 × 2-inch round cake ring on a parchment paper–covered baking sheet. Place the ladyfingers, flat side in, around the inside of the cake ring. Press them tightly next to one another, but do not overlap them. Cover the bottom of the cake ring with some of the remaining ladyfingers. You should not see any parchment paper between the ladyfingers. Gently press down on the ladyfingers to make an even layer. Generously soak the bottom layer of ladyfingers with some flavored simple syrup.

Prepare the strawberry Bavarian: Clean and hull the strawberries and place them in a tall container. Use a hand-held immersion blender, food processor, or blender to puree the strawberries until smooth. Set aside. I usually do not strain the puree to remove the strawberry seeds because I like the texture they add. You can strain it if you prefer.

Place the heavy cream and sugar in a large mixing bowl and whip to soft peaks with an electric mixer set on medium-high speed. Whipped cream contains the most volume when whipped to soft peaks. Place in the refrigerator until ready to use.

If you are using gelatin sheets, place them in a medium-size mixing bowl with enough cold water (about 2 cups) to cover. Let stand for about 5 minutes to allow the gelatin to soften and hydrate. Cold water hydrates the gelatin without letting it absorb too much liquid. Remove the gelatin from the bowl and squeeze out the excess water with your hands. If you are using powdered gelatin, sprinkle it over ¼ cup (2 ounces; 60 grams) of cold water. Let the gelatin bloom until it has absorbed all the water, about 1 minute.

Place the hydrated gelatin and the strawberry vodka (or water if you prefer) in a 1-quart heavy-bottomed saucepan and set over medium heat until the gelatin dissolves. Pour the gelatin mixture into the cold strawberry puree and immediately whisk to combine. It is important to whisk immediately so the gelatin does not set into small pieces, which would leave lumps in the Bavarian. Make the Bavarian by carefully folding the strawberry puree into the whipped cream with a rubber spatula. Fold gently, being careful not to deflate the whipped cream.

Assemble the cake: Fill the cake ring halfway with the strawberry Bavarian. Add another layer of ladyfingers, covering the Bavarian as completely as possible. Press down gently. Soak this layer with the remaining flavored simple syrup. Fill the cake mold to the top with the remaining Bavarian. I like to leave about a ¼-inch piece of ladyfinger showing at the top of the cake. Place the cake in the refrigerator or freezer for several hours to set. This will make it easier to unmold.

Unmold the cake: Simply lift off the cake ring; it should release quite easily. I like to decorate the top of the cake with some strawberries and ladyfingers. You can decorate it any way you prefer.

Lemon Upside-Down Cake

Yield: One 9-inch cake; 8 to 10 servings

My dad's lemon tree is his pride and joy. It is a four seasons tree, which means at any given time you can find on it light pink buds, five-petal white flowers, small green fruits, and tasty ripe yellow lemons. It grows right in front of the house in a very cherished spot between the front door and his bedroom window. He is so protective of the tree, he won't even let the gardener trim it. When we grill fish, all we have to do is lean back in the chair and pluck a lemon off the tree.

I'm not sure if this is one of my dad's favorite cakes because he really likes it or because I use his lemons to make it.

For the preserved lemons

3 large lemons			
Granulated sugar	Generous 2¼ cups	18 ounces	500 grams
Water	Generous 1 cup	9 ounces	250 grams

For the pound cake

½ recipe Basic Pound Cake (page 87) flavored with Stoli Limonaya vodka			

For the lemon curd mousseline

Lemon Curd (page 37)			
Heavy cream	1 cup + 1½ tablespoons	9 ounces	250 grams
3 gelatin sheets or 1 envelope powdered gelatin			
Stoli Limonaya vodka or water	¼ cup	2 ounces	50 grams

For the soaking syrup

Simple Syrup flavored with Stoli Limonaya vodka (page 86)			

To finish the cake

Apricot Glaze (page 27)			

Prepare the preserved lemons: To do this, you will poach the lemons in sugar. The recipe is simply two parts sugar to one part water by weight. Use a serrated knife to slice the lemons very thinly, about 1/16 inch thick. Remove the seeds. Pour the sugar and water into a nonreactive 4-quart heavy-bottomed saucepan and place over medium-high heat. Stir to combine and to dissolve the sugar. Place the lemon slices in the syrup and bring the mixture to a boil. Remove the saucepan from the heat. Pour the lemons and syrup into a nonreactive container and let cool for a couple of hours. The heat softens the peel and the sugar sweetens it to make a tasty treat. Thirty minutes before you are ready to use them, drain the lemon slices and place on a wire rack placed over a parchment paper–covered baking sheet.

Prepare the pound cake: Make the pound cake batter as directed in the recipe, but flavor it with the lemon vodka when you add the eggs. This will intensify the flavor of the cake. Bake in a 9 × 2-inch cake pan. Unmold and let the cake cool on a wire rack until ready to

Place a layer of plastic wrap in the cake pan.

Line the bottom and side of the cake pan with the lemon slices.

use. You will need to slice the cake horizontally into ½-inch-thick layers. To do this easily, use a knife to mark the layers into the side of the cake. Place the cake on a revolving cake stand. Use a long, serrated knife to begin to slice the cake as you turn the stand. This will help keep the layer even as you cut it. Do not try to cut all the way through on the first rotation. When you finish the first turn, keep turning while gradually cutting deeper into the layer until you are all the way through it. Separate the layers by sliding each one onto a flat plate or cake circle. You only use two cake layers for this recipe. Store the others in the freezer, well wrapped in plastic wrap, for up to 4 weeks.

Coat the inside of a 9 × 2-inch cake pan with vegetable cooking spray. Place a layer of plastic wrap over the spray into the cake pan. Be sure to allow excess plastic wrap to drape over the side of the cake pan; this will make it easier to unmold the finished cake. The spray causes the plastic wrap to adhere to the side of the pan. Press the plastic wrap completely into the side and bottom of the pan. Line the bottom of the cake pan with the lemon slices. Arrange the slices any way you like and cover as much of the cake pan bottom as you like. Remember that the bottom of the cake pan will become the top of the cake when unmolded, so try to make a nice design. Line the side of the cake pan with the lemon slices. You may overlap the lemons if you wish.

Prepare the lemon curd mousseline: Make the lemon curd as directed in the recipe and let it cool. Whip the heavy cream to soft peaks with an electric mixer set on medium-high speed. Place in the refrigerator until ready to use.

If you are using gelatin sheets, place them in a medium-size mixing bowl with enough cold water (about 2 cups) to cover. Let stand for about 5 minutes to allow the gelatin to soften and hydrate. Cold water hydrates the gelatin without letting it absorb too much liquid. Remove the gelatin from the bowl and squeeze out the excess water with your hands. If you are using powdered gelatin, sprinkle it over ¼ cup (2 ounces; 60 grams) of cold water. Let the gelatin bloom until it has absorbed all the water, about 1 minute. Place the hydrated gelatin in a 1-quart saucepan with the lemon vodka (or water if you prefer not to use alcohol) and a small scoop of lemon curd. Place over medium heat and stir gently to combine as the gelatin dissolves. Immediately pour the dissolved gelatin into the remaining lemon curd and fold in quickly but gently with a rubber spatula. The dissolved gelatin will begin to set immediately upon contact with the cold lemon curd. Fold the gelatin in as quickly as possible to prevent lumps. When the gelatin is fully combined, use a rubber spatula to fold the lemon curd into the whipped cream. Do not do this with a whisk, or you risk overwhipping the cream, causing it to lose volume and lightness.

Assemble the cake: Pour about half of the lemon mousseline into the cake pan. Use the back of a large spoon or a rubber spatula to gently spread it around the bottom and up the side of the cake pan. Push the mousseline into the side of the pan between the lemon slices to prevent air pockets. You should not see the bottom or side of the cake pan. Place one layer of pound cake over the mousseline and press down gently. Soak the cake layer evenly with the flavored simple syrup. If you prefer not to add alcohol to your cake, you can use some of the strained lemon-poaching liquid as simple syrup. Fill the cake pan almost to the top with lemon mousseline. Leave only enough room for the second cake layer to close the cake. Soak this layer with the simple syrup. Place this cake layer on top of the mousseline soaked side down and press down gently. Place the cake in the refrigerator for a few hours to set. This will make it easier to unmold and allow the cake to hold its shape once unmolded.

Unmold the cake: Carefully dip the bottom of the pan in hot water for about 5 seconds. Center a flat plate facedown over the top of the cake pan. Flip over the plate and cake pan at the same time so the pan is on top of the plate. Gently lift off the cake pan. It should lift off easily because of the plastic wrap. If necessary, pull gently on the plastic wrap while lifting off the cake pan. Carefully peel away the plastic wrap.

Finish the cake: Prepare the apricot glaze as directed in the recipe and apply it to the cake with a pastry brush. This will protect the cake from drying and keep it shiny. I like to garnish with any remaining preserved lemon slices. Use a serrated knife to cut this cake. You can serve this cake chilled or at room temperature.

Sunflower Ice Cream Cake

Yield: 8 to 10 servings

If you want to make a cake that's fun and do not have time to go to the store, you might be able to make this cake with items you already have in your house. I think it is worth your effort to make the pound cake but you could use any store-bought cake. If you do that, the recipe does not require baking. You can also make the ice cream if you like.

Use an 8-inch glass or stainless-steel mixing bowl for this recipe. I used the bubble wrap with extra tiny bubbles in it. That is what really helps to make the cake look like a sunflower. If you want to omit this step, you can use something like the point of a capped pen to make the indentations.

½ recipe **Basic Pound Cake (page 87)**

1 pint chocolate ice cream, softened

1 pint vanilla ice cream, softened

Simple Syrup flavored (optional) with dark rum or Grand Marnier (page 86)

1 large ripe pineapple

Prepare the pound cake: Make the pound cake batter as directed in the recipe and bake on a parchment paper–covered baking sheet instead of in a loaf or cake pan. Place on a wire rack to cool. When cool, invert onto the work surface and peel off the parchment paper. Use an 8-inch plain cutter to cut one disk from the cake. Store the remaining cake in the freezer for up to 3 weeks, or serve it plain.

Prepare the mold: If you are doing this step, line the bowl with bubble wrap. The textured side of the wrap should be facing up to give the ice cream the appearance of seed pockets. Be sure the bubble wrap lies as smoothly as possible, since any creases will show in the ice cream. Also make sure the bubble wrap comes all the way up the side of the bowl and hangs over the side by an inch or two. This will make it easier to unmold.

Assemble the cake: Fill the bottom of the bowl with the chocolate ice cream. Use the back of a large spoon or a rubber spatula to gently spread the chocolate ice cream up the side of the bowl. This will be easier to do if the ice cream is soft. To soften it, I usually refrigerate it for about 30 minutes and then stir it with a spoon so the consistency is even. Spread the ice cream almost to the rim of the bowl. If you try to keep the layer of chocolate ice cream the same thickness on the bottom as up the sides, the dessert will look nicer when cut. Make sure the chocolate ice cream completely covers the bubble wrap. Fill the inside of the dessert with the vanilla ice cream. Leave enough room at the top for the cake layer. If you really like cake, you could add another layer between the chocolate and vanilla ice creams. Soak the top layer of pound cake with the simple syrup. I like to flavor it with rum or Grand Marnier if the dessert is for adults. Place the cake in the freezer for a couple of hours to set.

Prepare the pineapple petals: Use a serrated knife and cut a ¾-inch-thick slice from the top and bottom of the pineapple. Stand the pineapple upright on a cutting board and place the blade of the knife at the top center of the pineapple. Use the blade of the knife at a 45-degree angle to cut a straight line from the top to the outside edge about halfway down the pineapple. Repeat on the other side. Then cut about ¼ inch in from the skin along the natural curve of the bottom of the pineapple. Repeat until all of the skin is removed. Cut off as many of the eyes as possible. Slice the pineapple in half down the center. Stand one half on its end and hold the top with one hand. Cut very thin slices, about ⅛ inch thick, by cutting along the core. Repeat with the other half. Arrange the slices in a circle on a large platter. If you do this more than 30 minutes prior to serving, cover the fruit with plastic wrap to keep it from drying and place in the refrigerator until ready to use.

Unmold the cake: Dip the bottom of the bowl in hot water for about 5 seconds. As you gently pull on the bubble wrap, the cake should easily release. If not, you may need to dip it again. Carefully peel away the bubble wrap. If you did not use the bubble wrap, this is the time to make the indentations in the ice cream. Place the dessert in the center of the pineapple petals and serve.

Variation: Sometimes I make an ice cream or sorbet caterpillar to go with the sunflower. This is very easy to do. Make balls of ice cream or sorbet with an ice cream scoop and place on a parchment paper–covered baking sheet in the freezer to let harden. Your caterpillar will have more character if you use different flavors of ice cream or sorbet. When you are ready to serve the dessert, remove the balls from the freezer. Arrange them like a caterpillar body on top of the pineapple petals. Use "M&M's"® Milk Chocolate Mini Baking Bits for the eyes. To make the antennae, fill a cornet (page 16) with some tempered bittersweet chocolate (page 8) and draw the antennae onto a sheet of parchment paper. Let set, then place on top of the caterpillar's head.

Jacques's Favorite Cheesecake

Yield: One 8-inch cheesecake; 8 to 10 servings

I discovered cheesecake ten years ago, and I really like it. We do not have anything like it in France, and since it is an American institution, I don't have too much to add to the recipe. It is fun to bring a little something different to the presentation, so that is how I came up with the idea listed in the variation to do a triple-layer, multicolored and multiflavored cheesecake.

If you like a drier cheesecake, use less sour cream. If you like your cheesecake softer, use the same amount of sour cream, 3 whole eggs, and 2 yolks.

For the crust

Cookie crumbs	1½ cups	5.5 ounces	150 grams
Granulated sugar	2 tablespoons	1 ounce	25 grams
Walnuts, crushed	¼ cup	1.6 ounces	40 grams
Unbleached all-purpose flour	2 tablespoons	0.6 ounce	15 grams
Unsalted butter, melted	2½ tablespoons	2.6 ounces	75 grams

For the batter

Cream cheese, softened		32 ounces	960 grams
Granulated sugar	1½ cups	11.5 ounces	330 grams
4 large eggs			
1 vanilla bean			
Sour cream	1 cup	8.3 ounces	235 grams

Prepare the pan: I find that it is easier to unmold the baked cheesecake if you place a square of parchment paper over the bottom of the springform pan. Cut the square so it overlaps the bottom of the pan by about 1 inch. Then attach the side, leaving the extra parchment paper hanging out of the side of the pan. Wrap a piece of aluminum foil around the bottom and halfway up the side of the outside of the pan. If the bottom and side do not fit together tightly, this will prevent batter from leaking all over your oven. Set the prepared pan aside.

Prepare the crust: Using your hands, combine the cookie crumbs, sugar, walnuts, and flour in a medium-size mixing bowl until well mixed. Add the melted butter slowly, using a rubber spatula or your hands to incorporate. You may not need all of the butter; when the crust is just wet enough to stick together as you grab a handful, enough butter has been added. It should feel like wet sand. Place the crust in the bottom of the springform pan and use your fingers to pat it into an even layer. Set the crust aside.

Prepare the batter: Preheat the oven to 300°F (148°C).

Place all of the cream cheese in a large mixing bowl and soften it by beating with an electric mixer set on medium-high speed for about 3 minutes. This will be easier if you allow the cream cheese to soften at room temperature for at least 1 hour before you use it. Add the sugar to the mixture and combine on medium-high speed until light and fluffy, about 5 minutes, scraping down the side of the bowl as needed. Add the eggs one by one, incorporating fully after each addition. Use a sharp knife to slice the vanilla bean in half lengthwise. Separate the seeds from the skin by scraping the blade of the knife along the inside of the bean. Add the vanilla bean seeds and sour cream to the cream cheese mixture and mix with an electric mixer on medium-high speed until fully combined. The mixture should be smooth. If there are any lumps, use a whisk to break them.

Pour the batter into the prepared pan. (If you are using a convection oven, bake the cheesecake at 250°F/121°C.) Bake the cheesecake until the center ripples only slightly when the pan is jiggled, about 2 hours. The cheesecake will continue to set in the refrigerator, so you do not want to bake it until it is completely firm.

Remove the cheesecake from the oven and cool on a wire rack. Remove the foil around the bottom of the pan to allow the cake to cool more efficiently. When the cheesecake and pan are cool to the touch, lightly and carefully cover the pan with plastic wrap (you do not want it to stick to the top of the cake) and allow the cheesecake to rest in the refrigerator for about 8 hours or overnight.

Unmold the cake: When you are ready to serve the cheesecake, remove from the refrigerator and run a hot paring knife around the inside of the pan to loosen the cake from the side. Unsnap the side of the pan and remove it. Cover the top of the cheesecake with a sheet of parchment paper. This will prevent the cake from sticking to the plate as you unmold it. Center a flat plate upside down over the cheesecake. Place one hand on either side, grasping both the plate and the bottom of the pan, and flip them both over so that the bottom of the springform pan is now on top. Gently lift off the pan bottom and peel away the parchment paper. Place a second flat plate upside down over the bottom of the cheesecake. Once again, flip both plates so that the cheesecake is right side up. Remove the first plate and the parchment paper.

The cheesecake will keep in the refrigerator, well wrapped in plastic wrap, for up to 3 days or in the freezer for up to 4 weeks.

When ready to serve, heat a sharp chef's knife by running it under hot water and wiping it dry. Use the hot knife to slice the cheesecake.

Variations: Prepare the batter as directed. Leave half of it plain. Flavor one quarter of it by folding in ⅓ cup (3.2 ounces; 90 grams) raspberry jam and flavor the other quarter by folding in 90 grams (3.2 ounces) melted, warm bittersweet chocolate. Place the plain batter in the prepared pan on top of the crust. Then drop in large dollops of the raspberry batter and swirl it into the plain batter. Repeat with the chocolate batter. Be careful not to mix them too much; you want to be able to see and taste the swirl pattern. Bake, cool, and serve as directed.

To make a triple-layer cheesecake, pour each of the three batters into separate 8-inch springform pans. The chocolate layer should be poured into the pan containing the crust. Freeze each layer solid. Use a hot knife to loosen the side of the plain and raspberry layers from the sides of the pans. Unsnap the springform sides and remove the plain and raspberry layers. Place the plain layer on top of the chocolate layer. Top with the raspberry layer. Bake and refrigerate as directed.

Refrigerated Cheesecake

Yield: One 8-inch cake; 8 to 10 servings

Gaston LeNôtre is a legendary French pastry chef. He is certainly one of the most famous and well-respected chefs in our industry. He makes a cheesy cake called *Schuls* in French. It is made with fromage blanc, which is similar to cream cheese, but its taste is not as intense and the consistency is more like that of yogurt. My refrigerated cheesecake recipe follows LeNôtre's *Schuls* recipe, but I have substituted American cream cheese, which I think works quite well.

If you make this in a cake ring instead of a cake pan, it will be easier to unmold.

½ **recipe Pâte Sablée (page 32)**			
½ **recipe Basic Pound Cake (page 87)**			
Linda's Red Raspberry Jam (page 26) or store-bought	½ **cup**	**7 ounces**	**200 grams**
For the filling			
8 gelatin sheets or 2⅔ envelopes powdered gelatin			
Cold cream cheese		**14.5 ounces**	**415 grams**
Granulated sugar	¾ **cup**	**5.6 ounces**	**160 grams**
Whole milk	⅓ **cup**	**2.9 ounces**	**85 grams**
Grated zest of 1 lemon			
Cold heavy cream	**Scant 2¼ cups**	**18 ounces**	**500 grams**
Stoli Razberi vodka or water	¼ **cup**	**1.8 ounces**	**50 grams**

Prepare the pâte sablée: Make the dough as directed in the recipe and let rest in the refrigerator for 30 minutes. Preheat the oven to 375°F (190°C). Remove the dough from the refrigerator. Lightly give it a few quick raps with the rolling pin to slightly soften the dough. This will make it easier to roll. Lightly flour the work surface and each side of the dough. Roll the dough into a 9-inch circle about ⅛ inch thick. Transfer the dough to a parchment paper–covered baking sheet by rolling it up and around the rolling pin. Unroll the dough onto the baking sheet. Use an 8-inch plate as a guide to cut a circle from the dough. Remove the scraps. Dock the bottom of the tart shell with a fork. Bake until the dough is an even light golden brown, about 15 minutes. The dough may rise unevenly in

sections; if that happens, release the air by gently piercing the dough with the tip of a paring knife. Remove the baked dough from the oven and allow to cool completely on a wire rack. (At this stage the baked dough can be stored in the freezer, well wrapped in plastic wrap, for up to 4 weeks.)

Prepare the cake: Make the pound cake batter as directed in the recipe and bake it on a parchment paper–covered baking sheet instead of in a loaf or cake pan. Place on a wire rack to cool. When cooled, invert onto the work surface and peel off the parchment paper. Use a 6-inch plate as a guide to cut one disk from the cake. Store the remaining cake in the freezer, well wrapped in plastic wrap, for up to 3 weeks.

Prepare the jam: Make the jam as directed in the recipe. You can set aside the amount needed for this recipe and let cool. Can the rest.

Prepare the filling: If you are using gelatin sheets, place them in a medium-size mixing bowl with enough cold water (about 1 quart) to cover. Let stand for about 5 minutes to allow the gelatin to soften and hydrate. Cold water hydrates the gelatin without letting it absorb too much liquid. Remove the gelatin from the bowl and squeeze out the excess water with your hands. If you are using powdered gelatin, sprinkle it over ¾ cup (6 ounces; 180 grams) of cold water. Let the gelatin bloom until it has absorbed all the water, about 1 minute.

Place the cream cheese in a medium-size mixing bowl and beat with an electric mixer set on medium-high speed until softened, about 1 minute. Add the sugar and milk and beat on medium-high speed until well incorporated and light, about 5 minutes. Scrape down the side of the bowl using a rubber spatula as needed. Add the lemon zest and continue to mix. The batter should be completely smooth. Pour in the heavy cream and whip to barely soft peaks, about 1 minute.

Place the hydrated gelatin in a small heavy-bottomed saucepan and place over medium heat. Add the flavored vodka or water and a small scoop of the cream cheese mixture. Stir the gelatin as it heats and dissolves. Add the dissolved gelatin mixture to the cream cheese mixture and whip to soft peaks, about another 1 to 2 minutes.

Assemble the cake: Place an $8 \times 2\frac{1}{2}$-inch cake ring on a parchment paper–covered baking sheet. Set the baked tart dough inside the cake ring. You may need to shave it slightly with a sharp paring knife to make it fit. Use a small offset spatula to cover the dough with an ⅛-inch-thick layer of raspberry jam. Top with the cake layer and cover with another layer of raspberry jam. Then fill the cake ring to the top with the cream cheese filling. Use a large offset spatula to smooth the top and make it as flat as possible.

Place the cake in the freezer to set for about 2 hours. (At this stage the cake can be stored in the freezer, well wrapped in plastic wrap, for up to 2 weeks.)

Unmold the cake: Remove the cake from the freezer. Use a small offset spatula to spread an even layer of jam around the top of the cake. If you do this before you unmold it, the cake will have a nice clean edge. Unmold the cake by running the blade of a knife around the inside of the cake ring to loosen the cake from the side. Then simply lift off the cake ring. Sometimes I like to top this cake with fresh raspberries.

Mochaccino Cake

Yield: One 9 × 3-inch cake; 8 to 10 servings

During the taping of our show, our producer, Charlie Pinsky, asked me to make a mochaccino cake like his mom makes. This is my adaptation of her recipe.

For the cake layer

Angel Food Cake (page 64) or ½ recipe Basic Pound Cake (page 87)

For the coffee syrup

Strong brewed coffee	1 cup	7.7 ounces	220 grams
Granulated sugar	1 tablespoon	0.6 ounce	15 grams
Stoli Kafya vodka	1 tablespoon	0.3 ounce	10 grams

For the truffle ganache

DOVE® PROMISES® Dark Chocolate, finely chopped		9 ounces	250 grams
Heavy cream	Scant 2¼ cups	18 ounces	500 grams

To finish the cake

Heavy cream	2 cups	16 ounces	450 grams
Chocolate shavings (optional; page 288)			
Cinnamon sugar (optional)	¼ cup	1.9 ounces	55 grams
Dutch-processed unsweetened cocoa powder (optional)	¼ cup	1.2 ounces	30 grams

Prepare the pound cake or angel food cake: Make the batter and bake in a cake pan as directed in the recipe. Let cool on a wire rack until ready to use, then unmold. You will need to slice the cake horizontally into 1-inch-thick layers before you use it. To do this easily, use a knife to mark the layers into the side of the cake. Place the cake on a revolving cake stand. Use a long, serrated knife to begin to slice the cake as you turn the cake stand. This will keep the layer even as you cut it. Do not try to cut all the way through on the first rotation. When you finish the first turn, keep turning while gradually cutting deeper into the layer until you are all the way through it. Separate the layers by sliding each one onto a flat plate or cake circle. You will only use one layer for this cake. Store the remaining cake in the freezer for up to 3 weeks. *continued*

Place a 9 × 3-inch cake ring on a parchment paper–covered baking sheet. Shave the outside edge of the cake layer slightly so it fits just inside the ring and place it at the bottom. If you use angel food cake, fill in the center with extra cake.

Prepare the coffee syrup: Pour the coffee into a medium-size mixing bowl. Stir in the sugar and allow to cool to room temperature. Once the coffee is cool, add the flavored vodka and stir to combine. Pour the coffee syrup into a squeeze bottle or cover well with plastic wrap to keep the alcohol from evaporating until you are ready to use the syrup. Soak the cake layer well with the syrup and set aside.

Prepare the truffle ganache: Place a 1-quart saucepan half filled with water over medium heat and bring it to a simmer. Make a double boiler by setting a large mixing bowl over the simmering water. Place the chocolate in the bowl and allow it to melt, stirring occasionally. The chocolate must be fully melted and very warm.

Pour the heavy cream into a medium-size mixing bowl and whip with an electric mixer set on medium speed until it barely holds its peaks. Be careful; if the cream is whipped too much, it will separate when the chocolate is added.

Remove the melted, warm chocolate from the double boiler. Use a rubber spatula to immediately fold the slightly whipped cream into the warm chocolate. If the cream appears to be melting because the bowl and the chocolate are too hot, immediately pour the entire mixture into the cold bowl that held the cream. Fold until the mixture is smooth and homogenous.

Assemble the cake: Fill the cake ring with the truffle ganache. Smooth with an offset spatula. Place the cake in the freezer for a few hours until set.

Finish the cake: Pour the heavy cream into a small mixing bowl and whip with an electric mixer set on medium-high speed to soft peaks. Remove the cake from the freezer and place on a flat platter. Use an offset spatula to spread the whipped cream over the top of the cake. If you do this before you remove the cake ring, the edge of the cake will be smooth and clean. Pat the back of the spatula gently up and down on the whipped cream to create peaks. This will make it look like the foam on top of a cup of cappuccino. Sprinkle the top of the cake with any of the following ingredients: coarsely grated chocolate shavings, cinnamon sugar (this is just cinnamon and sugar combined), or cocoa powder.

Unmold the cake: Run the blade of a hot knife around the inside of the cake ring to loosen the cake from the side. Gently and carefully lift off the cake ring. If the side of the cake is not completely smooth, you can use a hot offset spatula to smooth it. It will be easier to cut the cake if you heat the blade of the knife in hot water and dry it before each slice.

Birthday Cake

Yield: One 8 × 4-inch cake or two 8 × 2-inch cakes

here is no doubt that the occasion for which I make the most cakes is the birthday. Over the years I have had the pleasure of making cakes for celebrities like Tom Hanks and Bill Cosby, government figures like the mayor of New York, my boss and everyone in his family, my family, and, it seems, most everyone else in the world. The story that stands out most in my mind is the night I made a cake for Lee Iacocca. He was dining with my boss at Le Cirque. I wanted to make the Chrysler emblem for the top of the cake but could not remember the design. Finally, I asked one of the workers to find a Chrysler on the street and draw the emblem on paper. I was mortified when the person came back to me with an actual hood ornament. I did not want to ask where he got it, and I was really worried about the possibility of Mr. Iacocca's car missing this item. I never heard anything from anyone, so I assume the best.

For the cake

Almond paste	¾ cup	5.6 ounces	160 grams
Granulated sugar	Generous ½ cup	4.5 ounces	125 grams
1 large egg			
5 large egg yolks			
Cake flour	⅓ cup	1.8 ounces	50 grams
Dutch-processed unsweetened cocoa powder	Scant ½ cup	1.8 ounces	50 grams
5 large egg whites			
Unsalted butter, melted	Scant ¼ cup	1.8 ounces	50 grams

For the chocolate mousse

Heavy cream	Scant ½ cup	3.5 ounces	100 grams
Bittersweet chocolate, finely chopped		6 ounces	170 grams
Heavy cream	Generous 1⅓ cups	11.5 ounces	330 grams

For the soaking syrup

Simple Syrup flavored (optional) with dark rum (page 86)	

For the ribbon, bows, and flowers

White chocolate, tempered (page 8)	8 ounces	230 grams
Bittersweet chocolate, tempered (page 8)	8 ounces	230 grams

continued

Prepare the cake layers: Preheat the oven to 350°F (176°C). Line the bottom of an 8 × 3-inch cake pan with a sheet of parchment paper. Spray the parchment paper–covered bottom and the side of the pan with vegetable cooking spray. Be sure to apply an even layer of spray. This will make it easier to unmold the baked cake.

Place the almond paste in a medium-size mixing bowl and beat with an electric mixer set on medium speed to soften it, about 3 minutes. Add a scant ⅓ cup (2.6 ounces; 75 grams) of the sugar and continue to mix, allowing the sugar to dissolve into the almond paste. The almond paste will not soften completely. Mix until it is somewhat smooth. Add the egg and yolks one at a time, mixing well after each addition. If you take the time to incorporate each egg yolk fully, you will avoid lumps in the batter. Remember to scrape the side of the bowl down as needed. After all of the egg yolks and the egg have been added, the mixture should be loose and have no lumps. Keep mixing at medium-high speed until the batter is light in color and fluffy, about 5 minutes.

Sift the flour and cocoa together onto a sheet of parchment paper.

Place the egg whites in a large mixing bowl and whip with an electric mixer set on medium speed until foamy, about 2 minutes. Make a French meringue by adding the remaining 2½ tablespoons (1.8 ounces; 50 grams) sugar 1 tablespoon at a time. When all of the sugar has been added, increase the mixer speed to medium-high and whip to stiff but not dry peaks, about 5 minutes.

Use a rubber spatula to fold about one third of the meringue into the almond mixture. This will lighten the consistency of the almond mixture and make it closer to that of the meringue. Then fold all the almond mixture into the meringue. Fold gently to avoid deflating the meringue and remember to fold all the way to the bottom of the bowl. Slowly add the sifted mixture to the meringue mixture, folding gently. It helps to have a friend pour in the sifted mixture while you keep folding. Fold gently. If the batter deflates, the cake will be flat.

Add the melted butter all at once when the flour mixture is almost fully incorporated. Fold to the bottom of the bowl until the butter is fully combined. Fill the cake pan with the batter and gently smooth the top. Bake until the cake is well risen and springs back when pressed gently, about 45 minutes.

Remove the cake from the oven and let cool on a wire rack for about 10 minutes. Run the blade of a knife around the inside of the cake pan to loosen the cake from the side. Invert a flat plate over the cake pan. Place one hand on each side, grasping both plate and pan, and flip them both over so that the cake pan is on top. Gently lift off the cake pan and peel away the parchment paper. Invert a second flat plate over the bottom of the cake. Once again, flip both plates so that the cake is right side up. Remove the first plate.

Once the cake has cooled completely, you will need to cut it into four layers. To do this easily, use a knife to mark the layers into the side of the cake. Place the cake on a revolving cake stand. Use a long serrated knife to begin to slice the cake as you turn the stand. This will help keep the layer even as you cut it. Do not try to cut all the way through on the first rotation. When you finish the first turn, keep turning while gradually cutting deeper into the layer until you are all the way through it. Separate the layers by sliding each one onto a flat plate or cake circle. If necessary, trim the cake layers so they will fit inside the cake ring. Choose the flattest, most even layer (usually the bottom) to be used as the top of the cake. Set the cake layers aside while you prepare the filling.

Prepare the chocolate mousse: Heat the scant ½ cup (3.5 ounces; 100 grams) of heavy cream in a 1-quart heavy-bottomed saucepan until bubbles begin to form around the edge of the pan. Place the chopped chocolate in a medium-size mixing bowl. Make a ganache by pouring the hot cream over the chocolate and letting it sit for 30 seconds to melt the chocolate, then slowly whisking until smooth and homogenous. Transfer the ganache to a cool bowl.

Pour the remaining heavy cream into a medium-size mixing bowl. Use an electric mixer set on medium-high speed to whip the cream to soft peaks. Use a rubber spatula to fold about one third of the whipped cream into the ganache. Then fold all of the ganache into the remaining whipped cream.

Assemble the cake (for 2 cakes): Place an 8 × 2-inch cake ring on a parchment paper–covered baking sheet. Place one of the cake layers in the bottom of the ring. Soak the cake layer with some of the flavored simple syrup. Fill the cake ring half full with the chocolate mousse and spread it evenly with a rubber spatula. Top with the second cake layer and press down gently. Soak this cake layer with the flavored simple syrup. Fill the cake ring with mousse and use an offset spatula to smooth the top. Be careful not to press down on the mousse as you spread it. Repeat to make a second 8 × 2-inch cake. Place the cakes in the refrigerator until set, about 2 hours. To make one high cake, use a higher ring mold and all four layers of cake, remembering to end with a layer of mousse.

Unmold the cake: Place the cake on a platter. Run the heated blade of a paring knife around the inside of the cake ring to loosen the cake from the sides. Gently lift off the ring. Set aside while you prepare the ribbon and flowers.

continued

Spread a layer of white chocolate over the acetate strip.

Draw a cake comb through the white chocolate from top to bottom, the full length of the strip.

Spread a layer of bittersweet chocolate over the white stripes.

Prepare the chocolate ribbon: Use a large offset spatula to spread an ⅛-inch-thick layer of tempered white chocolate over a 2 × 30-inch-long strip of acetate (page 2). Draw a cake comb (see illustration) through the white chocolate from top to bottom, the full length of the strip. Pick up the strip of acetate by opposite corners and move it to a clean spot on your work surface. Clean the excess white chocolate with an offset spatula and return it to the bowl of white chocolate. Allow the chocolate lines on the acetate to set. When set, spread an ⅛-inch-thick layer of tempered bittersweet chocolate over the strip of acetate. You should not be able to see any white chocolate. The bittersweet chocolate will fill in the lines between the white chocolate, creating stripes. Allow the chocolate to set just until it begins to harden. The strip should still be pliable. Pick up the strip by opposite corners and wrap it around the unmolded cake, acetate side out. The strip will be slightly longer than the diameter of the cake. To close the ribbon, peel back enough of the acetate and press the two overlapping chocolate ends together tightly to form a seal. There is a good chance your acetate will be longer than the diameter of the cake. You can cut off this extra piece later when it hardens. Allow the ribbon to set completely before removing the acetate. The acetate is ready to be removed when it looks slightly cloudy and begins to pull away from the chocolate. Gently remove the acetate. Cut any extra ribbon using the blade of a paring knife. Heat the blade under some hot water and dry it off completely. Then simply press the edge of the blade against the part you want to cut, and let the heat melt it. You should end up with a nice clean cut where the ribbon connects.

Prepare the bows: Make a striped chocolate ribbon as just described using a 2 × 30-inch-long strip of acetate. Allow the chocolate to set until barely hardened. Cut the strip into 2 × 5-inch strips. Fold over each of these strips to make a loop and press the ends together tightly to seal. Rest the bows on edge and allow to fully set. Prepare another 2 × 14-inch-long strip. Allow the chocolate to set. Use the blade of a hot paring knife to cut the strip into 2 × 7-inch pieces for the tails of the ribbon. When all of the chocolate has completely set, peel away the acetate. Assemble the bow on top of the cake. Set aside while you make the flowers.

To make a bow: Fold the strip to make a loop and press the ends together tightly.

Prepare the flowers: This is easiest to do on a marble, granite, or stainless-steel surface because the surface is cool. If you do not have any of these, place a baking sheet in the freezer for several minutes and allow it to get cold. Place it upside down on your work surface and make the flowers on the back of the cold baking sheet. Cut a small square from a sheet of acetate and place a dab of chocolate in the center of the square. This will be the base of the flower. Use an offset spatula to spread an ⅛-inch-thick layer of tempered bittersweet chocolate in a large rectangle on the work surface. Let the chocolate set until slightly firm. Hold a 3-inch plain cutter flat against the chocolate rectangle and pull it toward you through the chocolate. The chocolate should curl to form abstract petals. Dip the end of each petal in the bowl of chocolate and "glue" them to the base. These flowers are very abstract. Let your eye guide you as you arrange the petals. Make as many petals and flowers as you like. I like to dust the tops of the flowers with some powdered sugar before I place them on the cake. Remember to remove the acetate from the bottom of the flower before you place it on the cake.

To make a flower: Hold a 3-inch plain cutter against the chocolate and pull it toward you through the chocolate to form abstract petals.

A finished flower.

Variation: If you are short on time, you can decorate the cake with a real ribbon and edible flowers like apple blossoms, tulips, lilacs, roses, and violets.

Crêpe Cake

Yield: One 9-inch cake; 8 to 10 servings

The first time I was asked to make a crêpe cake was for my friend Jacques Maximin's cookbook. That was years ago, and every once in a while someone comes across my name in that book. Since that time I have revised the recipe and made it lighter. I think it's great to use leftover crêpes this way. For this recipe I just combine all of my favorite tastes: pastry cream, chocolate, Grand Marnier, and crêpes.

½ recipe Basic Pound Cake (page 87)			
Crêpes (page 210)			
For the filling			
Pastry Cream (page 20)			
Heavy cream	1⅓ cups	10.5 ounces	300 grams
4 gelatin sheets or 1⅓ envelopes powdered gelatin			
DOVE® PROMISES® Dark Chocolate, finely chopped		7 ounces	200 grams
Grated zest of 1 orange			
Grand Marnier	¼ cup	1.8 ounces	50 grams
Apricot Glaze (page 27)			

Prepare the cake: Make the pound cake batter as directed in the recipe and bake it in a cake pan. Place on a wire rack to cool. When cooled, invert onto your work surface and peel off the parchment paper. You will need to slice the cake horizontally into ½-inch-thick layers. To do this easily, use a knife to mark the layers into the side of the cake. Place the cake on a revolving cake stand. Use a long, serrated knife to begin to slice the cake as you turn the stand. This will help keep the layer even as you cut it. Do not try to cut all the way through on the first rotation. When you finish the first turn, keep turning while gradually cutting deeper into the layer until you are all the way through it. Separate the layers by sliding each one onto a flat plate or cake circle. You only use one cake layer for this recipe. Store the rest in the freezer, well wrapped in plastic wrap, for up to 4 weeks.

Prepare the crêpes: Make the crêpes as directed in the recipe and let cool. These can be made ahead of time and stored in the refrigerator, well wrapped in plastic wrap, for up to 2 days. If the crêpes stick together when cold, simply warm them slightly in the

microwave for 10 to 15 seconds on high power. This will allow them to separate easily.

Line the bottom of a 9 × 2-inch cake pan with a sheet of parchment paper. Cut 4 to 5 crêpes in half. Line the bottom and side of the pan with the crêpe halves, allowing the tips to overlap the rim of the pan. The unmolded cake will look nicest if all of the crêpes are placed in the cake pan in the same direction. Overlap the crêpes slightly to completely cover the bottom and side of the pan. Set aside.

Prepare the filling: Make the pastry cream as directed in the recipe and allow it to cool. Pour the heavy cream into a medium-size mixing bowl and whip to soft peaks with an electric mixer set on medium-high speed. Place in the refrigerator until ready to use.

If you are using gelatin sheets, place them in a medium-size mixing bowl with enough cold water (about 1 quart) to cover. Let stand for about 5 minutes to allow the gelatin to soften and hydrate. Cold water hydrates the gelatin without letting it absorb too much liquid. Remove the gelatin from the bowl and squeeze out the excess water with your hands. If you are using powdered gelatin, sprinkle it over ¼ cup (2 ounces; 60 grams) of cold water. Let the gelatin bloom until it has absorbed all the water, about 1 minute.

Place a 1-quart saucepan half filled with water over medium heat and bring to a simmer. Make a double boiler by setting a large mixing bowl over the simmering water. Place the chocolate in the mixing bowl and allow it to melt completely, stirring occasionally to dissolve any lumps. The chocolate should be completely melted and warm.

Fold the orange zest and Grand Marnier into the cold pastry cream and mix well. Use a rubber spatula to fold the pastry cream mixture into the warm chocolate. I like to do this over the simmering water because the combined mixture should be slightly warm. If the chocolate is too cold, it will seize (harden) when combined with the pastry cream. Remove the chocolate pastry cream from above the simmering water. Place the hydrated gelatin in a small heavy-bottomed saucepan and place over medium heat. Add a small amount of water or a little Grand Marnier if you have it and a small scoop of pastry cream and allow the gelatin to dissolve, stirring gently. Fold the dissolved gelatin mixture into the chocolate pastry cream and mix until well combined.

Fold the whipped cream into the chocolate pastry cream, remembering to fold all the way to the bottom of the bowl. If the bowl containing the chocolate pastry cream is too hot when you fold in the whipped cream, only add half of the whipped cream, then fold the chocolate mixture into the colder bowl of remaining whipped cream. The mixture should be smooth and homogenous.

Assemble the cake: Fill the prepared cake pan about one-quarter full with the chocolate pastry cream mixture. Add a layer of crêpes, this time arranging them within the pan so they do not hang over the side. Add another quarter of the pastry cream and top this with a layer of crêpes. Repeat this procedure until you reach the top of the cake pan. Leave enough room at the top to close the cake with the pound cake disk. If necessary, trim the cake disk to fit inside the pan. Soak this disk with some Grand Marnier and place it on top of the cream, pressing down gently. Use a sharp paring knife to slice the overhanging crêpes flush with the rim of the cake pan. Place the cake in the refrigerator for 1 hour to set.

Unmold the cake: Place a flat plate upside down over the cake pan. Place one hand on each side, grasping both plate and cake pan, and flip over both so that the cake pan is on top. Gently tap the bottom of the cake pan and lift off the pan.

Use a pastry brush to brush the hot apricot glaze over the cake. This will add shine to the cake and keep it from drying. Serve!

Bee's Nest

Yield: One 10-inch cake; 8 to 10 servings

Kris and I were exploring Saint-Tropez one summer when I discovered the *Tropézienne*, which was the inspiration for this recipe. The *Tropézienne* is a brioche disk that is cut in half, soaked with an alcohol-flavored simple syrup, and filled with light pastry cream. It is a wonderful treat to have in the late afternoon when you return from the beach. One of the variations of this dessert is to top it with caramelized almonds instead of sugar. I love this cake because the flavors are very intense and really delicious. You can make it with leftover unbaked brioche dough.

⅓ **recipe Brioche (page 192)**

¾ **recipe Pastry Cream flavored with**
    Stoli Strasberi vodka (page 20)

For the topping

Unsalted butter	7 tablespoons	3.5 ounces	100 grams
Granulated sugar	Scant ½ cup	3.5 ounces	100 grams
Honey	Scant ¼ cup	1.8 ounces	50 grams
Heavy cream	¼ cup	1.8 ounces	50 grams
Sliced blanched almonds, toasted (page 127)	1 cup	3.5 ounces	100 grams

To finish the bee's nest

Heavy cream	1⅓ cups	10.5 ounces	300 grams
Simple Syrup flavored with Stoli Strasberi vodka (page 86)			

Prepare the brioche: Make the dough as directed in the recipe and let rest in the refrigerator overnight.

Prepare the flavored pastry cream: Make the pastry cream, flavor it as directed in the recipe, and store in the refrigerator until ready to use.

Remove the dough from the refrigerator and place on a lightly floured work surface. Use a rolling pin to roll the dough into a 10-inch disk. Place on a parchment paper–covered baking sheet and set aside in the freezer for at least 30 minutes. You want the dough to be very cold and hard, or it will become too soft when the hot topping is added.

continued

Prepare the topping: Combine the butter, sugar, honey, and heavy cream in a 2-quart heavy-bottomed saucepan and place over medium-low heat. Stir occasionally and cook the mixture until it reaches a light caramel color, about 10 minutes. Add the almonds and stir until combined. Remove from the heat and spread evenly over the brioche disk, being sure to spread the topping all the way to the edge. Place the dough in a warm spot and let proof for a few hours. I usually place mine on top of the refrigerator, which is slightly warmer (about 80°F/27°C) than room temperature. You can also briefly warm the oven, turn it off, and then place the dough in the warm oven. The brioche will triple in height and appear light and full of air.

Preheat the oven to 350°F (176°C). Place the brioche cake in the oven and bake until well risen and evenly golden brown, about 25 minutes. Remove the cake from the oven and cool completely on a wire rack.

Assemble the cake: Use a serrated knife to slice off the top half of the cake and set aside. Transfer the bottom half to a flat serving platter.

Pour the heavy cream for the filling into a medium-size mixing bowl and whip to soft peaks with an electric mixer set on medium-high speed. Remove the pastry cream from the refrigerator and whisk it slightly to loosen it. Fold the whipped cream into the pastry cream until well incorporated. Soak the bottom half of the cake with the flavored simple syrup.

Use an offset spatula to spread a thick layer of the lightened pastry cream over the bottom of the brioche cake. Spread the pastry cream all the way to the edge. It will be easier to serve the cake if you cut the top before you place it back onto the pastry cream–covered cake bottom. Use a serrated knife to cut the top into eight or ten slices. Then place the slices in a circle on the top of the cake. If you replace the top without slicing it first, the pastry cream will ooze from the side of the cake when you cut it.

> **To toast nuts:** Preheat the oven to 300°F (148°C). Spread the nuts evenly on a baking sheet and place in the oven. Toast for about 30 minutes, until they are golden brown. You will be able to smell the nuts when they are ready. A good test is to break a nut in half and check to see if it is light brown on the inside. Toasting nuts brings out their natural flavor. Remove them from the oven and allow to cool completely on the baking sheet on a wire rack.

Peanut Brittle Meringue Cake

Yield: One 10-inch cake; 8 servings

There is a traditional meringue-based cake recipe in France called *Succès*. It is not a tall cake, but it is very rich and full of flavor. I think I have given it an American twist by adding the peanuts.

For the cake layers

7 large egg whites			
Granulated sugar	Scant 1 cup	7 ounces	200 grams
Powdered sugar, sifted, plus extra for dusting	⅔ cup	2.6 ounces	75 grams
Peanuts, toasted (page 127) and finely chopped	¾ cup	3.5 ounces	100 grams

For the buttercream

Whole milk	Scant 1 cup	7 ounces	200 grams
Granulated sugar	Generous 1¼ cups	10 ounces	280 grams
Cold unsalted butter, cubed	1¾ cups	14 ounces	400 grams

For the filling

Peanut brittle or 3 SNICKERS® MUNCH® Bars, finely chopped	About 1 cup	4 ounces	120 grams

Prepare the cake layers: Draw two 10-inch circles on a sheet of parchment paper by tracing around the outside of a 10-inch cake pan with a pen. Turn the paper over so the drawing is facedown (so that the ink does not bake into the meringue) and place on a baking sheet. Preheat the oven to 200°F (93°C).

Place the egg whites in a large mixing bowl and whip with an electric mixer set on medium speed until foamy. Make a French meringue by adding the granulated sugar 1 tablespoon at a time. Adding the sugar slowly allows the whites to gain some volume and the sugar to dissolve into the whites. When you have volume, add the rest of the granulated sugar. Increase the mixer speed to medium-high and whip to stiff but not dry peaks, about 5 minutes. When the whites are slightly stiff, reduce the mixer speed to low to allow more air to incorporate without overwhipping the egg whites. Continue to whip for about another 2 minutes. Stop whipping if the egg whites look dry or separated. Fold in the powdered sugar all at once. Fold gently so you don't lose too much volume. When the pow-

dered sugar is almost fully incorporated, gently fold in the peanuts. Place the peanut meringue in a pastry bag fitted with a ½-inch plain tip.

To pipe the cake layers, hold the pastry bag at a slight angle about 1½ inches above the parchment paper. This height and angle allows the piped meringue to hold the full shape of the ½-inch tip. Start at the center of the circle and pipe the meringue in a spiral to the edge of the outline. (I work counterclockwise because I am right-handed.) If the meringue breaks while you are piping it, just continue where it broke. If any air bubbles appear on the disk, go back and fill them in with the extra meringue left in the pastry bag. It takes practice to get the disks perfectly round. Don't worry if yours are slightly misshapen. You can gently scrape away the imperfections after the disks are baked. Don't forget to sprinkle the disks with powdered sugar. If you do not want to use a pastry bag, use an offset spatula to spread the meringue in a ½-inch-thick layer inside each drawn circle. Try to keep the top of each circle as smooth and even as possible.

Bake the meringue disks until they are firm to the touch, about 2 hours. If the meringue begins to take on color while baking, reduce the oven temperature by 50°F (10°C). Remove the baking sheet from the oven and place on a wire rack until the meringue disks have completely cooled. If you have the time, turn off the oven and cool the meringue on the baking sheet in the oven. This will take about 1 hour and will allow the meringue to dry completely.

Prepare the buttercream: Pour the milk and sugar into a 1-quart heavy-bottomed saucepan and place over medium-high heat. Stir to combine and to help the sugar dissolve and allow the mixture to come to a boil. Pour into a clean bowl and let cool until warm.

Place the cold butter in a medium-size mixing bowl. Use an electric mixer set on medium speed to whip the butter while slowly adding the warm milk mixture. When all of the milk has been added, increase the mixer speed to medium-high and whip until smooth, fluffy, and shiny, about 5 minutes. If the milk begins to separate when added to the butter, it is too cold. To fix this, place a small amount (about a cup) of the mixture in a small saucepan and place over medium heat. Allow the butter to melt and the mixture to soften. Combine the warmer mixture with the other and continue to whip. The separated mixture should come back together after a few minutes. If the buttercream becomes too liquid after the milk has been added, the milk was too hot. To fix this, place the mixture in the refrigerator for about 15 minutes to allow the butter to harden slightly, then continue to whip.

Assemble the cake: Place one of the meringue disks flat side down on a platter. I like to anchor the disk to the platter with a small dab of buttercream. This will keep the cake from sliding off the platter. Fill a pastry bag fitted with a ½-inch plain tip with the buttercream. Hold the pastry bag at a slight angle, with the tip about 1 inch from the meringue disk. Pipe large mounds shaped like kisses onto the disk, leaving a ¼-inch border around the edge of the disk. If you do not want to pipe it, you can use an offset spatula to spread the buttercream onto the disk. Top with about three quarters of the peanut brittle. Place the second disk spiral side up on top of the buttercream and press down very slightly to adhere. Lightly dust the top of the cake with powdered sugar. Use an offset spatula to spread the sugar around the meringue. This will ensure that sugar goes into all of the little air bubbles and creates a smooth surface. When smooth, dust liberally with more powdered sugar and peanut brittle.

To cut the cake, use a serrated knife in a sawing motion to cut through the top layer of meringue first. Then cut through the remaining cake layers. If you try to press down with the knife, the meringue will break.

Variation: Here is an easy way to decorate the top of the cake: Hold a piece of paper over part of the cake. Sprinkle the uncovered part with unsweetened cocoa powder. This will create a contrasting pattern. You do not have to use a straight edge. Be creative with your design!

Kid's Play

People who know me say I'm just a big kid. The recipes in this chapter are things you can make with the children in your life—grown-up or otherwise. The items are familiar, and kids really love them. Sometimes nothing will do like a favorite sweet from your childhood. Some call that *soul food*.

It is not important what you make; it is just important that you spend time with children. They offer a valuable perspective on life. Most kids will be more motivated to work with you in the kitchen than they would if you were mowing the lawn. I have a lot of memories of baking with my mom. There is something about pleasing your palate and sharing time with someone you love; both are nurturing.

Chocolate Chip Cookies

Yield: About 2½ dozen

Since I moved to this country, I have learned a lot about cookies. One thing is for sure: everybody has a favorite recipe. If you understand the ingredients and how they interact, you can adapt any recipe or create your own so your cookies will turn out exactly as you like them.

There are three basic flours in baking, and they all contain protein. When that protein is mixed with liquid, gluten (page 10) is formed. That is what gives dough its elasticity. Bread flour contains the most protein, cake flour the least. All-purpose flour is comprised of 50 percent bread flour and 50 percent cake flour. If you use a flour that is high in protein, the elasticity of gluten will cause the cookie to rise higher and the strength of the flour will allow the cookies to hold the rise. Cookies baked with cake flour will be flatter because the gluten is less elastic and strong.

Using melted butter will cause the cookies to bake flat and be chewy. This happens because the melted fat coats the protein molecules and keeps the liquid from interacting with the protein as efficiently, which inhibits gluten development. When you use softened butter, the butter still has an emulsion (page 17), which helps the cookies rise more.

Many cookie recipes call for a lot of sugar. You can replace up to 25 percent of the sugar with corn syrup. That will cut the sweetness. Corn syrup also helps the cookies to retain moisture, which keeps them fresh longer.

Egg yolks add fat to a recipe. If you want your cookies to be cakey, you can adjust the recipe by adding yolks. If the recipe calls for one egg, add a yolk and no white. If the recipe calls for two eggs, use one whole egg and two yolks. If the recipe calls for three eggs, use two whole eggs and two yolks. The egg white helps hold the mixture together.

If you want chocolate cookies, replace 25 percent of the flour (about ⅓ cup; 2.3 ounces; 65 grams) with unsweetened cocoa powder.

Unsalted butter, softened	**1 cup**	**8 ounces**	**126 grams**
Granulated sugar	**¼ cup**	**1.9 ounces**	**55 grams**
Light corn syrup	**¼ cup**	**3.5 ounces**	**100 grams**

Light brown sugar	Firmly packed ½ cup	2.5 ounces	70 grams
1 large egg			
½ vanilla bean, scraped			
Unbleached all-purpose flour	2 cups	9 ounces	250 grams
Pinch of baking soda			
Pinch of salt			
DOVE® PROMISES® Dark Chocolate, chopped, or "M&M's"® Milk Chocolate Mini Baking Bits		12 ounces	340 grams
Optional additions			
Grated chocolate	1 cup	4 ounces	120 grams
Chopped nuts	1 cup	4.7 ounces	130 grams

continued

Preheat the oven to 350°F (176°C). Combine the butter, granulated sugar, corn syrup, and brown sugar in a medium-size mixing bowl and beat with an electric mixer set on medium-high speed until light in color, about 3 minutes. Add the egg and vanilla bean seeds and beat until well incorporated.

Combine the flour, baking soda, and salt in a small mixing bowl (the salt will enhance the flavor of the chocolate). Reduce the speed of the mixer to medium, add the flour mixture to the sugar mixture, and mix until well combined. Don't overmix the batter, or the gluten will overdevelop and the cookies will be tough. Use a rubber spatula to fold in the chopped chocolate. If you want to add other ingredients, mix them in now. (At this point the dough can be stored in the freezer, well wrapped in plastic wrap, for up to 4 weeks.) When the cookie dough is well combined, drop 1-inch mounds onto a nonstick or parchment paper–covered baking sheet.

Place the baking sheets in the oven and bake until evenly golden brown, about 7 minutes. If the cookies bake too fast on the bottom but are still underbaked on top, double the baking sheet. Remove from the oven and cool on a wire rack. The baked cookies can be stored at room temperature, in an airtight container, for up to 5 days.

Brownies

Yield: One 12 × 18-inch baking sheet

I discovered brownies when I moved to the United States, and over the last ten years here I have eaten quite a few. There are many ways to make brownies, but they always have the same basic ingredients. When you learn how the ingredients interact, you will be able to adjust your recipe to make the brownies as you prefer them.

If you want soft, dense, fudgy brownies, use two parts cake flour and one part bread flour (cake flour has less gluten). If you want chewy brownies, use two parts bread flour to one part cake flour. The protein in the bread flour and the subsequent gluten in the batter will make the brownies chewy. If you want something between these two, use all-purpose flour.

The way butter is incorporated into the recipe will affect the texture of the brownies. If you melt the butter, it loses its emulsion, meaning the brownies will not rise as much and will be moister and dense. If you cream the butter with the flour, you keep the emulsion. This helps the brownies to rise and makes them more crumbly.

The more sugar you add to your brownies, the crustier and drier they will be. To add moisture and elasticity, replace one fourth of the sugar with the same amount of corn syrup.

Eggs bring fat to the recipe. If you want cakey brownies, add an extra yolk. If you use fewer eggs, the brownies will be dry and rubbery.

Whatever version you choose, invite me over when you make brownies. I can't get enough of these things!

Water	Generous 1 cup	9 ounces	250 grams
Unsalted butter	1 cup	8 ounces	230 grams
Granulated sugar	Generous 1 cup	8 ounces	230 grams
Bittersweet chocolate, chopped		21 ounces	600 grams
Unbleached all-purpose flour	2 cups	18 ounces	250 grams
Baking soda	1 teaspoon	0.18 ounce	6 grams
Pinch of salt			
Vanilla extract	2 tablespoons	1 ounce	25 grams
6 large eggs			

Optional additions

Nuts, chopped	1 cup	5.5 ounces	150 grams
Shredded sweetened coconut	1 cup	2.6 ounces	75 grams
"M&M's"® Milk Chocolate Mini Baking Bits	1 cup	7 ounces	200 grams

Preheat the oven to 375°F (190°C). Lightly spray a nonstick baking sheet with vegetable cooking spray and set aside.

Place the water, butter, and sugar in a 2-quart heavy-bottomed saucepan and place over medium-high heat. Whisk occasionally as the mixture melts. Add about half of the chocolate to the mixture and stir to combine. Allow the chocolate to melt while stirring occasionally. (In this recipe I melt half of the chocolate and add the other half as is so my brownies will have some crunchy texture.) When the chocolate has melted and the mixture is well combined, remove from the heat. Combine the flour, baking soda, and salt in a large mixing bowl. Pour the melted chocolate mixture into the flour mixture and combine well with a spatula. Mix in the vanilla.

Incorporate the eggs one at a time, whisking well after each addition. Do not overmix, or the brownies will develop too much gluten, causing them to be tough and elastic. If the mixture is not too warm, add the remaining chopped chocolate and fold to combine. If the mixture is too warm when the chocolate is added, it will melt.

Pour about half of the brownie batter onto the prepared baking sheet and use a large offset spatula to evenly spread it. At this point, sprinkle the chopped nuts, shredded coconut, or "M&M's"® Milk Chocolate Mini Baking Bits over the brownie batter. Choose any topping you like or make a combination as I do, but only use 1 cup of topping! Then cover with the remaining brownie batter.

Place the brownies in the oven and bake for about 40 minutes. When touched, they should be as firm as the palm of your hand. Let cool on a wire rack. Run a sharp paring knife around the inside of the baking sheet to loosen the brownies from the sides. Invert the baking sheet onto a sheet of parchment paper. Lift the baking sheet off the brownies. Use a sharp chef's knife to cut the brownies into the desired size. I imagine the brownies can be stored at room temperature, if well wrapped in plastic wrap, for up to 5 days, but they never last longer than one day at my house.

> Baking time is very important. I like my brownies slightly under-baked and fudgy. If you like them slightly drier, bake them a few extra minutes.

Marshmallows

Yield: About 54 pieces

In France we call these *Chamallows* and they are often colored pink, green, and white. This recipe is very similar to an old French recipe called *Guimauve*, which are long strips of marshmallows, sometimes twisted together with different flavors. I am sure your kids will have fun with this recipe.

9 gelatin sheets or 3 envelopes powdered gelatin

Water	⅓ cup	3.6 ounces	75 grams
Granulated sugar	Generous 1¼ cups	10.5 ounces	300 grams
Light corn syrup	¼ cup	3.5 ounces	100 grams
6 large egg whites			
1 to 2 drops liquid food coloring			
1 to 2 drops flavored oil (page 12)			
Powdered sugar for dusting	¾ cup	2.8 ounces	80 grams
Cornstarch for dusting	¾ cup	2.8 ounces	80 grams

If you are using gelatin sheets, place them in a medium-size mixing bowl with enough cold water (about 2 quarts) to cover. Let stand for about 5 minutes to allow the gelatin to soften and hydrate. Cold water hydrates the gelatin without letting it absorb too much liquid. Remove the gelatin from the bowl and squeeze out the excess water with your hands. If you are using powdered gelatin, sprinkle it over ¾ cup (6 ounces; 180 grams) of cold water. Let the gelatin bloom until it has absorbed all the water, about 1 minute.

Pour the water, granulated sugar, and corn syrup into a 2-quart heavy-bottomed saucepan and place over medium-high heat. When bubbles start to form around the edge of the pan, insert a candy thermometer in the mixture and begin to whip the egg whites.

Place the egg whites in a large mixing bowl and whip to stiff but not dry peaks with an electric mixer set on medium-high speed, about 5 minutes. Be careful not to overwhip.

The sugar is ready when it reaches 240°F to 250°F (115°C to 121°C). Make an Italian meringue by pouring the cooked sugar down the side of the bowl into the whipping egg whites. Do not pour the hot sugar onto the beaters or it will splatter. Place the hydrated gelatin in the hot pan that held the sugar mixture and swirl it around as it dissolves. Add the dissolved gelatin to the hot meringue and continue to whip until stiff, glossy, and fluffy, about 7 minutes. The gelatin will make the marshmallows lighter, hold their shape, and give them their trademark elasticity.

If you would like to color and/or flavor the meringue, add one to two drops of food coloring and/or flavored oil now. Be careful, though; they are very concentrated—one drop goes a long way. Whip the meringue until the coloring or flavoring is fully combined.

Spray the bottom and sides of a parchment paper–covered baking sheet with vegetable cooking spray to keep the marshmallows from sticking. Use a large offset spatula to spread the meringue evenly into the pan until the pan is completely full. Try to keep the meringue as level as possible, but do not press down on it as you spread it, or the meringue will deflate. To make the top very even, rest a long ruler on the two long sides of the pan and slide it across the top of the meringue.

Combine the powdered sugar and cornstarch in a small bowl. Use a fine-mesh sieve to sprinkle most of this mixture over the top of the meringue. Save a little for the next step. Let the meringue dry for 2 to 3 hours at room temperature.

Lightly dust your work surface with the powdered sugar mixture. Invert the meringue onto the work surface and remove the parchment paper from its bottom. Use a sharp chef's knife to cut the meringue into pieces of the desired size. It will be easier to cut the meringue if you dip the knife in hot water between each cut. The marshmallows will keep at room temperature, well wrapped in plastic wrap and dusted with the powdered sugar mixture, for up to 3 days.

Graham Crackers

Yield: 3 ½ dozen crackers

You might wonder what I am doing making my own graham crackers when the ones you can buy in the store are pretty good. I always try to do homemade things and think there is usually a place where I can improve a recipe. Sometimes all it takes is a different flour or an extra egg. This recipe is based on one that my friends from King Arthur shared with me. Let me know if you think my recipe stands up against the ones you can buy.

The dough is easy to make with your hands. If you have a stand mixer, use the paddle attachment and be careful not to overwork the dough.

Whole wheat flour	1 ½ cups	7.5 ounces	215 grams
Unbleached all-purpose flour	½ cup	2.5 ounces	70 grams
Powdered sugar	¼ cup	1.8 ounces	50 grams
Light brown sugar	¼ cup	1.7 ounces	45 grams
Baking powder	1 teaspoon	0.15 ounce	4 grams
Ground cinnamon	1 teaspoon	0.15 ounce	4 grams
Cold unsalted butter, cubed	½ cup	4 ounces	113 grams
Cold whole milk	4 to 5 tablespoons	2 to 2.5 ounces	60 to 75 grams
Water	1 tablespoon	1 ounce	25 grams
Light corn syrup	¼ cup	3.5 ounces	100 grams

Preheat the oven to 400°F (204°C). Combine the flours, sugars, baking powder, and cinnamon in a medium-size mixing bowl. Work in the butter with your hands until the mixture resembles coarse meal. The easiest way to do this is to grab a handful of flour mixture and butter, then gently rub the two between your hands to combine them. As you rub, the mixture drops back into the bowl. Keep doing this until most of the butter is combined. If your hands are too warm, the butter will melt. If necessary, wash your hands in ice-cold water every few minutes. Make sure your hands are dry when you return to the mixture. Stop working the mixture while you can still see small chunks of butter. This will make the dough softer and crumbly.

Add half of the milk and work it into the dough. The amount of liquid you use will always vary, depending on the humidity in the air. Add only enough liquid to hold the dough

together. Knead the dough gently in the bowl until it is smooth. Pat it into a disk and let it rest in the refrigerator for 1 hour. Turn the dough onto a lightly floured work surface. Use a rolling pin to roll the dough into a rectangle about ⅛ inch thick. Use a sharp paring knife to slice the rectangle into 2-inch squares and remove the scraps. Dock the squares using a fork. Place the squares on a parchment paper–covered baking sheet. Gently reroll the scraps and cut more squares, being careful not to overwork the dough.

Combine the water and corn syrup in a small bowl. Use a pastry brush to give each square a light coat of the corn syrup mixture. This will make them very shiny and give them a nice crust. Bake the crackers until evenly deep golden brown, about 10 minutes. Cool on a wire rack. The crackers can be stored at room temperature in an airtight container for up to 2 weeks.

> If the dough is slightly soft or sticky when you try to roll it, roll it
> out between two large pieces of plastic wrap or parchment paper.

Ice Cream Cones

Yield: 10 to 12 cones

When we visit my parents in the summer, the big debate every day is about who will pay for the ice cream that evening. My dad likes to celebrate my vacation every night by going down to the port in Bandol for ice cream. Our dinner conversations eventually lead to the flavors we anticipate having in our cones or sundaes. When I am not home, my dad buys those boxed ice cream treats from the grocery store. The cones are always soft and soggy. Here is my recipe for the cones.

You will need a template to make the cones. I cut mine from the side of a plastic bucket. Use a pen to trace the template outline on page 143 onto a square of stiff plastic and cut it out with an X-acto knife. The plastic piece with the cutout becomes your template and can be washed and used over and over again.

Unsalted butter, softened	**6 tablespoons**	**2.9 ounces**	**85 grams**
Powdered sugar	**Scant 1 cup**	**3.5 ounces**	**100 grams**
1 vanilla bean			
2 large egg whites			
Cake flour	**⅔ cup**	**3.5 ounces**	**100 grams**
For the topping (optional)			
Bittersweet chocolate, tempered (page 8)		**10.5 ounces**	**300 grams**
Shredded sweetened coconut, toasted (page 245)	**2 cups**	**5.5 ounces**	**150 grams**
Chopped toasted nuts (page 127)	**Scant 1 cup**	**4.5 ounces**	**125 grams**
12-ounce bag "M&M's"® Milk Chocolate Mini Baking Bits			

Place the butter and powdered sugar in a medium-size mixing bowl and beat with an electric mixer set on medium-high speed until creamy. Use a sharp knife to slice the vanilla bean in half lengthwise. Separate the seeds from the outside skin by scraping the blade of the knife along the inside of the bean. Add the vanilla seeds to the butter mixture and continue mixing until it lightens in color and gains volume. Add one of the egg whites and mix until combined. Add half of the cake flour and mix until the flour is no longer visible. Add the remaining egg white, again mixing until well combined. Mix in the remaining

cake flour just until incorporated and the dough is smooth. I add the egg whites and flour in two additions because it makes a more homogenous mixture. If your dough separates while you are adding the egg whites, don't worry. It should come back together smoothly with the final addition of flour. The separation happens when there are not enough dry ingredients to hold the liquid ingredients together. After the final addition of cake flour, do not overmix, or the dough will become tough and elastic. Let the dough rest at room temperature for 30 minutes.

Preheat the oven to 400°F (204°C). Lightly spray a nonstick baking sheet with vegetable cooking spray. Lay the template on the baking sheet. Use an offset spatula to spread about 2 tablespoons of the batter over the template. Carefully lift off the template. Repeat to make as many cones as needed. Place the baking sheet in the oven and bake just until the cones begin to take on color, about 6 minutes. The outside edges will brown first.

Remove the cones from the oven. To shape them, lift one off the baking sheet and place it on the work surface. Hold the bottom tip while you roll the wider end from one side to the other. Carefully hold the cone upright as it cools to keep its shape. Repeat with the remaining cones. It will be easier if you have a friend to help you do this. You need to work quickly, since the cones will cool within a couple of minutes. If they harden before you have removed all of them from the baking sheet, return the baking sheet to the oven for 1 to 2 minutes, until they are once again flexible enough to roll.

When all of the cones are rolled and cooled, you may choose to paint them with tempered chocolate. I like to paint chocolate around the rim and about 1 inch down the side. Leave enough room to be able to hold the cone without getting chocolate on your hands. You may add as much or as little chocolate as you like. Then I roll the top of each cone in a different topping—toasted coconut, toasted nuts, or "M&M's"® Milk Chocolate Mini Baking Bits. Have fun and create your own designs. The cones are now ready to be filled and eaten. The cones will keep for 3 days, stored in an airtight container at room temperature.

Variation: Spread the batter in a 4-inch circle on the baking sheet and bake. Immediately upon removal from the oven, use an offset spatula to lift the circle off the baking sheet and place it inside a 3-inch bowl. Allow the circle to fold against the side of the bowl, creating a "tulip cup" or basket, and let cool to set. Add a scoop of ice cream and *voilà*!

Fried Ice Cream

Yield: 8 to 10 balls

I love Japanese food, especially tempura. My favorite Japanese restaurant is right in my neighborhood. Tina and Kris met me for dinner one night. As usual, I was late getting out of my kitchen. By the time I joined them, they were ready for dessert. I ordered tempura. When the server brought their ice cream and my tempura, it reminded me of fried ice cream. Here is my recipe!

2 recipes Biscuit (page 283)			
1 pint chocolate ice cream			
1 pint strawberry ice cream			

For the coating

12 large eggs			
Whole milk	1 cup	7.8 ounces	225 grams
1 large box Kellogg's Corn Flakes			
Mango Sauce (page 24)			
Raspberry Sauce (page 24)			
Vegetable or canola oil for deep-frying			

Prepare the biscuit as described in the recipe and let cool. Use a 2½-inch plain cutter to cut 16 to 20 circles from the biscuit. Use a sharp paring knife to cut half as many 2½ × 10-inch strips from the biscuit. Set aside.

Prepare the ice cream balls: Use a large ice cream scoop to make balls of ice cream the size of tennis balls. Have fun with it. Use both ice creams to make some two-flavored balls by filling half the scoop with one flavor and then filling the remaining half with the other flavor. Place the balls on a parchment paper–covered baking sheet and place in the freezer to harden, about 2 hours.

Prepare the coating: Place the eggs and milk in a large mixing bowl and whisk to combine. Pour the cornflakes onto a parchment paper–covered baking sheet.

Coat the ice cream balls: Remove the frozen ice cream balls from the freezer. Wrap one biscuit strip completely around each ball. Squeeze gently to adhere it to the ice cream. Place one biscuit circle on each side of the strip, where the ice cream is not covered, and press gently to adhere. The ice cream ball should be completely covered with the biscuit. If the ice cream begins to melt, return the balls to the freezer for about 1 hour before proceeding. One by one, dip each ball into the egg mixture and immediately roll in the cornflake mixture. When all the balls have been covered, repeat with a second coating of egg mixture and cornflakes. It may be necessary to return the balls to the freezer between coatings. After the second coating, place the balls back in the freezer for a few hours to allow them to harden.

Decorate the serving plates: While the oil is heating, pour or squeeze a circle of mango sauce and a circle of raspberry sauce in the center of each plate. Use a wooden skewer to swirl them together to resemble flames.

Fry the ice cream: About 15 minutes before you are ready to serve the fried ice cream, heat the oil. Use an electric deep fryer or a 4-quart heavy-bottomed saucepan placed over medium-high heat to heat the oil to 350°F (176°C). If using a saucepan, you will need to fill it about halfway with oil and check the temperature with a candy thermometer. It is important to maintain this temperature, so you may need to turn down the heat or remove the pan from the burner briefly once the oil reaches the proper temperature. Fry the ice cream balls, two at a time, until they are golden brown, 3 to 5 minutes. It is important that they be frozen solid before you fry them, or they will melt during the time it takes for the coating to cook. Using a large slotted spoon or spider, remove the fried ice cream from the hot oil. Gently blot on a paper towel and center each over the decorated plates. Serve immediately.

Lollipops

Yield: 15 to 30 pieces, depending on your molds

I tend to attract a lot of children wherever I go. Kris calls me the Pied Piper of Pastry. You know how finicky kids can be about what they eat. I was invited to a big charity event for a children's foundation and wanted to make something especially for the kids that I could be sure they would all like. Tina found the most fantastic array of molds from the Apollo Company in Oklahoma and ordered them, knowing that I would go crazy when I saw them. I don't know who had more fun on the day of that event, the kids as they ate the lollipops or me as I made them!

You can use this recipe to make candy as well. Use candy molds or the Play-Doh technique described in this recipe. Be sure your food color is in liquid form. You should be able to find the lollipop molds, sticks, and flavored oils in a baking supply store, or see the Sources (page 296) for mail-order sources.

Water	Scant ¾ cup	5.5 ounces	150 grams
Granulated sugar	Generous 2¼ cups	18 ounces	500 grams
Light corn syrup	Scant ⅔ cup	7 ounces	200 grams
5 drops flavored oil: watermelon, apple, and/or lime			
1 drop food coloring			

Prepare the lollipop molds: Lightly spray each mold with vegetable cooking spray. Use your fingers to spread the spray around inside the mold and into all its little crevices. This will help the cooled lollipops release easily. Set the prepared molds aside while you cook the sugar.

Combine the water, sugar, and corn syrup in a 2-quart heavy-bottomed saucepan and place over medium-high heat. The corn syrup will make the cooked sugar harder and crunchier. It will also help prevent the cooked sugar from melting as quickly due to the humidity in the air. Insert a candy thermometer and cook the sugar mixture to 311°F (155°C), what is known as the hard crack stage (page 14). Stir the sugar mixture gently and slowly to ensure that it cooks evenly. If you do not stir it, the mixture will have hot spots where the sugar will cook faster than in the rest of the mixture. Use a pastry brush to keep the inside of the saucepan clean as the sugar cooks, or the sugar may recrystallize. To do this, dip a clean brush in cold water and brush the inside of the pan clean.

continued

Remove the cooked sugar from the heat and pour into a heatproof measuring cup with a spout. This will make it easier to pour the sugar into the molds. Add the desired flavoring and food coloring to the hot sugar and carefully stir it in using a wooden skewer or chopstick. Immediately pour the hot sugar into the molds, filling them to the top. Set the sticks in place by inserting them just far enough to be secure within the mold you are using. Set the molds aside to allow the sugar to cool completely. When cooled, simply pop out the lollipops. I suggest you make these no more than a few hours before you are going to use them. They won't last long, especially on a humid day, unless well wrapped in plastic.

If you do not have any lollipop molds, you can use Play-Doh. Roll fresh Play-Doh into a ½-inch-thick rectangle on top of a sheet of parchment paper. Use a sharp paring knife to cut out whatever shapes you like from the Play-Doh. Remove the cutout, leaving the homemade mold. Spray the inside edge of the Play-Doh with vegetable cooking spray. Pour the sugar syrup into the cut-out space. Insert the lollipop sticks and let cool completely before removing the Play-Doh. If the sugar syrup is still warm, the Play-Doh will stick to the side of the lollipops. When finished, the Play-Doh can be saved and reused for another day.

The Bread Basket

I like to work dough with my hands. The smell of the fermenting dough makes me feel close to the earth. Bread is a staple and it even has its own food group. Most everyone wants to try a hand at baking it.

It is very important to use the right flour for each recipe. When making cakes and tarts, the gluten in the flour is not overdeveloped, but in bread you need the strength of gluten. I hope you will refer to the flour technology section on page 10 for a detailed explanation of the whole process. Proof the dough in a warm place, such as on top of the refrigerator.

The craft of baking is very different from the craft required to make pastry. There is an art to making bread and the techniques are quite unique to it. The French Culinary Institute dedicates a whole curriculum to bread making. Never assume that a bread baker is a pastry chef and vice versa. Bread bakers have a feel for the dough, and they are quite passionate about the touch and smell. My friend Michel Peden is the most amazing baker I know. Fortunately, his bakery is not far from my house.

Pizza Dough

Yield: Enough for 3 pizzas

When I make pizza dough, I use bread flour. Its high protein content helps it develop more gluten strands. The gluten retains the gas that is released during fermentation, which helps the dough rise.

Kris is a very finicky eater. She has very specific likes for almost every dish. This is her favorite pizza dough. She prefers it rolled very thinly and baked well. I guess living with a pastry chef has a few advantages!

Bread flour	4 cups	18 ounces	500 grams
Fresh compressed yeast	2 tablespoons	0.75 ounce	20 grams
Salt	2½ teaspoons	0.5 ounce	12 grams
Granulated sugar	2½ teaspoons	0.5 ounce	12 grams
Extra virgin olive oil	¼ cup	1.8 ounces	50 grams
Water	Generous 1¼ cups	10.25 ounces	290 grams

Place the flour, yeast, salt, sugar, and olive oil in a large mixing bowl. I like to put the flour in the bottom of the bowl and all of the other ingredients in separate piles on top of it. That way, before I begin to mix it all together, I can double-check that I have added all of the correct ingredients. Beat with an electric mixer set on medium speed just until the ingredients are dispersed, about 5 seconds. If you have a stand mixer, use the paddle attachment. Add part of the water and continue to mix on medium-high speed. Flour

never absorbs the same quantity of liquid. The amount of water needed for the dough depends on the humidity in the air, so you will always need to adjust the recipe slightly. If too much liquid is added, just add a little more flour. Be careful; if too much flour is added, the recipe will become unbalanced and you will need to start again. It is better to add the water slowly and conservatively at the beginning. During the mixing process when the liquid is added, the gluten begins to work and the flavors in the dough develop. When ready, the dough will be fairly smooth and slightly sticky. Turn it onto a lightly floured work surface and gently knead it until smooth, about 30 seconds. Divide the dough into three equal pieces. Pat each piece into a disk, cover lightly with a dish towel or plastic wrap, and set aside in a warm place to ferment for about an hour. I usually place mine on top of the refrigerator, which is slightly warmer than room temperature (about 80°F/27°C). You can also briefly warm the oven, turn it off, and then place the dough in the warm oven. (At this point the dough can be stored in the freezer, well wrapped in plastic wrap, for up to 2 weeks.)

Preheat the oven to 480°F (250°C). Place the rested dough on a lightly floured work surface. Dust the top of each piece with flour. Use a rolling pin to roll each piece into a 10-inch circle. If you rotate the dough a quarter of a circle after every few passes with the rolling pin, it will be easier to maintain a circular shape. It will also help ensure that you are rolling the dough evenly. The dough may snap back as you roll it due to the gluten development. If the dough is too elastic, let it rest for about 5 minutes before you continue to roll.

Lightly coat a perforated baking sheet with olive oil or a pizza stone with cornmeal. If using a pizza stone, preheat it in the hot oven for 15 minutes before using. A nonperforated baking sheet can also be used, but the pizza won't bake as well. Place the rolled-out pizza dough on the baking sheet and add your toppings. Place in the oven and bake for 15 minutes. The crust will be golden brown, and the bottom should be fully baked and crunchy. Let cool slightly and enjoy.

> If you want to make your pizza crust ahead of time, you can prebake the rolled dough for 2 to 3 minutes on a perforated baking sheet lightly coated with olive oil. (The prebaked pizza crust can be stored in the freezer, well wrapped in plastic wrap, for up to 2 weeks.) When it is cool, add the toppings and finish baking it a few hours later. This is great when you have a party and prefer to spend your time with the guests rather than in the kitchen.

Sweet Pizza

Yield: One 10-inch pizza; 8 servings

This is a great dessert if you have some leftover pizza dough and jam in your refrigerator. I believe food has to be fun and this is a fun dessert. If you cut the dough into the size of cookies, no one would be surprised at the presentation, but most people would not expect you to serve a pizza for dessert. Go ahead. Push the limit. Do the unexpected.

Linda's Red Raspberry Jam (page 26) or store-bought	¾ cup	7 ounces	200 grams
⅓ recipe Pizza Dough (page 150)			
Mascarpone cheese	Generous ¼ cup	3.5 ounces	100 grams
Grated zest of ½ lemon			
Granulated sugar	1 tablespoon	0.6 ounce	15 grams
1 ripe mango, peeled, halved, and pitted			
5 fresh strawberries, cleaned and hulled			
10 fresh mint or basil leaves, cleaned and chopped			

Prepare the jam as directed in the recipe. You can set aside the amount needed for this recipe and let cool. Can the rest. I think the flavor of Linda's jam is really what makes this recipe.

Preheat the oven to 350°F (176°C). Prepare the pizza dough as specified in the recipe and roll it into a 10-inch circle. Prebake the dough on a perforated baking sheet that has been lightly coated with olive oil for a few minutes. It should be firm but without color. Set on a wire rack and let cool.

Combine the mascarpone cheese, lemon zest, and sugar in a medium-size mixing bowl and mix until softened and combined. Use an offset spatula to spread a ¼-inch-thick layer of jam over the prebaked crust. Use a tablespoon to drop large dollops of the mascarpone mixture onto the jam-covered pizza crust. Place in the oven and bake until the crust is light golden brown and the mascarpone mixture has melted slightly, about 20 minutes. Remove the pizza from the oven and let cool slightly. While the pizza is cooling, dice the mango halves and the strawberries. Sprinkle these over the pizza. Garnish with the chopped mint or basil leaves and serve.

continued

Sweet Pizza

Variation: Use a pastry brush to brush both sides of the mint or basil leaves with egg whites. Immediately press each side of the leaves into some granulated sugar. Place the coated leaves on a parchment paper–covered baking sheet and let dry overnight at room temperature. Use them to garnish the pizza.

Schiacciata

Yield: One 12 × 18-inch baking sheet or about 3 dozen rolls

I really enjoy making bread and this bread is made with a yeast starter. A starter is simply flour and water, and you will need to make your own. This can take eight to twelve days for the longer version or four to six hours if you use the shortcut. I am very protective of my starter, since it is seven years old and has a wonderful flavor. When Le Cirque moved, I divided my starter, into three pieces. I gave one to my sous-chef, Ken, one to Francisco, who makes the crème brûlée, and I took home the third. That way our starter was protected in case anyone's freezer broke during the time the restaurant was closed.

To make a starter the long way, mix together the flour and just enough water to make a liquid dough. If the dough is too liquid, add a little more flour. Whisk well to incorporate it

completely. Cover the bowl with plastic wrap and set aside for two to three days at room temperature. During this time, natural fermentation (bubbles) will occur and the dough will be a little more liquid. Throw away about 75 percent of the mixture. Refresh the dough by adding a cup of flour and some water to the remaining dough and mix. Let it ferment for another two to three days. The fermentation of the second dough will be stronger. Throw away 75 percent. Refresh and let ferment for an additional two to three days. The dough will continually grow and ferment. It is best to refresh the dough at least four times before it is used for the first time. If you are going to make bread often, keep it refreshed every two to three days so you always have starter.

If you don't make bread often and need to store your starter, just place it, well wrapped in plastic wrap, in the freezer. When you are ready to use it, allow it to defrost in the refrigerator. Refresh it at least one time and then you are ready to go.

There is a faster way to make a starter and this is the shortcut. Add 1 teaspoon of fresh yeast to the flour and water. Let it rest for one day. Then you are ready to make the bread. The flavor will be less intense than with a natural starter, but it is a lot quicker!

I never use a hand-held electric mixer for this recipe because the motor will not hold up to the strength of the dough.

You will need 4.5 ounces (130 grams) of starter for this dough. It will be a lot easier if you use a scale with this recipe.

For the starter

Bread flour	½ cup	2.3 ounces	65 grams
Water	⅓ cup	2.6 ounces	75 grams
Fresh compressed yeast	1 teaspoon	0.15 ounce	4 grams

For the dough

Bread flour	4 cups	18 ounces	500 grams
Salt	1 tablespoon	0.6 ounce	15 grams
Granulated sugar	2 teaspoons	0.2 ounce	8 grams
Extra virgin olive oil	⅓ cup	2 ounces	60 grams
Fresh compressed yeast	2 tablespoons	0.75 ounce	20 grams
Water	1¼ cups	9.6 ounces	275 grams

Extra virgin olive oil	**Generous 1 ½ tablespoons**	**0.75 ounce**	**20 grams**
Coarse salt	**1 tablespoon**	**0.6 ounce**	**15 grams**
Pinch of fresh rosemary or thyme leaves			
Cold water	**¼ cup**	**2 ounces**	**60 grams**

Prepare the starter: Place all three ingredients in a large mixing bowl. Mix well with a rubber spatula until completely combined. Tightly cover the mixing bowl with plastic wrap. (Do not allow the plastic wrap to touch the starter, or it will stick.) Allow the starter to ferment at room temperature for 4 to 6 hours before using. You will need 4.5 ounces (130 grams) of starter for this dough. The fermentation in the starter will add flavor to the bread.

Prepare the bread dough: Place the starter, flour, salt, sugar, olive oil, and yeast in the bowl of a stand mixer. I usually put the flour in the bottom of the bowl and place the other ingredients in small piles on top of the flour. That way I can double-check that everything has been added before I begin to mix it. Add part of the water and mix on medium speed with the dough hook. Flour never absorbs the same quantity of liquid. Its moisture content is dependent on the humidity in the air, so you will always need to adjust the recipe slightly. If too much liquid is added to the recipe, you can fix it by adding a little more flour. If too much flour is added, the recipe will become unbalanced and you will need to start again. Be careful and add the water slowly when you begin.

The gluten (page 10) begins to form when the liquid is added during the mixing process. This is also when the flavors in the dough develop. Bread dough needs to be soft and elastic. If the dough separates and breaks, not enough water has been added; the dough needs water to be able to expand. If too much water is added, the dough will be flat. Mix until the dough is smooth and forms a ball on the bottom of the bowl, about 3 minutes. Then increase the mixer speed to medium-high. Continue to mix until the dough pulls away from the side of the mixing bowl, another 10 minutes. The dough should be elastic and not too sticky.

Remove the dough from the mixer and knead gently on a lightly floured surface. Fold it onto itself several times as you knead it to give the dough some strength. Knead the dough for a few minutes until it becomes very smooth. Pat the dough into a disk and set it aside on a parchment paper–covered baking sheet. Cover with plastic wrap or a dish towel and let the dough rest at room temperature for 30 to 45 minutes. The towel will help retain the warmth of the dough and protect it from drafts.

Divide the dough as indicated for the recipe you are making: For a baking sheet size, you will need all the dough. For individual rolls, divide the dough into 1-ounce (28-gram) pieces.

If you use a baking sheet, use a rolling pin to roll the dough on a lightly floured work surface into a 12 × 17-inch rectangle that is about ¼ inch thick. Transfer the dough to a baking sheet that has been lightly coated with olive oil. Gently pull the dough from the center until the edges reach the sides of the baking sheet.

To make individual-size rolls, lightly dust the work surface and the palms of your hands with some flour. Cover a piece of dough with your hand so it touches the middle of your palm. Slowly roll the ball with the palm of your hand, pressing down slightly as you roll. (Roll clockwise if you are left-handed, counterclockwise if you are right-handed.) Gradually pull your fingers toward your palm so you begin to cup your hand around the ball of dough. At this point the ball of dough should roll freely under your cupped hand. Set the ball aside to rest while you roll the remaining pieces. This rolling technique helps to ensure that the ball is tight and contains no trapped air.

When all of the dough has been rolled, transfer the balls to a lightly oiled baking sheet. Space the balls a couple of inches apart, since they will grow when proofed and baked. Cover the baking sheet loosely with plastic wrap to keep the dough from developing a skin while proofing and to trap the heat generated from fermentation, which helps it rise. Allow the dough to proof at room temperature for about 2 hours. When fully proofed, the dough will have doubled in size and appear full of air.

About 30 minutes before the dough is ready, put a baking sheet on the bottom of the oven and preheat the oven to 450°F (232°C). When it is time to bake the bread, water will be added to this pan to create steam. When the dough has finished proofing, lightly rub the dough with some olive oil.

If making the baking sheet size, lightly dock the dough with your fingers, indenting the dough slightly. Be careful not to poke through the dough. For the rolls, use the tips of your fingers to very, very gently press down on each ball so it is not quite so high as you rub on the olive oil.

Sprinkle the coarse salt and chopped rosemary or thyme on the bread or rolls. Immediately before placing the dough in the oven, pour the cold water into the bottom of the hot baking sheet that is already in the oven. This will create steam in the oven and help the dough develop a nicer crust. Immediately place the bread dough in the oven and close the oven door. You want to keep as much of the steam in the oven as possible. For the rolls, bake until well risen and golden brown, about 15 minutes. For the baking sheet size, bake for about 25 minutes. Remove the bread from the oven and cool on a wire rack. For safety reasons, I always allow the oven to cool before I remove the water-covered baking sheet from the bottom of the oven. While the bread is still warm, brush or rub with more olive oil. Slice the bread using a serrated knife.

Variation: Top the bread with thinly sliced fresh tomatoes or onions before baking.

Schiacciata Plum Tart

Yield: One 12-inch tart; 8 servings

Egidiana Maccioni is the chef/consultant of the restaurant Osteria del Circo in New York. She is also the wife of my boss. One afternoon she invited me to her house to experiment with schiacciata dough. We used several kinds of olive oils, flours, and different starters and made six different types of breads. At the end of the day we were tired of making bread and craving something sweet, so we decided to turn the bread dough into a tart.

⅓ recipe Schiacciata dough (page 155)

Extra virgin olive oil	1 tablespoon	0.6 ounce	15 grams

For the crumble topping

Cake flour	⅔ cup	3.5 ounces	100 grams
Granulated sugar	⅓ cup	2.6 ounces	75 grams
Almond flour (page 6)	Scant ¼ cup	1 ounce	25 grams
Cold unsalted butter, cubed	7 tablespoons	3.5 ounces	100 grams

To finish the tart

10 fresh plums

Prepare the schiacciata dough as directed in the recipe. After allowing the dough to proof for 30 minutes, place it on a lightly floured work surface. Use a rolling pin to roll the dough into a 12-inch circle. Place the circle on a perforated baking sheet that has been

Schiacciata Plum Tart

lightly coated with olive oil. Set aside and let proof for 30 minutes at room temperature.

Prepare the crumble topping: Combine the cake flour, sugar, and almond flour in a medium-size mixing bowl. Work in the cold butter with your hands. To do this, grab a handful of flour mixture and butter, then gently rub the two between your hands to combine them. As you rub, the mixture drops back into the bowl. Keep doing this until most of the butter is combined. If your hands are too warm, the butter will melt. If necessary, wash your hands in ice-cold water every few minutes. Make sure your hands are dry when you return to the mixture. Stop working the mixture while you can still see small chunks of butter. Place the crumble topping in the freezer until ready to use. (At this stage it can be stored in the freezer, covered tightly with plastic wrap, for up to 2 weeks.)

Assemble the tart: Preheat the oven to 450°F (232°C). Pit the plums and slice them into eighths. Lightly coat the proofed dough disk with some olive oil. I usually use my hands to do this, but be careful not to press down on the dough and deflate it. Lay the plum slices on top of the tart and cover with the crumble topping. Place in the oven and bake until evenly golden brown and crispy, about 20 minutes. Cool on a wire rack before serving.

Castagnaccio

Yield: 4 individual tarts

This Italian specialty is very easy to make. The recipe leaves a lot of room for error, which is why it is a confidence builder for any beginner. The measurements do not have to be exact. If you add too much or too little water to the batter, it only means the castagnaccio may need more or less time to bake, but it will still be good! You can find chestnut flour at a specialty gourmet or health food store.

continued

Chestnut flour (page 7)	2 cups	7 ounces	200 grams
Pinch of salt			
Water	Generous 1 cup	8 ounces	230 grams
Extra virgin olive oil	2½ tablespoons	1.3 ounces	36 grams
Pine nuts	1½ tablespoons	0.5 ounce	12 grams
Pinch of fresh rosemary leaves			
Ricotta cheese or heavy cream whipped to firm peaks	¼ cup	2 ounces	60 grams

Preheat the oven to 375°F (190°C).

Place the flour and salt in a medium-size mixing bowl. Add the water slowly while whisking constantly with a hand whisk. Watch the consistency; it should be similar to that of pancake batter. If you add too much or too little water, don't worry. You'll get the hang of this after you make it a few times.

Spread about 1 teaspoon of the olive oil over the bottom of each 4 × 1-inch tartlet mold. Fill each mold three quarters full with the chestnut batter. Sprinkle the top of each with the pine nuts and rosemary. Top each with another teaspoon of olive oil and place in the oven. Bake until browned on top and set, about 20 minutes.

Remove from the oven and run the blade of a sharp paring knife around the inside of each tart pan to separate the castagnaccio from the side of the pan. Invert the pan and allow the cake to drop out of the mold. Serve warm with a dollop of ricotta cheese or whipped cream.

Signature Desserts

When someone asks me to name my signature dessert, I am happy to offer a number of choices. I prefer to be known more for a style than for one dessert. That's why I try to teach the basics. If you master those, you can develop your own style, and that way we will all contribute a lot more to the field of pastry.

My signature desserts usually represent some twist on a classic recipe. I would like my trademark to be presenting the basics in a less obvious fashion. I get inspiration from the everyday things I see in my life and from the stress of my usual workday. That phrase about necessity being the mother of invention really applies to my job. No matter what, I think it is important to have fun with dessert. Be whimsical. Go out on a limb. You can always say your zany design was the result of ingesting too much sugar!

Coconut Cookie Dreams

Yield: 12 desserts

Oreos can always be found in my cupboard at home. I love the idea of two cookies sandwiched together. I especially like the concept of dunking the cookie in milk, but I never time it right and usually end up dropping it in my glass.

I love Oreos so much that I was inspired to try to improve on the recipe. My recipe is a long way away from an Oreo cookie, but I am pretty happy with the result. I added the milk (coconut milk) to the center of the cookie and eliminated the need to dunk it!

For the chocolate cookies

Cake flour	2⅔ cups	14 ounces	400 grams
Dutch-processed unsweetened cocoa powder	½ cup	1.9 ounces	55 grams
Pinch of nutmeg			
Cold unsalted butter, cubed	1¾ cups	14 ounces	400 grams
Powdered sugar	1⅓ cups	5.6 ounces	160 grams
Salt	1 teaspoon	0.2 ounce	5 grams
1 large egg			

For the coconut filling

3¾ gelatin sheets or 1⅓ envelopes powdered gelatin			
Unsweetened coconut milk	3¼ cups	27 ounces	750 grams
Granulated sugar	¾ cup	5.5 ounces	150 grams
Dark rum	2½ tablespoons	1.5 ounces	35 grams
Grated zest of ½ lime			
¾ vanilla bean			
7 large egg whites			

continued

Prepare the cookie dough: Place the flour, cocoa powder, nutmeg, butter, powdered sugar, and salt in a medium size mixing bowl and beat with an electric mixer set on medium-high speed just until the butter is incorporated. This can also be done by hand. (The nutmeg will enhance the flavor of the chocolate.) Add the egg and mix just until the ingredients hold together in a dough. The egg is the "glue" that holds everything together. Do not overmix the dough, or the gluten will overdevelop (page 10) and the cookies will be tough and elastic instead of crumbly. Pat the dough into a disk and let it rest in the refrigerator for 2 hours. (At this stage the dough can be stored in the refrigerator, well wrapped in plastic wrap, for up to 5 days or in the freezer for up to 4 weeks.) The dough will darken as it rests in the refrigerator due to the maturation of the chocolate flavor.

Prepare the coconut filling: Preheat the oven to 310°F (154°C). If you are using gelatin sheets, place them in a medium-size mixing bowl with enough cold water (about 2 cups) to cover. Let stand for about 5 minutes to allow the gelatin to soften and hydrate. Cold water hydrates the gelatin without letting it absorb too much liquid. Remove the gelatin from the bowl and squeeze out the excess water with your hands. If you are using powdered gelatin, sprinkle it over ¼ cup (2 ounces; 60 grams) of cold water. Let the gelatin bloom until it has absorbed all the water, about 1 minute.

Pour the coconut milk, sugar, rum, and zest into a 2-quart heavy-bottomed saucepan and place over medium-high heat. Use a sharp knife to slice the vanilla bean in half lengthwise. Separate the seeds from the skin by scraping the blade of the knife along the inside of the bean. Add the seeds and skin to the mixture. Add the hydrated gelatin and stir occasionally as the mixture heats. Heat the mixture until bubbles begin to form around the edge of the saucepan. Do not allow the mixture to boil. Remove it from the heat. Remove the vanilla bean skin.

Pour the hot liquid into a tall container or large measuring cup and mix with a hand-held immersion blender for about 30 seconds just to give it an emulsion. If you don't have an immersion blender, whisk the mixture very, very well. Gelatin is an emulsifier and will help keep the fat in the coconut milk from separating during baking. Slowly add the egg whites while continuing to blend. Blend until smooth and homogenous, about 45 seconds.

Pour the mixture into 4 × 1-inch individual tartlet pans and place on a baking sheet with 1-inch-high sides. Place the baking sheet in the oven. Using hot water from the tap, fill the baking sheet with enough water to come halfway up the side of the tartlet pans. The custard is baked in a hot water bath to insulate it from the direct heat of the oven and to keep the eggs from cooking too fast, which would cause them to separate. If you are using a convection oven, a water bath is not needed because the even circulation of the air insulates the custard from the direct heat of the oven. If using a convection oven, bake at 200°F (93°C). When baked correctly, the custard should tremble slightly when gently shaken. If you detect any liquid under the skin, the custard is underbaked. Put it back in the oven and shake it every 5 minutes until it is ready. The total baking time is about 40 minutes. Remove the tartlet pans from the oven and the water bath and place on a wire rack for 30 minutes. Refrigerate for 2 hours before serving; it will finish setting in the refrigerator. Let the water bath cool before removing it from the oven.

Bake the cookies: Preheat the oven to 400°F (204°C). Remove the dough from the refrigerator. Divide in half and place half on a lightly floured work surface. Return the other half to the refrigerator. Lightly give it a few quick raps with the rolling pin to soften the dough slightly. This will make it easier to roll. Lightly flour the work surface and each side of the dough. Roll the dough into a ¼-inch-thick rectangle. If you have a textured rolling pin, you may choose to pattern the dough. Use a 4-inch fluted cutter to cut 12 circles from the dough. Combine the scraps. These can be used to make more cookies if you are careful not to overwork the dough. Place the circles well spaced on a parchment paper–covered baking sheet. Repeat with the second half of dough. Bake until firm to the touch, about 10 to 15 minutes. It is hard to tell when the cookies are done because the chocolate conceals the color they take on when baked. Cool on a wire rack and set aside until ready to use. (At this stage the cookies can be stored at room temperature, well wrapped in plastic wrap, for up to 1 week or in the freezer for up to 4 weeks.)

Assemble the cookie sandwiches: Place one cookie in the center of a plate. Run a paring knife around the edge of the tartlet pan and tilt it to see if it will unmold. Then invert the tartlet pan over a cookie and allow the coconut filling to drop on top of the cookie. (If it does not unmold easily, you can dip the bottom of the tartlet pan in hot water.) Cover with another cookie. Serve immediately. Sometimes I garnish this with fresh fruit and fruit sauces.

Variation: If you are short on time, make the cookies, but fill them with vanilla or coconut ice cream instead of the coconut filling.

The Clown Hat

Yield: 8 desserts

This dessert is one of my new signature desserts. I created it for my menu at Le Cirque 2000. It is made up of everything I like—caramel, fruit, ice cream, crispy dough, and chocolate—for a texture that's crunchy and creamy. Everything about it is yummy. Not too long ago, my friend Bill Bellody sent me a bag of "M&M's"® Milk Chocolate Mini Baking Bits. They are the perfect size and give the clown hat the right finish. Sticking the candies onto the hat is somewhat therapeutic, but I have to admit I take a shortcut when the banquet manager chooses this dessert for a party of 150 people!

Some of the components of this recipe can be prepared a day in advance, such as the clown hats and the hydrated raisins. I actually keep a container of hydrating raisins in the refrigerator at all times. You may want to do the same.

To make the clown hats

White chocolate, tempered (page 8)		10.5 ounces	300 grams
"M&M's"® Milk Chocolate Mini Baking Bits			

For the raisin crème brûlée

Golden raisins, hydrated in dark rum (page 28)	Scant ⅔ cup	3.5 ounces	100 grams
Heavy cream	1½ cups	12.6 ounces	360 grams
Whole milk	½ cup	4 ounces	120 grams
½ vanilla bean			
2 large eggs			
2 large egg yolks			
Granulated sugar	Scant ½ cup	3.2 ounces	90 grams

For the puff pastry circles

½ recipe Classic Puff Pastry (page 33) or store-bought			
Light corn syrup	Generous ⅓ cup	4.7 ounces	130 grams
Water	1½ tablespoons	1.2 ounces	30 grams

For the caramelized banana sauté

4 large ripe bananas			
Dark rum or Grand Marnier	½ cup	3.5 ounces	100 grams

Granulated sugar	**Scant 1 cup**	**7 ounces**	**200 grams**
Unsalted butter (optional), cubed	**1½ tablespoons**	**1.1 ounces**	**30 grams**

To finish the desserts

Vanilla ice cream

Raspberry Sauce (page 24)

Mango Sauce (page 24)

Prepare the chocolate clown hats: I used to use plastic molds to make these hats, but then I discovered that the cone-shaped paper cups found at water dispensers were an easier alternative. Fill each cup all the way to the top with tempered white chocolate. Invert the paper cup over the bowl of tempered chocolate and allow the excess chocolate to drip back into the bowl. Place the paper cups upside down on a wire rack placed over a parchment paper–covered baking sheet and allow the chocolate to set. When set, use a sharp paring knife to gently trim the chocolate off the bottom (opening) of each hat. Then peel off the paper cone.

To adhere the "M&M's"® Milk Chocolate Mini Baking Bits to the hats, heat the tip of a paring knife in boiling water. Dry it off and gently press it against the chocolate hat to melt the spot for the candy. Immediately press an "M&M's"® Mini Baking Bit into the chocolate hat. Use as many as you like to decorate the hat.

Prepare the raisin crème brûlée: Preheat the oven to 320°F (160°C). Sprinkle the hydrated raisins over the bottom of a 9-inch round cake pan with 2-inch-high sides. Pour the heavy cream and milk into a nonreactive 2-quart heavy-bottomed saucepan and set over medium heat. Use a sharp paring knife to slice the vanilla bean in half again, this time lengthwise. Separate the seeds from the outside skin by scraping the bean with the knife. Place the skin and seeds in the heating cream. Scald the cream by heating it until bubbles start to form around the edge of the pan. Remove from the heat.

Place the whole eggs, egg yolks, and sugar in a large mixing bowl and whisk until well incorporated. Continue to whisk as you slowly pour the hot cream into the egg mixture. Whisk until the mixture is smooth and homogenous in color. Strain the mixture through a fine-mesh sieve to remove the vanilla bean pieces and any overcooked eggs. Your next step will be made easier if you strain the mixture into a large measuring cup with a spout.

Place the cake pan on a baking sheet with 1-inch-high sides. Fill the cake pan with the custard and set the baking sheet in the oven. Traditionally, crème brûlée is baked in a hot water bath to insulate the custard from the direct heat of the oven and to keep the eggs from cooking too fast, which would cause them to separate. Use hot water from the tap and pour enough water onto the baking sheet to reach halfway up the side of the pan. If you are using a convection oven, a water bath is not needed because the even circulation of the air insulates the custard from the direct heat of the oven. If using a convection oven, preheat to 200°F (93°C). Baking time is about the same for either oven, about 50 minutes.

When baked correctly, the custard should tremble slightly when gently shaken. If you detect any liquid under the skin, the custard is underbaked. Put it back in the oven and shake it every 5 minutes until it is ready. Remove the mold from the oven and the water bath and place on a wire rack to cool for 30 minutes. Refrigerate for 2 hours before serving; it will finish setting in the refrigerator. Let the water bath cool before removing it from the oven.

Prepare the puff pastry circles: Make the puff pastry as directed in the recipe. Preheat the oven to 360°F (182°C). Place the puff pastry on a lightly floured work surface. Lightly dust the top of the puff pastry with flour. Use a rolling pin to roll the puff pastry into a rectangle 1/4 inch thick. Use a 4-inch fluted cutter to cut 8 circles from the puff pastry. Remove the scraps and space the circles 2 inches apart on a parchment paper–covered baking sheet. Combine the corn syrup and water in a small mixing bowl and mix well. Use a pastry brush to coat the top of each circle with the corn syrup mixture. This will give each baked circle a nice, shiny glaze; it will also enhance the flavor of the baked puff pastry. Place the puff pastry circles in the oven until well risen and evenly browned, 20 to 25 minutes. To keep the circles from rising unevenly, I place six 3-inch-high timbale molds (one in each corner and two in the center) on the baking sheet with the circles. Then, I place a wire rack on top of the molds. As the puff pastry rises, the rack will keep it level. You can also place another sheet of parchment paper directly on top of the puff pastry circles and bake. The slight weight of the parchment paper will keep the puff pastry even as it bakes and rises. Remove the baked puff pastry circles from the oven and place on a wire rack to cool.

Prepare the caramelized banana sauté: Peel and dice the bananas into 1/4-inch cubes. Place them in a small mixing bowl with the rum or Grand Marnier and about one third of the sugar and let macerate for 10 minutes.

Heat a medium-size heavy-bottomed frying pan over medium-high heat. If it starts to smoke, the pan is too hot and you need to run it under cool water, dry it, and start again. When warm, sprinkle the remaining sugar into the pan. Try to keep the sugar in an even layer to allow it to caramelize at the same time. As soon as you see the sugar begin to melt, start moving the pan over the burner to keep the sugar from burning. Tilt the pan from side to side so that the melted sugar runs over the unmelted sugar. Cook until all of the sugar is light golden brown. I usually add the butter at this stage because it makes the caramel smoother. Add the banana mixture and spread it evenly in the pan. Let cook over medium-high heat until most of the liquid has evaporated and the bananas are soft but not mushy. If the bananas are still firm when most of the liquid has evaporated, add a few tablespoons of water and continue cooking until they are ready. Remove from the heat and pour the caramelized bananas onto a plate. Cover with plastic wrap and set aside. Covering the hot bananas with plastic wrap keeps the caramel from drying as it cools. I do not make the bananas too far in advance because this dessert tastes better when the bananas are still warm. If you want to prepare the bananas more than an hour ahead of time, you can cover them with plastic wrap and reheat in the microwave for 1 to 2 minutes on high power.

Assemble the clown hats: Use a paring knife to carefully cut a small circle from the top of each puff pastry shell. Set the top aside to use later. Use your fingers to remove the doughy inside from the shell. Fill the shell with a large scoop of the raisin crème brûlée. Cover with a generous layer of the warm caramelized bananas. Top with a scoop of vanilla ice cream and reposition the puff pastry circle. Place the clown hat on top of the puff pastry.

I like to decorate the plate with raspberry and mango sauces. Serve.

The Porcupine

Yield: 6 servings

Kris always calls me "Dr. Doolittle" because of my love for all creatures great and small. There is a cute little animal called the *hérisson* that can be found all over Provence. It resembles the American hedgehog, but it is tiny and its spines seem shorter. Like most kids, I made great adventure of "hunting" for the "wild animals." When confronted, this shy little creature curls into a ball and probably hopes kids like me will leave it undisturbed. The adventure was to scoop the animal into your hands and feel the spines against your palms. When I make this dessert, I am reminded of the wild adventures of my childhood.

I like to use a 6-inch plastic dome mold to make this dessert. You can also use a glass or stainless-steel mixing bowl.

½ **recipe Basic Pound Cake (page 87)**			
½ **recipe Pastry Cream (page 20)**			
Heavy cream	1⅓ **cups**	10.5 **ounces**	300 **grams**
3 gelatin sheets or 1 envelope powdered gelatin			
Grand Marnier or dark rum	¼ **cup**	1.8 **ounces**	50 **grams**
Golden raisins, hydrated with dark rum (page 28)	Scant ⅔ **cup**	3.5 **ounces**	100 **grams**
Simple Syrup flavored with Grand Marnier or dark rum (page 86)			

4 large egg whites			
Granulated sugar	**Generous ½ cup**	**4 ounces**	**120 grams**
Powdered sugar, sifted	**1 cup**	**4 ounces**	**120 grams**

Prepare the pound cake batter as directed in the recipe and bake it on a parchment paper–covered baking sheet instead of in cake or loaf pans. Place on a wire rack until

completely cooled. Invert onto the work surface, peel off the parchment paper, and use a 6-inch plate to cut two circles from the cake layer. Set aside until ready to use. Store the remaining cake in the freezer for up to 3 weeks.

Prepare the pastry cream as directed in the recipe. Let cool and store in the refrigerator, tightly covered with plastic wrap, until ready to use.

Pour the heavy cream into a medium-size mixing bowl and whip to soft peaks with an electric mixer set on medium-high speed. Do not overwhip, or the cream will lose volume. Keep in the refrigerator until ready to use.

If you are using gelatin sheets, place them in a medium-size mixing bowl with enough cold water (about 2 cups) to cover. Let stand for about 5 minutes to allow the gelatin to soften and hydrate. Cold water hydrates the gelatin without letting it absorb too much liquid. Remove the gelatin from the bowl and squeeze out the excess water with your hands. If you're using powdered gelatin, sprinkle the gelatin over about ¼ cup (2 ounces; 60 grams) cold water. Let the gelatin bloom until it has absorbed all the water, about 1 minute.

Place the hydrated gelatin and about ½ cup of the pastry cream in a 1-quart heavy-bottomed saucepan. Cook over medium heat, stirring gently, until the gelatin has dissolved. Whisk the dissolved gelatin and hot pastry cream together until well combined. Add this mixture to the cold pastry cream. Immediately whisk to distribute the dissolved gelatin throughout the cold pastry cream. The dissolved gelatin will begin to set as soon as it comes in contact with the colder pastry cream, so whisk quickly and vigorously. Whisk in the Grand Marnier or rum and fold in the raisins. When evenly dispersed, gently fold in the whipped cream.

Fill the dome mold almost half full with the pastry cream mixture. Use the back of a large spoon to spread the pastry cream around the bottom and up the side of the mold. This will make the finished dessert look smooth. Place a cake circle in the center of the mold. If necessary, trim the cake layer to fit. Soak the cake with flavored simple syrup. Then fill the mold almost to the top with more pastry cream. Soak the remaining cake circle with simple syrup. Top with the soaked cake circle, soaked side down, and press down slightly. Place the filled mold on a parchment paper–covered baking sheet. Place the baking sheet in the freezer to allow the filling to set, about 2 hours. The filling can be stored in the freezer, well wrapped in plastic wrap, for up to 3 weeks. Keep it in the mold to help protect it from freezer burn.

Unmold by dipping the mold in hot water for 5 seconds. Press against one side of the frozen filling to slide the filling out of the dome mold. Return the unmolded filling to the freezer while you prepare the meringue.

Place the egg whites in a large mixing bowl and whip with an electric mixer set on medium speed until foamy. Make a French meringue by adding the granulated sugar 1 tablespoon at a time. Once all of the granulated sugar has been added, increase the mixer speed to medium-high and whip to stiff but not dry peaks, about 5 minutes. Use a rubber spatula to gently fold the sifted powdered sugar into the meringue. Place the meringue into a large pastry bag fitted with a ½-inch plain tip.

Remove the filling from the freezer and place it on a baking sheet or ovenproof platter. To achieve the porcupine effect, hold the pastry bag perpendicular to the molded filling so the tip of the bag is approximately ½ inch from the surface. Squeeze gently until a dime-size dot of meringue sticks to the surface of the filling. Stop squeezing and quickly pull back (pull up if you are decorating the top). The meringue should stretch slightly and end in a point. Repeat this technique until the filling is completely covered in meringue porcupine quills. Pipe a squiggly tail covered in small spikes at one end. Pipe a small mound of meringue at the other end for the face. Return the decorated dessert to the freezer for 15 minutes. It needs to be well frozen before the meringue is baked in the oven. If the dessert is too soft, the filling will melt before the meringue is finished baking. (At this point the porcupine can be stored in the freezer for up to 1 day.)

Preheat the oven to 450°F (232°C). Place the porcupine in the oven until the meringue takes on color, 2 to 3 minutes. Watch it closely. Once it begins, the meringue browns very quickly. Remove from the oven and, if necessary, transfer to a platter. Serve immediately. I like to use "M&M's"® for the eyes, nose, and mouth. If you like, you can decorate with crème anglaise and chocolate sauce.

Variation: Instead of golden raisins, fold "M&M's"® Milk Chocolate Mini Baking Bits into the pastry cream. The kids will love it!

Chocolate Moose

Yield: 10 desserts

The first time I ever saw a moose was in Atlanta. Kris and I were in an antiques store. I saw antlers out of the corner of my eye and wondered if there was a real moose in the store. I am sad to tell you that while he was real, he was not alive. I promised myself I would visit a place where I would be able to see moose in their natural habitat. I think they are such magnificent animals and I adore their comical faces. I'm making this moose until I get to see them for real!

For the moose

Bittersweet chocolate, tempered (page 8)		16 ounces	454 grams

For the chocolate mousse

Bittersweet chocolate, chopped		8.9 ounces	250 grams
1 large egg			
5 large egg yolks			
Water	Scant ¼ cup	2 ounces	60 grams
Granulated sugar	Scant ½ cup	3.7 ounces	105 grams
Heavy cream	1⅔ cups	14 ounces	400 grams
Grand Marnier (optional)	2½ tablespoons	1 ounce	30 grams

To finish the moose

Sour cream	2 tablespoons	1 ounce	28 grams
10 fresh raspberries			
5 large fresh strawberries			

Prepare the moose: I use dome molds (page 4) to make the moose. Any type of half-sphere or round mold will work. If you use a sheet of molds, like I do, make sure the tempered chocolate is in a wide bowl. Fill each mold with chocolate and tap the sides with the handle of an offset spatula to remove any air bubbles. Invert the molds over the bowl of chocolate and allow the excess chocolate to drip back into the bowl. Scrape the top of the molds clean with the edge of the spatula and place the molds upside down on a wire rack set over a baking sheet. The excess chocolate will drip from the molds. When the chocolate has begun to harden but is not completely set, about 5 minutes later, scrape the edge

of each chocolate shell clean with a sharp paring knife. This makes it easier to unmold the shells, keeps the chocolate from breaking as it contracts, and gives the dome a clean rim. Place the molds on a baking sheet in the refrigerator until completely set, about 5 more minutes. Remove from the refrigerator and unmold. The molds I use allow me to just push against one edge of the shell and slide it out of the mold. Depending on your mold, you may need to lift the chocolate from the mold. Set the chocolate shell aside.

continued

Signature Desserts

To make the antlers: You will need two antlers for each moose. Use a small offset spatula to spread some tempered chocolate over a maple leaf template (page 5) placed on a parchment paper–covered baking sheet. Keep the thickness of the chocolate as even as possible, about ⅛ inch thick. Repeat until you have enough antlers for each moose.

To make the eyes: Pour a small amount of the tempered chocolate into a cornet (page 16). Use the cornet to draw small horseshoe-shaped eyes onto a sheet of parchment paper. Fill in the center of the horseshoe completely. Make two eyes for each moose and set aside to finish later.

Prepare the mousse: Place a 1-quart saucepan half filled with water over high heat and bring it to a simmer. Make a double boiler by setting a large mixing bowl over the simmering water. Place the chopped chocolate in the bowl and heat until completely melted, stirring occasionally. Make sure no water or steam comes in contact with the chocolate, because it can cause the chocolate to seize (harden). It is important to allow the chocolate to melt completely, or you will have lumps in the finished mousse. As soon as the chocolate is melted, remove it from the heat and set aside until ready to use.

Place the whole egg and egg yolks in a medium-size mixing bowl and beat with an electric mixer set on medium-high speed until light in color and thick, about 7 minutes. The egg mixture will gain in volume due to the incorporation of air. Keep whipping while the sugar cooks.

Place the water and sugar in a 1-quart heavy-bottomed saucepan over medium-high heat. Insert a candy thermometer and cook the sugar mixture until it reaches 250°F (121°C), what is called the soft ball stage (page 14). Remove it from the heat and pour the hot sugar down the side of the mixing bowl into the whipping eggs. Be careful not to pour the hot sugar directly onto the beaters, or it will splatter. Continue to whip with the electric mixer set on medium-high speed until the outside of the bowl is warm but not hot, 2 to 3 minutes.

Pour the heavy cream into a medium-size mixing bowl and whip to soft peaks with an electric mixer set on medium speed. At this stage the whipped cream has the most volume. If you overwhip the cream, you will lose volume and the mousse will not be as light and airy as it should be. If you are using Grand Marnier, fold it in with a rubber spatula, being careful not to deflate the cream.

Fold the egg mixture into the whipped cream. If the egg mixture is too hot, it will melt the whipped cream. If it is too cool, it will not fold well. Use a rubber spatula and fold gently just until the two are combined. You should still see streaks of each in the mixture. Carefully pour the warm melted chocolate into the mixture. If the chocolate is too warm, it will melt the whipped cream. If it is too cool, the chocolate will seize (harden) upon contact with the cooler mixture and you will have pieces of chocolate in your mousse. Use a rubber spatula to gently fold in the chocolate until completely incorporated. The chocolate mousse should be the same color throughout, with no streaks.

Assemble the moose: Fill each shell with the chocolate mousse, filling almost to the rim. Place them in the refrigerator until set, about an hour. Remove from the refrigerator. Invert the filled shell and place on the center of a plate. Use a sharp paring knife to trim the antlers where they will stick to the shell. Use a small amount of tempered chocolate to "glue" two antlers to the head of each moose. Loosen the eyes from the sheet of parchment paper. Melt the bottom of each eye with the blade of a hot paring knife and stick the eyes onto the moose head, under the antlers. Fill a cornet with the sour cream and draw a pupil in the center of each eye. Place one raspberry, tip side out, in the front for the nose. To make the mouth, lay a large strawberry on its side and slice it into ¼-inch-thick slices. Slice as many strawberries as necessary to make ten mouths. Place one slice under each nose.

Frozen Soufflé

Yield: 5 individual soufflés

f you do not have an ice cream maker and you want to serve a frozen dessert, this is the best solution. When I started in this profession, I always thought a frozen dessert had to contain ice cream. I was wrong. The parfait in this recipe does not require an ice cream maker.

½ recipe Basic Pound Cake (page 87)			
8 large egg yolks			
I large egg			
Water	**2 tablespoons**	**1.5 ounces**	**35 grams**
Granulated sugar	**Scant ½ cup**	**3.5 ounces**	**100 grams**
Light corn syrup	**Generous 2 tablespoons**	**1.8 ounces**	**50 grams**
Heavy cream	**Generous 2 cups**	**16 ounces**	**475 grams**
Grated zest of I orange			
Grand Marnier	**¼ cup**	**1.8 ounces**	**50 grams**
Simple Syrup flavored with Grand Marnier (page 86)			

continued

Prepare the cake: Make the pound cake batter as directed in the recipe and bake it on a parchment paper–covered baking sheet instead of in loaf or cake pans. Place on a wire rack to cool. When cooled, invert onto the work surface and peel off the parchment paper. Use a 3-inch plain cutter to cut 5 disks from the cake. Cut the circles as close together as possible to avoid waste.

Prepare the soufflé molds: Cut a 2-inch-wide sheet of parchment paper the length of the circumference of the mold. (I use 4 × 2-inch molds.) Butter the short end of one side of the paper strip. Wrap the strip around the outside of the mold so that it stands 1½ inches taller than the mold. "Glue" the paper closed with the buttered side. Repeat for each mold and set aside.

Prepare the soufflé: Place the egg yolks and whole egg in a large mixing bowl and whip with an electric mixer set on medium-high speed until thick, light, and tripled in volume, 5 to 7 minutes. Continue to whip the eggs while you cook the sugar.

Pour the water, sugar, and corn syrup into a 1-quart heavy-bottomed saucepan and place over medium heat. Insert a candy thermometer into the mixture. The sugar is ready when it reaches 250°F (121°C), what is known as the soft ball stage (page 14). Make a *pâte à bombe* by pouring the cooked sugar down the side of the bowl into the whipping eggs. Be careful not to pour the hot sugar onto the beaters, or it will splatter. Continue whipping the *pâte à bombe* until the outside of the bowl is cool, about 5 minutes.

Pour the heavy cream into a large mixing bowl and whip to soft peaks with an electric mixer set on medium-high speed. Use a rubber spatula to fold in the zest and Grand Marnier until incorporated. Use a rubber spatula to fold the *pâte à bombe* into the whipped cream. Remember to fold all the way to the bottom of the bowl and be gentle. You don't want to deflate the *pâte à bombe* or the whipped cream.

Use a large spoon to fill the prepared molds about half full with the soufflé mixture. Place a cake circle over the soufflé mixture and soak the cake circle with the flavored simple syrup.

Fill the molds with the remaining soufflé mixture to about 1 inch above the actual rim of the mold. Use the back of the spoon to smooth the tops of the soufflés, making them as flat and even as possible. Place the molds in the freezer for a few hours to set.

To serve the soufflés: Peel away the parchment paper and serve. When I want to make the presentation a little fancier, I use a small ice cream scoop to remove several scoops from the top of each soufflé. Then I fill in the scoops with raspberry or mango sauce or some strawberry jam.

Variation: You can make a simple version of the soufflé without the cake layer. Use 1-ounce disposable aluminum molds to make miniature soufflés. Pour the soufflé mixture into a pastry bag fitted with a ½-inch plain tip and fill each mold almost to the top. Place in the freezer for a few hours to set. Unmold by dipping the bottom of each mold into hot water for about 5 seconds. Squeeze the bottom of the mold and pop out the frozen soufflé. Insert a long wooden skewer into the top of each soufflé. Use the skewer to lift the soufflé and dip it halfway into tempered bittersweet chocolate (page 8). Place on a parchment paper–covered baking sheet to allow the chocolate to set, and remove the skewer. Decorate the top of each with a piped rosette of whipped cream. Drizzle some of the tempered chocolate over the top of each soufflé (makes about 30).

Frozen Nougat Parfait

Yield: One 10-inch loaf pan; 8 servings

This is a dessert I used to make often when I worked at the Hotel Negresco in the South of France. It is good to serve in the summer and is a wonderful recipe for a beginner, since it does not require much cooking. The recipe is a little like the Italian *cassata*, a dessert usually served individually instead of in a terrine as shown here. I added "M&M's"® to give it an American twist.

For the praline

Granulated sugar	Scant ½ cup	3.5 ounces	100 grams
Water	¼ cup	2 ounces	60 grams
Hazelnuts, blanched	¾ cup + 2 tablespoons	4.5 ounces	125 grams

For the filling

Heavy cream	Scant 2¼ cups	18 ounces	500 grams
Grated zest of ½ orange			
Grand Marnier	1 tablespoon	0.5 ounce	13 grams
Golden raisins, hydrated with dark rum (page 28)	⅓ cup	2 ounces	60 grams
"M&M's"® Milk Chocolate Mini Baking Bits	1 cup	7 ounces	200 grams

For the Italian meringue

2 large egg whites			
Water	1 tablespoon	0.75 ounce	20 grams
Granulated sugar	¼ cup	1.8 ounces	50 grams
Light corn syrup	1½ tablespoons	1 ounce	25 grams

Prepare the praline: Place the sugar and water in a copper pot or 2-quart heavy-bottomed saucepan over medium-high heat and bring the mixture to a boil. Add the hazelnuts and stir to coat them evenly in the sugar syrup. Your goal is to cook the hazelnuts until the sugar crystallizes and caramelizes. Let me explain what happens as you keep stirring.

When we added water to the sugar, we dissolved the crystals. As it boils, the syrup becomes thicker as the water evaporates and big soaplike bubbles begin to form. Soon all the mois-

ture evaporates and the mixture becomes sandy. The sandiness is the sugar recrystalliz-ing. It only takes the reformation of one sugar crystal to recrystallize the others. Keep stir-ring! Next you see the sugar closest to the heat change from sandy to a clear liquid. The melted sugar clings to the hazelnuts. When the sugar changes from clear to golden brown, the nuts are caramelized. Once this happens, pay close attention; the time it takes to pass from caramelized to burned is only a matter of seconds, especially when making smaller batches. You know the nuts are finished when most of the sandy sugar is gone.

The first few times you make these, I suggest you try the following: When the sugar clos-est to the heat changes from sandy to liquid, remove the pan from the burner and con-tinue to stir. The residual heat in the sugar and nuts will continue to cook the mixture while you stir it. Reduce the heat to medium-low and continue to stir the nuts while mov-ing the saucepan on and off the heat at 10-second intervals. This will give you more control as it cooks. When the nuts begin to caramelize, remove them from the heat and finish stirring.

Use a wooden spoon to spread the caramelized nuts onto a parchment paper–covered baking sheet. Do not touch the nuts; they are extremely hot. Let the nuts cool completely. If your freezer will accommodate the baking sheet, you can place the nuts in the freezer for about 30 minutes to speed up the cooling process. When completely cooled, break apart any nut clusters that may have formed. Use a rolling pin and roll over the nuts to crush them. Another technique is to hold one end of the rolling pin on the table and crush the nuts by bringing the other end of the rolling pin up and down on top of them. Be gentle, or the nuts will fly all over the place. Set the praline aside until ready to use.

Prepare the filling: Place the heavy cream in a medium-size mixing bowl and whip to soft peaks using an electric mixer set on medium-high speed. Store the whipped cream in the refrigerator until ready to use.

Prepare the Italian meringue: Place the egg whites in a medium-size bowl and whip with an electric mixer set on medium speed for about 5 seconds. Pour the water, sugar, and corn syrup into a 1-quart heavy-bottomed saucepan and place over medium-high heat. Insert a candy thermometer and cook the mixture until it reaches 250°F (121°C), what is known as the soft ball stage (page 14). Remove the cooked sugar from the heat.

Increase the mixer speed to medium-high and make an Italian meringue by pouring the hot sugar down the side of the mixing bowl into the whipping whites. Be careful not to pour the hot sugar directly onto the beaters, or it will splatter. Whip the meringue until stiff and glossy, about 5 minutes.

Finish the filling: Fold the orange zest and Grand Marnier into the whipped cream using a rubber spatula. Then fold the meringue into the whipped cream, being careful not to deflate either mixture. Fold in the crushed praline, raisins, and "M&M's"® Milk Chocolate Mini Baking Bits. When you use "M&M's"®, don't mix them too much, or they will lose their color.

Pour the mixture into the loaf pan and use an offset spatula to smooth the top. Place in the freezer for a few hours to set.

Unmold the loaf: Dip the loaf pan in hot water for about 5 seconds. Invert a flat plate over the loaf pan. Place one hand on either side, grasping both plate and loaf pan, and flip them so that the loaf pan is on top. Gently lift off the loaf pan. Use a hot chef's knife to slice the dessert. To heat the knife, dip it in hot water and wipe it dry before each slice. Sometimes I like to serve this dessert with raspberry and mango sauce, although chocolate sauce is good, too.

Breakfast and Tea

The first year Kris visited my parents in France, my mom bought eggs, ketchup, bacon, and potatoes to serve her for breakfast. She had heard about the big farmers' breakfasts and thought that was a typical meal for all Americans. Like most people, Kris is happy with a muffin and a cup of coffee.

Every culture seems to have set aside a time for a light afternoon snack: the British have tea, Germans serve coffee, and Americans seem to offer breakfast and tea around the clock. In this country the nicer hotels serve tea, there are coffee bars on every corner, and even bookstores serve muffins all day long. I like to eat these things any time of the day, and for that, it's great to be in America.

9C's Muffins

Yield: 12 regular or 6 large muffins

Rarely would you find muffins in a French bakery. I don't know why France missed the muffin phenomenon. I really like them but I don't get a chance to make them very often. This recipe comes from my friend Nancy Stark. I call her "9C." When we were taping the second series of our television show, "9C" was my sous-chef.

We tape in front of a live audience, and I like to make it interactive, so at the beginning of the show on which we made muffins our producer planted an egg with an audience member. The idea was to have the person throw the egg to me when I reached the point in the recipe that I needed it. I made the whole recipe from start to finish, baked the muffins, and invited someone from the audience to taste them. When the segment was finished and we stopped the tape, I realized that I had forgotten to call for the egg and never added it in my recipe! We had to shoot the whole show over again.

Unbleached all-purpose flour	2 cups	9 ounces	250 grams
Baking powder	Generous ½ tablespoon	0.3 ounce	10 grams
Pinch of salt			
Pinch of ground cinnamon			
Granulated sugar	¾ cup	5.5 ounces	150 grams
Unsalted butter, melted	½ cup	4 ounces	113 grams
2 large eggs			
Whole milk	Generous ½ cup	4.5 ounces	125 grams
Fresh fruit	About ¾ cup	4.5 ounces	125 grams
Crumble topping (page 159)			

Preheat the oven to 375°F (190°C). Lightly spray a muffin pan with vegetable cooking spray.

Place the dry ingredients in a large mixing bowl and mix until well combined. Use a wooden spoon or rubber spatula to mix in the butter. Add the eggs and mix until well incorporated. Mix in the milk until fully combined. Use a rubber spatula to gently fold in the fresh fruit. If you are using soft fruit like raspberries or strawberries, place them in the freezer just until they begin to freeze, then add them to the batter. This way they will be firm enough to withstand the gentle mixing without breaking. Divide the batter evenly among the muffin cups, filling each three quarters full. Cover with the crumble topping and place the muffin pan in the oven. Bake until the muffins are well risen and golden brown, about 30 minutes. When the tops of the muffins spring back slightly when pressed, they are ready. Cool the muffins on a wire rack. The muffins should fall out of the muffin pan quite easily when cool. The muffins will keep, well wrapped in plastic wrap, for up to 3 days.

Variation: Sprinkle the tops of the muffins with cinnamon sugar (which is just cinnamon and sugar mixed together) instead of the crumble topping and then bake.

Dieter's Danish

Yield: About 18 Danish

This recipe makes the best Danish I have ever eaten. My friend Chef Dieter Schorner taught me how to make these wonderful pastries. He has accomplished many great things in his pastry career. He is the chairman of the Pastry Arts Program at the French Culinary Institute, and he was Le Cirque's first pastry chef.

Dieter advises that one should never ask for a Danish in Denmark. If you ask for a Danish, they will think you want a person from Denmark! I never use a hand-held mixer for this recipe because the motor will not hold up to the strength of the dough.

For the dough

Cold whole milk	½ cup	4 ounces	120 grams
Fresh compressed yeast	Scant ¼ cup	1.5 ounces	35 grams
Granulated sugar	2 tablespoons	1 ounce	25 grams
Pinch of salt			
Pinch of ground cardamom			
Unsalted butter, softened	2 tablespoons	1 ounce	25 grams
1 large egg			
Bread flour	1½ cups	6 ounces	170 grams
Cake flour	Generous ⅔ cup	3.8 ounces	110 grams
Cold unsalted butter	¾ cup	6 ounces	170 grams

For cinnamon rolls

¼ recipe Almond Cream (page 23)			
Golden raisins, hydrated with dark rum (page 28)	Scant 1⅓ cups	7 ounces	200 grams
Nuts, chopped	1¼ cups	3.5 ounces	100 grams
Cinnamon sugar	¼ cup	1.8 ounces	50 grams

For the egg wash

2 large egg yolks			
1 large egg			
Whole milk	¼ cup	1.8 ounces	50 grams

For the cheese filling

Cream cheese, softened		8.5 ounces	240 grams
Golden raisins, hydrated with dark rum (page 28)	Scant 1⅓ cups	7 ounces	200 grams
Grated zest of 1 lemon			
Granulated sugar	2 tablespoons	1 ounce	25 grams

For the fruit Danish

½ recipe **Pastry Cream (page 20)**

15 canned peeled apricot halves, drained, or fresh

Prepare the dough: Pour the milk into the bowl of a stand mixer fitted with the paddle attachment. Add the yeast and stir to dissolve. When the yeast is fully dissolved, add the sugar, salt, cardamom (this is the secret ingredient), softened butter, and egg and beat on medium speed just until combined. Add the flours and incorporate on low speed. Mix just until the dough holds together and it is firm enough to be rolled. Increase the mixer speed to medium for

about 10 seconds before you remove the dough from the mixer. The dough will be rough and ropy looking. Pat it into a disk and place it on a parchment paper–covered baking sheet. Let the dough rest in the refrigerator for 30 minutes to allow the gluten to relax.

Remove the dough from the refrigerator and place it on a lightly floured work surface. Roll it into an 8 × 16-inch rectangle, flouring lightly as needed to keep the dough from sticking to the table. Lay the dough on the table with the long side facing you and roll one end slightly wider than the other.

Mold the cold butter into a square and give it a few quick raps with the rolling pin. Gently knead it and give it a few more raps. Your goal is to make the cold butter the same consistency as the cold dough; this will make it easier to incorporate. If the butter is too cold, it will tear the dough when you try to spread it. If the butter is too warm, it won't distribute evenly and this will affect the layers in the dough. Use an offset spatula to spread the butter over the wider half of the dough. Then fold the dough in half, placing the narrower top on the wider bottom, leaving about a ½-inch border all around. Fold this border over onto the top half, creating a seam. This will ensure that the edges are well sealed. Press the dough with your fingers to seal it tight.

Turn the dough over onto the lightly floured work surface and roll it into an 8 × 16-inch rectangle. Place the dough on the table with a long side facing you. You will now give the dough what is called a *single*, or *letter, fold*. Fold the right third of the dough over the center, then fold the left third of the dough to the right. Now the dough should resemble a folded letter. The seam should now be on your right. Place the dough on a parchment paper–covered baking sheet and mark it with one indentation of your finger to represent one turn, meaning you have rolled it and folded it once. Let it rest in the refrigerator for 20 minutes. You will need to give the dough two more single, or letter, folds, starting each time with an 8 × 16-inch rectangle. Lightly flour the dough and the work surface as needed. Try to keep the dough an even thickness as you roll, and always begin to roll out the rectangle with the seam of the dough on your right. After each fold, make an indentation in the dough with your fingertips to correspond to the number of folds you have given the dough (two folds, two indents; three folds, three indents). This way you will not forget and miss a fold. After each fold, return the dough to the refrigerator and let it rest for 20 minutes. When the dough has all three folds, you can wrap it well in plastic wrap and store it in the refrigerator for up to 1 day or in the freezer for up to 2 weeks. If frozen, thaw the dough in the refrigerator before using.

After the third fold and rest, the dough is ready to be formed. Remove it from the refrigerator and place on the lightly floured work surface. Use the rolling pin to roll the dough into a 12 × 22-inch rectangle. Place the dough on the work surface with the long side facing you. At this stage you can make any of the following varieties of Danish:

To make cinnamon rolls: Use an offset spatula to spread an ⅛-inch-thick layer of almond cream over the dough, spreading it all the way to the edges of the rectangle. Sprinkle the top of the almond cream with the hydrated raisins. Add a layer of the chopped nuts and sprinkle with the cinnamon sugar. Roll the dough toward you, starting at the long side. Try to keep the roll tight and even. Cut the roll into 1-inch-thick slices. You will have a tail on each slice. To close the Danish, simply tuck the tail under the dough. Place the Danish on a parchment paper–covered baking sheet, spaced about 2 inches apart.

To make cheese Danish: Use a sharp chef's knife to cut the rectangle of dough into 15 squares. To do this, cut the rectangle in thirds from left to right. Then make four equally spaced cuts from top to bottom. Mix the egg wash together, then use a pastry brush to brush the outside edge of each square with the egg wash. The center of each square should be dry. Combine all of the ingredients for the cheese filling in a medium-size mixing bowl and mix with a wooden spoon until softened and combined. Place a large tablespoon of the cheese mixture in the center of each square, then take two opposite corners on each square and fold them in toward the center to partially cover the cheese mixture. Press the tips of the corners together to seal and then brush egg wash on top of each Danish. Place on a parchment paper–covered baking sheet.

To make fruit Danish: Cut the rectangle as if you were making cheese Danish and brush the edge of each square with egg wash. Place a large tablespoon of pastry cream in the center of each square. Top with an apricot half that has been drained on a wire rack placed over a parchment paper–covered baking sheet. Place the apricot half, cut side down, onto the pastry cream. Close the Danish the same as you would a cheese Danish and brush the egg wash on top. Place on a parchment paper–covered baking sheet.

When all of the Danish have been rolled or formed, place them in a warm spot like on top of the refrigerator. Cover lightly with plastic wrap and let proof until doubled in size. The Danish will appear light and full of air. This should take about 1½ hours. About half an hour before the Danish finish proofing, preheat the oven to 375°F (190°C). Just before baking, use a pastry brush to gently and lightly brush the top of the Danish with more egg wash. Be careful not to press down on the proofed dough with the brush, or it will deflate.

Place the Danish in the oven and bake until well risen and evenly golden brown, about 20 minutes. Cool on a wire rack. I like to eat Dieter's Danish right out of the oven when they are still slightly warm. Traditionally they are served with coffee at breakfast, but these are so good, I eat them all day long. The Danish can be stored at room temperature, well wrapped in plastic wrap, for up to 2 days, or in the freezer for 2 weeks. Thaw in the refrigerator and warm up in the oven before eating.

Brioche

Yield: 38.5 ounces or 1,100 grams; enough for: 22 small brioche à tête or 3 large brioche à tête or 4 couronne or 2 brioche loaves or 22 long brioche rolls or 22 chocolate rolls

During my apprenticeship, my boss gave me 17 kilos (37½ pounds) of flour and asked me to make croissants. I scaled all of the ingredients, placed them in the bowl, made the dough, let it ferment, and placed it in the refrigerator. The next day I gave the dough the required turns and baked the croissants. The delivery trucks arrived, we packed up the croissants, and sent them on their way to the local bakeries and restaurants. Thirty minutes later the trucks started to return to the bakery. The customers had refused the croissants. When I tasted them, I realized I made a mistake with the quantities of sugar and salt. That is how I came up with the technique of placing each ingredient in a small pile on top of the flour. Now, whenever I make breads, I can double-check the recipe before I mix it!

You can make the recipe without a scale, but it will be much easier to work the dough into the various forms if you weigh it. Rock sugar is available in any baking supply store.

Bread flour	4 cups	18 ounces	500 grams
5 large eggs			
Salt	2½ teaspoons	0.5 ounce	12 grams
Granulated sugar	Generous ⅓ cup	2 ounces	60 grams
Fresh compressed yeast	3 tablespoons	1 ounce	25 grams
Water	Scant ¼ cup	2 ounces	60 grams
Cold unsalted butter, cubed	1 cup	8 ounces	227 grams
22 pieces DOVE® PROMISES® Dark Chocolate (optional)			
For the egg wash			
2 large egg yolks			
1 large egg			
Whole milk	¼ cup	1.8 ounces	50 grams
Rock or crystal sugar (page 14)	¼ cup	1.6 ounces	40 grams

Place the flour, eggs, salt, granulated sugar, and yeast in a large mixing bowl. I usually put the flour in the bottom of the bowl and all of the other ingredients in separate small piles

on top of the flour. That way I can double-check that I have added all of the correct ingredients before I begin to mix it all together. Beat with an electric mixer set on medium speed just until the ingredients are dispersed, about 5 seconds. If you are using a stand mixer, use the dough hook. Add part of the water and continue to mix on medium-high speed. Flour never absorbs the same quantity of liquid; the amount of liquid that will be needed for this recipe is dependent on the humidity in the air. You will always need to adjust the recipe slightly. If too much liquid is added, just add a little more flour. Be careful; if too much flour is added, the recipe will become unbalanced and you will need to start again. It is better to add the water slowly at the beginning to avoid having to compensate with more flour. When the liquid is mixed with the flour, the gluten starts to work (page 10) and the flavors in the dough develop. When the dough is homogenous and begins to hold together, it is time to add the butter. This will take about 4 to 5 minutes. The butter is cubed so it will incorporate into the dough quickly. The butter needs to be cold to compensate for the friction (heat) created by mixing the dough. If too much heat develops during the mixing process, it can kill the fermentation in the dough. It is added at this time because the butter (fat) coats the protein in the flour, which inhibits further gluten development. You want gluten to develop before you add the butter. Add the cubed butter all at once and continue mixing on medium-high speed until the butter is fully incorporated. At this point the dough should hold together and appear smooth and elastic. It will be slightly sticky to the touch. Turn the dough onto a lightly floured baking sheet and pat into a disk. Let the dough rest at room temperature for 30 minutes, then cover the dough with plastic wrap and place it in the refrigerator for a couple of hours or overnight. Once the butter in the dough is cold, the dough will be easier to work. Remove the dough from the refrigerator. It is now ready to be formed.

For individual *brioche à tête:* To make these, you will need to use the *brioche à tête* molds made of stainless steel. Lightly butter the molds. Divide the dough into 1.8-ounce (50-gram) pieces. Fold each piece into itself several times, each time pressing out the air with the heel of your palm. Lightly flour the bottom of each piece. Place each piece on the work surface and roll it into a tight ball. The technique to do this is to cover a piece with your hand so it touches the middle of your palm. Slowly roll the ball with the palm of your hand, pressing down slightly as you roll. (Roll clockwise if you are left-handed, counterclockwise if you are right-handed.) Gradually pull your fingers toward your palm so you begin to cup your hand around the ball of dough. At this point the ball of dough should roll freely under your cupped hand. Set the ball aside to rest while you roll the remaining pieces. This rolling technique helps to ensure that the ball is tight and contains no trapped air.

Place the side of your hand on the ball and use a sawing motion as you press about one-third of the dough (the head) away from the rest of the ball (the body). Do not cut through the dough.

When all of the dough has been rolled, return to the first ball. Place the side of your hand on the ball and use a sawing motion as you press about one third of the dough (the head) away from the rest of the ball (the body). This will help form the "head" of the brioche. Do not cut through the dough. Place the brioche body into the prepared mold so the head is at the top. Gently press about one third of the head into the body.

To make a large *brioche à tête:* To make this, you will need to use the 2-quart *brioche à tête* mold made of stainless steel.

Lightly butter the mold. Work with about 12.5-ounce (350-gram) pieces of the dough. The procedure is the same as for the individual size, but use both hands to roll the dough into a tight ball. Mark the head the same way and place the brioche in the prepared mold. Anchor the head as you would for the individual-size brioche.

Place the brioche body into the prepared mold so the head is on top.

To make a *couronne* (crown): Work with about 9-ounce (250-gram) pieces of dough. Roll the dough into a tight ball. Make a hole in the center of the ball. Gently and evenly pull the dough to increase the hole until it is about 6 inches in diameter. I would suggest that you pull the dough partway and then let it rest for 5 to 10 minutes before you continue. This will keep the elasticity of the dough to a minimum and make it easier to pull. Set on a parchment paper–covered baking sheet.

To make a brioche loaf: Lightly butter an 8-inch loaf pan. Work with about 2.6-ounce (75-gram) pieces of dough. You will need six pieces for each loaf pan. Roll each piece into a tight ball. Place six balls next to each other in the center of the loaf pan and set aside.

Use your fingers to gently press about one third of the head into the body to anchor the head in place.

To make long brioche rolls: Divide the dough into 1.8-ounce (50-gram) pieces. Roll each piece into a tight ball and then roll each ball into a 4-inch length. Place on a parchment paper–covered baking sheet.

To make chocolate rolls: Divide the dough into 1.8-ounce (50-gram) pieces. Roll each piece into a tight ball. Flatten each ball with the palm of your hand and place a piece of chocolate in the center. Close the dough completely around the chocolate and roll the dough into a tight ball once again. Place on a parchment paper–covered baking sheet.

For a chocolate roll, close the dough completely around the chocolate.

Once all of the dough is formed and placed on a parchment paper–covered baking sheet, cover with plastic wrap. This will trap the heat created during fermentation and help the dough rise. It will also protect the dough from any cold air while it is proofing. Place the baking sheet in a warm spot and let the dough proof for several hours. When fully proofed, the brioche will have doubled in size and appear light and full of air.

Preheat the oven to 350°F (176°C).

Prepare the egg wash: Place the egg yolks, whole egg, and milk in a small mixing bowl and whisk to combine. Lightly brush the top of the brioche with the egg wash. Be careful not to press on the dough as you apply the egg wash, or the dough will deflate.

If you choose to cut the tops of the brioche, use a sharp pair of scissors to do it. The cuts will open as the brioche bakes. For the brioche loaf, the long brioche rolls, and the *couronne,* make small ¼-inch-deep cuts down the center of each. Sprinkle the long rolls and the *couronne* with some rock sugar. Use a sharp paring knife to lightly score the tops of the chocolate brioche.

Place the brioche in the oven and bake until evenly golden brown. This will take about 20 minutes for the smaller pieces and 35 minutes for the larger ones. To test for doneness of the large *brioche à tête* and the brioche loaves, tap the bottom of the mold when the brioche appears fully baked. If it sounds hollow, the brioche is ready. Remove from the oven. Unmold the *brioche à tête* and the brioche loaves while they are still warm. To unmold, lightly tap the molds against the side of the work surface and invert the molds. The brioche should release easily. Cool all on a wire rack.

> The ingredients for the brioche are all very dependent on one another. Each serves a purpose as they work together. Flour contains protein. When liquid is added, the protein becomes gluten. Gluten gives dough elasticity, which helps it retain the gas released during fermentation. Gas is produced by the yeast, and that is what causes the dough to rise. Salt enhances the flavor and helps the gluten hold the gas. Sugar adds color and helps form the crust. Egg is a liquid that also adds fat, and since it is a French recipe, of course it contains butter!

Scones

Yield: 30 scones

Tea is such a lovely tradition. I think I like it so much because it reminds me of the time in Provence when we have our cake and coffee after the siesta. The little sandwiches and cookies are so delicate. My friend Peter Marengi shared with me the wonderful experience of having tea at The Lanesborough in London. I was amazed by all of the silver serving utensils that accompanied our tea. Having tea was only slightly more fun than being in my room and ringing for the butler!

Bread flour	**4 cups**	**18 ounces**	**500 grams**
Cake flour	**1⅔ cups**	**9 ounces**	**250 grams**
Baking powder	**3 tablespoons + 1 teaspoon**	**1.6 ounces**	**40 grams**
Granulated sugar	**Generous ½ cup**	**4 ounces**	**120 grams**
Salt	**2 teaspoons**	**0.3 ounce**	**10 grams**
Heavy cream	**3⅓ cups**	**27 ounces**	**750 grams**
Golden raisins	**¾ cup**	**4 ounces**	**120 grams**
Blanched almonds, toasted (page 127) and chopped	**1 cup**	**3.5 ounces**	**100 grams**
To finish the scones			
Whole milk	**¼ cup**	**2 ounces**	**60 grams**

Preheat the oven to 400°F (204°C).

Place the flours, baking powder, sugar, salt, and heavy cream in a medium-size mixing bowl. Use an electric mixer set on medium speed to mix the ingredients just until combined. This is also an easy dough to make by hand. Stir in the raisins and almonds. When fully incorporated and the dough holds together, turn it onto a lightly floured work surface. Knead gently for about 1 minute, just until the dough is smooth. If you overwork the dough, it will shrink during baking. Use a rolling pin to gently roll the dough into a ½-inch-thick rectangle. Use a 2¼-inch fluted cutter to cut circles from the dough. Cut the circles as close together as possible to avoid waste. When all of the circles have been cut from the dough, push the scraps back together. Gently reroll them into a ½-inch-thick piece. Cut as many circles from this piece as possible. Repeat until all of the dough has been used. Place the circles on a parchment paper–covered baking sheet.

continued

Use a pastry brush to brush some milk over the tops of the scones. This will give them a nice golden color. Place the baking sheet in the oven and bake until the scones are well risen and evenly golden brown, about 15 minutes. Remove from the oven and cool on a wire rack. Traditionally scones are served with clotted cream and jam. I think they are good with just about anything!

Babka

Yield: Two 12-inch loaves; 16 servings

Babka is an Eastern European specialty. The first time I made it was with my colleague Dan Leader from the French Culinary Institute. He heads the bread baking program at the school. My office is right next to the bakery and I think I've put on a few pounds due to the proximity. I just can't resist the bread when it is still hot from the oven.

Use a stand mixer to make this recipe. A hand-held mixer may not stand up to the dough.

For the dough

Unbleached all-purpose flour	4 cups	18 ounces	500 grams
Whole milk	Scant ½ cup	3.5 ounces	100 grams
Water	1½ tablespoons	1.2 ounces	30 grams
Granulated sugar	½ cup	3.8 ounces	110 grams
Salt	2 teaspoons	0.3 ounce	10 grams
Fresh compressed yeast	¼ cup	1.6 ounces	40 grams
3 large eggs			
Cold unsalted butter, cubed	¾ cup + 2 tablespoons	7 ounces	200 grams

For the chocolate filling

Heavy cream	Generous ¼ cup	2.8 ounces	80 grams
DOVE® PROMISES® Dark Chocolate, finely chopped		3.5 ounces	100 grams

For the French meringue

1 vanilla bean			
Granulated sugar	Generous ¼ cup	2 ounces	60 grams
2 large egg whites			

continued

Prepare the dough: Place the flour, milk, water, sugar, salt, yeast, and eggs in the bowl of a stand mixer fitted with the paddle attachment. I usually put the flour in the bottom of the bowl and all of the other ingredients in separate small piles on top of the flour. That way I can double-check that I have added all the correct ingredients before I begin to mix it all together. Beat on slow speed until the ingredients are dispersed and the dough begins to come together, about 5 minutes. You will see the gluten strands develop and the dough become elastic. Add the butter all at once and increase the mixer speed to medium-high. Continue to mix the dough until it is smooth and pulls away from the side of the bowl, another 8 minutes. You want this dough to be slightly on the wet side. If necessary, add another teaspoon of water as it mixes. Remove the dough from the mixer and pat into a disk. Let the dough rest for 30 minutes at room temperature to start the fermentation. Wrap the disk well in plastic wrap and let rest in the refrigerator for a couple of hours. This will allow any gluten strands to relax and the butter to harden, making the dough easier to work. You can actually make the dough the evening before and let it rest overnight in the refrigerator.

Prepare the chocolate filling: Heat the heavy cream in a 1-quart heavy-bottomed saucepan until bubbles begin to form at the edge of the pan. Place the chopped chocolate in a medium-size mixing bowl. Make a ganache by pouring the hot cream over the chocolate and letting it sit for 30 seconds to melt the chocolate. Then slowly whisk until smooth and homogenous. Allow the chocolate mixture to cool at room temperature until it has the consistency of toothpaste.

Lightly spray two nonstick 12-inch loaf pans with some vegetable cooking spray. You can also use regular 12-inch loaf pans if you butter and flour them. Remove the dough from the refrigerator and divide it in half. Place one half on a lightly floured work surface. Lightly flour each side of the dough. Use a rolling pin to roll the dough into a 12 × 15-inch rectangle. Repeat with the second piece of dough.

Prepare the meringue: Use a sharp knife to slice the vanilla bean in half lengthwise. Separate the seeds from the skin by scraping the blade of the knife along the inside of the bean. Add the seeds to the sugar and mix to combine. Place the egg whites in a medium-size mixing bowl and whip with an electric mixer set on medium speed until foamy, about 3 minutes. Make a French meringue by adding the sugar mixture 1 tablespoon at a time. Once all of the sugar has been added, increase the mixer speed to medium-high and whip to stiff but not dry peaks, about 5 minutes.

Assemble the babkas: Use a large offset spatula to spread half of the cooled ganache evenly over each of the dough rectangles. Be sure to spread it all the way to the edges. Cover the chocolate layer with the meringue, spreading it all the way to the edges. Roll each dough into a cylinder starting from a short end. Remember that the rolled cylinder needs to fit inside the loaf pan. Place each babka, seam side down, in the pan. Place in a warm spot and allow the babkas to proof until they have doubled in size. They should rise slightly higher than the rim of the mold. If you allow the babkas to proof in the refrigerator overnight, the taste and texture will be better because the slow fermentation gives the flavors time to develop.

About half an hour before the babkas have finished proofing, preheat the oven to 350°F (176°C). Place the proofed babkas in the oven and bake until evenly golden brown, about 40 minutes. Remove from the oven and let cool on a wire rack for about 10 minutes. Unmold by inverting the loaf pans and letting the babkas drop from them. If necessary, run the blade of a knife around the inside of the pan to loosen the babka from the sides. The babkas will keep at room temperature, well wrapped in plastic wrap, for up to 2 days.

Crumpets

Yield: About 8 crumpets

Crumpets are a yeast-risen bread cooked in a frying pan. They resemble English muffins. You can usually find fresh yeast in some grocery stores or gourmet shops. You can also check with your local bakery or pizza parlor.

Fresh compressed yeast	1 teaspoon	0.15 ounce	4 grams
Lukewarm water	⅓ cup	2.5 ounces	70 grams
Whole milk	⅔ cup	5.7 ounces	165 grams
Granulated sugar	1 teaspoon	0.15 ounce	4 grams
1 large egg			
Unbleached all-purpose flour	1¾ cups	8.3 ounces	235 grams
Pinch of salt			
Unsalted butter, melted and cooled slightly	2 tablespoons	1 ounce	25 grams

continued

Combine the yeast and lukewarm water in a medium-size mixing bowl and allow the yeast to dissolve. Add the remaining ingredients and whisk well to combine. Use an electric mixer set on medium-high speed to incorporate air into the mixture. Whip until smooth, about 5 minutes. You want to encourage the creation of air bubbles because they will give the crumpets their characteristic texture and appearance. When well whipped, the dough will be smooth, strong, and elastic. Cover the bowl with plastic wrap. Set the bowl in a warm spot and allow the mixture to ferment for about 1 hour. It should double in size and be full of air bubbles before you cook the crumpets.

Spray a frying pan lightly with vegetable cooking spray. Place the pan over medium-high heat. Spray the insides of four 3-inch stainless-steel rings or plain cutters with cooking spray and place these in the frying pan. Vigorously mix the batter with a wooden spoon. The batter will deflate and you will see air bubbles. Drop a large tablespoon of the crumpet batter into each ring. The batter should cover the bottom of the rings. The rings will keep the batter from spreading too far, ensuring the round shape of the crumpets. I've been told that you can also use clean tuna fish cans for the rings. Just remember to remove the top and bottom lids, remove the paper from the side, and clean them very, very well.

When you see the air bubbles rise to the top of each cooking crumpet and burst, the crumpets are ready to be flipped. Remove each ring (careful, they are hot!) and use a spatula or pancake flipper to flip each crumpet to the other side. The crumpets should be evenly golden brown. If they brown more in some spots than in others, turn the heat down slightly and continue cooking. Watch the side to be sure it is cooked thoroughly. Place the cooked crumpets on a wire rack to cool.

I like to eat these in the morning with my sister-in-law Linda's Red Raspberry Jam (page 26).

Rugelach

Yield: 4 dozen

My friend Arthur Schwartz has a radio show called "Food Talk." One day we were talking about Eastern European specialties when he told me about rugelach. Rugelach is a Yiddish word meaning "crescent." These remind me of mini fruit-filled croissants. One of the things I like best about New York is the variety of cultures and all the foods I get to try because all of those cultures are right here in my neighborhood. Another friend Joan Nathan shared her recipe with me.

For the dough

Cold cream cheese		8 ounces	230 grams
Cold unsalted butter, cubed	I cup	8 ounces	230 grams
Powdered sugar	Scant ⅔ cup	2.3 ounces	65 grams
Pinch of salt			
Splash of fresh lemon juice, strained			
Unbleached all-purpose flour	Generous 2 cups	9.5 ounces	270 grams

For the strawberry filling

Strawberry jam	½ cup	5.5 ounces	155 grams
Cake crumbs	I tablespoon	0.175 ounce	5 grams

For the chocolate filling

DOVE® PROMISES® Dark or Milk Chocolate, finely grated	½ cup	2 ounces	60 grams
Granulated sugar	¼ cup	1.8 ounces	50 grams

For the egg wash

2 large egg yolks			
I large egg			
Whole milk	¼ cup	1.8 ounces	50 grams

To finish the rugelach

Rock or crystal sugar (page 14)	¼ cup	1.6 ounces	40 grams

Prepare the dough: Place the cream cheese, butter, sugar, salt, lemon juice, and vanilla in a medium-size mixing bowl and beat just until incorporated with an electric mixer set on medium speed, about 5 minutes. I use powdered sugar because it will dissolve and mix into the dough faster than granulated sugar. Use a rubber spatula to scrape down the side of the bowl as needed. Add the flour and mix just until it forms a dough, about 30 seconds. Don't overmix, or gluten will develop and the rugelach will be chewy instead of crumbly. You can also mix this dough by hand to ensure that you don't overmix it. When ready, the dough will be slightly sticky. Remove the dough from the mixing bowl and pat it into a disk. Wrap it well in plastic wrap and let it rest in the refrigerator for about 1 hour. This will allow any gluten that may have developed to relax.

Prepare the strawberry filling: Combine the strawberry jam and cake crumbs in a small mixing bowl. Mix with a rubber spatula until well combined. Set aside.

Prepare the chocolate filling: Combine the grated chocolate and granulated sugar in a small mixing bowl and mix well with a rubber spatula. Set aside.

Prepare the rugelach: Preheat the oven to 350°F (176°C). Remove the dough from the refrigerator and divide it in half. You will only roll one half at a time, so return the other to the refrigerator. This will ensure that the unused dough does not become too soft before you roll it. Place the first half on a lightly floured surface and pat it into a rectangle. I pat it into a rectangle at the beginning because that is the shape I want the rolled dough to be in when I have finished rolling it. Starting with a similar shape makes it easier to end that way. Use a rolling pin to roll the dough into an 8 × 18-inch rectangle about ⅛ inch thick, flouring as needed to keep the dough from sticking. Place the rectangle on the work surface with the long side facing you. Use an offset spatula to spread the strawberry filling in an even layer over the rectangle, spreading it all the way to the edges. Cut the rectangle in half from left to right. Cut each half into 12 triangles. Then roll each of the 12 triangles into a small crescent. To do this, pick up one triangle and place it on the work surface with the tip facing you. Gently pull the tip toward you; this light stretch adds layers to the finished rugelach without adding density. Use the tips of your fingers to roll the triangle from the base toward the tip. Place it on a parchment paper–covered baking sheet and repeat with the remaining triangles.

Remove the remaining dough from the refrigerator and pat this into a rectangle. Repeat the entire procedure, making another 24 rugelach, this time with the chocolate filling.

Prepare the egg wash: Place the egg yolks, whole egg, and milk in a small mixing bowl and whisk to combine. When all of the rugelach have been rolled, use a pastry brush to brush the egg wash on top of each one. Sprinkle each with some of the rock or crystal sugar. Place in the oven and bake until golden brown, about 15 minutes. Cool on a wire rack and serve. If the strawberry filling has oozed out of the rugelach, you might find it is easier to remove them from the parchment paper before they have fully cooled. The rugelach can be stored for 2 days if kept in an airtight container.

Homemade and Heavenly

This chapter is dedicated to everyone who has ever made a recipe that has been handed down through the generations. Most of the desserts are somewhat traditional. There are specialties from all countries; the Crème Caramel comes from France, the Sabayon is Italian, Apple Crisp is American, and the Tempura is Japanese.

These are the traditional desserts most people remember from their childhood. They are simple and recognizable, the kinds of desserts you are likely to find at a church fair or at someone's house when you are invited for dinner.

Strawberry Shortcake
and Scones (page 197)

Strawberry Shortcake

Yield: 8 to 10 shortcakes

This is the *Dessert Circus* version of this summertime favorite. The traditional strawberry shortcake is made with pastry cream or, in the case of Kris's family, just biscuits, berries, and whipped cream. I think the chocolate complements the strawberries for a very tasty shortcake alternative. I use tea to infuse the flavor of orange into the ganache. You could use another flavor if you prefer. Now you can find so many different flavors of tea at the grocery store!

Scones (page 197)

For the tea ganache

Heavy cream	1⅓ cups	10.5 ounces	300 grams
Loose orange pekoe tea	3 tablespoons	0.75 ounce	20 grams
Bittersweet chocolate, finely chopped		11.5 ounces	330 grams
Grand Marnier	2 tablespoons	1.2 ounces	30 grams

To assemble the shortcake

Heavy cream	2 cups	16 ounces	450 grams
Powdered sugar	¼ cup	1 ounce	25 grams
Fresh strawberries	About 3 cups	14 ounces	400 grams

Preheat the oven to 350°F (176°C).

Prepare the scones: Make and roll out the dough as directed in the recipe, but use a 4-inch fluted cutter to cut circles from the dough. Place them on a parchment paper–covered baking sheet. Brush the tops of the scones with the milk or egg wash and place in the oven. Bake until well risen and evenly golden brown, about 20 minutes. Remove from the oven and cool on a wire rack until ready to use.

Prepare the tea ganache: Heat the heavy cream and tea together in a 2-quart heavy-bottomed saucepan until bubbles begin to form around the edge of the pan. Make sure you have chopped the chocolate as finely as possible so it will melt quickly and easily. Place the chopped chocolate in a medium-size mixing bowl. Make a ganache by straining the hot cream mixture through a fine-mesh sieve into the chocolate and letting it sit for 30 seconds to melt the chocolate. Then slowly whisk until smooth and homogenous. I use a hand-held immersion blender to ensure a smooth ganache and to keep the emulsion of the chocolate. Mix until all of the hot cream is incorporated and the ganache is smooth and homogenous. If the ganache separates, it is very easy to fix. It should come back together when you add a small amount of cold cream and whisk well. The ganache should be thick, shiny, and smooth. Add the Grand Marnier and mix until fully incorporated. Pour the ganache into a bowl. Cover with plastic wrap and allow it to cool for at least 4 hours at room temperature. I usually make this at the end of the day and let it cool overnight. As it cools, it will thicken and set. The ganache is ready to be used when the consistency is similar to that of toothpaste.

Assemble the shortcake: Pour the heavy cream and powdered sugar into a medium-size mixing bowl and whip to soft peaks with an electric mixer set on medium speed. Place the whipped cream in a pastry bag fitted with a ½-inch star tip.

Use a serrated knife to slice each scone in half. Sometimes I sprinkle each half with a little Grand Marnier, but that is totally optional. Spread a ¼-inch-thick layer of ganache over the bottom half of the scone. Hull and halve the strawberries. Cover the ganache with the strawberries. Pipe the whipped cream on top of the strawberries. (You can also do this with a spoon.) Cover with the top half of the scone and place on a plate. *Voilà!*

Crêpes Suzettes à la Jacques

Yield: 12 crêpes; 6 servings

This crêpe recipe is an adaptation of a very traditional one. Classic Crêpes Suzettes are served with an orange sauce made from a reduction of orange juice and Grand Marnier. I make my sauce differently, and I like to have a little pastry cream filling, too.

In my hometown, crêpes are sold at the crêpe stand on the port. Whenever we don't have ice cream on our evening outings, we enjoy crêpes as our treat. You can get them with other fillings, but they are mostly served with Grand Marnier. My dad is always the one who can eat the most crêpes.

continued

Pastry Cream (page 20)			
Candied orange peel	I cup	7.7 ounces	220 grams
Grand Marnier	¼ cup	1.8 ounces	50 grams

For the crêpes

3 large eggs			
Granulated sugar	¼ cup	1.8 ounces	50 grams
½ vanilla bean			
Unbleached all-purpose flour	Scant ½ cup	2.6 ounces	75 grams
Grated zest of ½ orange			
Grated zest of ½ lemon			
Whole milk	Scant ⅔ cup	5.5 ounces	150 grams
Heavy cream	Scant ½ cup	3.5 ounces	100 grams
Unsalted butter for cooking	I to 2 tablespoons	0.5 to I ounce	14 to 28 grams

For the orange butter sauce

Granulated sugar	I tablespoon	0.6 ounce	15 grams
Fresh orange juice, strained	I cup	9 ounces	250 milliliters
Cold unsalted butter, cubed	7 tablespoons	3.5 ounces	100 grams

Prepare the pastry cream: Make the pastry cream as described in the recipe and let cool. Fold in the candied orange peel and Grand Marnier. Store the pastry cream in the refrigerator, tightly covered with plastic wrap, until ready to use.

Prepare the crêpes: Place the eggs and sugar in a large mixing bowl and beat with an electric mixer set on medium speed until thoroughly combined, about 1 minute. Use a sharp knife to slice the vanilla bean in half again, lengthwise. Separate the seeds from the outside skin by scraping the blade of the knife along the inside of the bean. Add the vanilla seeds, flour, citrus zests, and half of the milk to the egg mixture and beat on medium speed until well incorporated. (I add the milk in two additions to keep the dry ingredients from clumping together.) Add the remaining milk and the heavy cream and continue to beat until the crêpe batter is smooth and homogenous. If the batter is lumpy, use a handheld immersion blender to make it smooth. Otherwise, use a blender and then strain it through a fine-mesh sieve.

Grease an 8-inch nonstick crêpe pan (a nonstick frying pan will also work) with about 1 teaspoon of the butter and place over medium-high heat. Once it is hot, wipe away any excess butter with a paper towel. Then pour a small amount of crêpe batter, about 2 tablespoons, into the pan and tilt the pan to spread the batter evenly. The batter should barely cover the bottom of the pan. Cook until it browns around the edges, about 30 seconds. Use a large spatula or pancake flipper to gently lift one side of the crêpe and carefully turn it. Cook the crêpe until the other side starts to brown, about another 30 seconds. You may need to adjust the level of heat if the crêpe cooks too quickly and burns in places. The crêpe should be thin, light, and unevenly browned. Slide the crêpe onto a plate and continue to make crêpes until all of the batter is used. If the crêpes begin to stick to the bottom of the pan, you should lightly butter the pan again.

The finished crêpes may be stacked directly on top of each other and can be made 1 or 2 days in advance if kept well wrapped in the refrigerator. When the crêpes are cold, they may stick together due to the butter residue on the surface of the crêpes. If you warm the crêpes slightly in the microwave for 10 to 15 seconds on high power, they will separate easily.

Prepare the orange butter sauce: Place the sugar in a small nonreactive heavy-bottomed saucepan and place over medium-high heat. Allow the sugar to cook until it is an evenly golden caramel color, stirring occasionally with a wooden spoon. Watch the sugar closely—once it begins to melt, it will caramelize quickly. Carefully (it may splatter) pour in the orange juice and whisk to combine. The caramel will harden when the orange juice is added. Keep whisking until all of the caramel has dissolved into the orange juice. Allow the mixture to boil until it has reduced to about half of its original volume. Pour the mixture into a tall container. Use a hand-held immersion blender or stand blender to mix in the cold butter. Add the butter in several additions, combining it almost completely each time. The butter is added slowly to keep the emulsion, which is what holds the sauce together and gives it a nice thick texture. When all of the butter has been added, mix until the sauce is thick, smooth, and homogenous.

Assemble the dessert: Spread a couple of tablespoons of the pastry cream filling in the center of each crêpe. Fold the crêpes into quarters and place on a plate. You can determine how many crêpes you would like to serve each person, but I usually serve two. Cover the crêpes with the sauce and serve.

The sauce will hold for about 2 hours if you place it in a double boiler over very low heat.

Caramel-Walnut Soufflé

Yield: 8 to 10 individual soufflés

This is a good dessert to serve in the fall. When the soufflés bake in the oven, the aroma reminds me of roasted nuts. I like the combination of caramel and walnuts; the tastes complement each other. I made this recipe on my show with my friend Mary Manksch.

Caramel-Walnut Base (page 47)	Generous 1½ cups	14 ounces	400 grams
Splash of rum (optional)			
13 large egg whites			
Meringue powder (optional)	Scant ½ cup	1.6 ounces	40 grams
Juice of ½ lemon, strained			
Water	2 tablespoons	1.5 ounces	35 grams
Granulated sugar	¾ cup + 1 tablespoon	6.3 ounces	180 grams
Light corn syrup	¼ cup	3.5 ounces	80 grams

Preheat the oven to 375°F (190°C). Use a pastry brush to coat the inside of eight to ten 1-cup soufflé molds evenly with softened butter. Fill each mold with granulated sugar, then pour out the excess. If you have properly buttered the molds, the sugar will stick to the bottom and side of them.

Prepare the soufflé base: Place a 1-quart saucepan half filled with water over medium heat and bring it to a simmer. Make a double boiler by setting a large mixing bowl over the simmering water. Place the caramel-walnut base in the bowl and heat until warm. If the base is too thick, you can add the rum to loosen it slightly. You'll know the base is too thick if its consistency is similar to that of peanut butter. The base will be easier to incorporate into the warm meringue if they are each about the same temperature.

Prepare the Italian meringue: Pour the egg whites, meringue powder, and lemon juice into a medium-size mixing bowl and whisk to combine. Old egg whites whip better than fresh ones because some of the water has evaporated and the albumen (page 16) is more concentrated. By adding meringue powder to fresh egg whites, I get the same result. The lemon juice will keep the egg whites from separating and having a crumbly texture.

While the base is heating, pour the water, sugar, and corn syrup into a 1-quart heavy-bottomed saucepan and place over medium-high heat. Insert a candy thermometer and cook the mixture until it reaches 250°F (121°C), what is known as the soft ball stage (page 14). Remove the cooked sugar from the heat.

Use an electric mixer set on medium speed to whip the egg whites for about 5 seconds. Increase the mixer speed to medium-high and make an Italian meringue by pouring the hot sugar down the side of the mixing bowl into the whipping whites. Be careful not to pour the hot sugar directly on the beaters, or it will splatter. I add the cooked sugar when I start to whip the meringue to give the meringue more strength and elasticity while making it heavier. This will help the soufflé hold up for 2 to 3 hours before being baked. Continue to whip the meringue until stiff and glossy, about 5 minutes.

Prepare the soufflé: Combine about one third of the meringue with the caramel-walnut mixture and use a rubber spatula to gently fold them together. Adding part of the meringue to the caramel-walnut mixture makes the two textures more similar, which helps them blend more evenly. Fold the remaining meringue into the mixture. Remember to fold to the bottom of the bowl to evenly distribute the walnut mixture.

Use a rubber spatula to fill the prepared soufflé molds. I usually round the tops because I think it looks nicer when baked. Place the soufflés in the oven on the center rack. Remove the top oven rack if necessary to allow enough room for them to rise. If the soufflé is too close to the top of the oven or under a rack, it will stick when it rises. If the soufflé is too close to the bottom of the oven, the bottom of the soufflé will burn before the inside is properly baked. Bake until the soufflés have risen to about one and a half times their original height and start to brown on top, about 20 minutes. I prefer the center of the soufflé to be soft and a little wet. If you like a drier soufflé, bake it a few minutes longer. Serve immediately with a side of whipped cream or crème anglaise, if desired.

Crème Caramel

Yield: One 8-inch dessert; 8 to 10 servings

Crème caramel is a classic dessert. It is baked at a low temperature because it contains no starch; it depends on the eggs for structure. If you bake it at a temperature that is too high, the eggs will scramble and the texture will not be smooth and creamy. When you unmold it, the melted caramel runs over it.

Granulated sugar	Scant ½ cup	3.5 ounces	100 grams
Water	1 tablespoon	0.6 ounce	15 grams

For the custard

Whole milk	4½ cups	32 ounces	900 grams
Granulated sugar	Generous 1½ cups	12.5 ounces	350 grams
1 vanilla bean			
5 large eggs			
8 large egg yolks			

Preheat the oven to 300°F (148°C).

Prepare the caramel: Pour the sugar into a medium-size heavy-bottomed frying pan and place over medium-high heat. Make a dry caramel by letting the sugar cook until evenly light golden brown, 3 to 5 minutes. Remember, the caramel will continue to cook in the oven, so do not make it too dark, or it will taste bitter. Occasionally stir the sugar with a wooden spoon to remove any lumps. When the caramel has reached the proper color, I carefully add a little water (it may splatter) to keep it from becoming too hard. Mix in the water and remove the caramel from the heat. Carefully pour the hot caramel into the bottom of a 2-quart mold. It may be necessary to tilt the mold from side to side so that the caramel completely covers the bottom.

Prepare the custard: Pour the milk and half of the sugar into a nonreactive 2-quart heavy-bottomed saucepan. While the milk is heating over medium-high heat, use a sharp paring knife to slice the vanilla bean in half lengthwise. Separate the seeds from the outside skin by scraping the bean with the knife. Place the skin and seeds in the heating milk. Scald the milk mixture by heating it until bubbles start to form around the edge of the pan. Remove from the heat.

Place the remaining sugar, the whole eggs, and egg yolks in a large mixing bowl and whisk until well incorporated. When you add sugar to eggs (especially to egg yolks), it is important to create an emulsion quickly, or a chemical reaction that produces heat will occur. If you do not whisk immediately, this heat will cook the egg yolks and create lumps in the custard. Continue to whisk while slowly pouring the hot milk into the egg mixture and whisking until the mixture is smooth and homogenous in color. Try not to create air bubbles on the surface of the custard when you whisk, as these can form a crust on the baked

custard. Pour the mixture through a fine-mesh sieve to remove the vanilla bean pieces and any overcooked eggs. Then pour it into the mold and place in a roasting pan in the oven.

Traditionally, custard is baked in a hot water bath to insulate it from the direct heat of the oven and to keep the eggs from cooking too fast, which would cause them to separate. Use hot water from the tap and pour enough water into the roasting pan to reach halfway up the side of the mold. (If you are using a convection oven, a water bath is not needed because the even circulation of the air insulates the custard from the direct heat of the oven. In a convection oven, bake the custard at 250°F [121°C].) When baked correctly, the custard should tremble slightly when gently shaken. In a conventional oven, this should take about 2½ hours. Baking time is about 1 hour in a convection oven. If you detect any liquid under the skin, the custard is underbaked. Put it back in the oven and shake it every 5 minutes until it is ready. If the custard begins to bubble during baking, reduce the oven temperature 25°F (14°C).

Remove the mold from the oven and the water bath and place on a wire rack for 30 minutes. Refrigerate for 2 hours before serving; it will finish setting in the refrigerator. It is safer to let the water bath cool before removing it from the oven.

Unmold the crème caramel: Carefully run a sharp paring knife around the inside of the mold to loosen the custard. Invert a flat plate over the crème caramel. Place one hand on either side, grasping both plate and mold, and flip them both so that the mold is on top. Gently lift off the mold. You may need to tap the bottom of the mold to release the custard. Sometimes I like to serve this dessert with whipped cream. Crème caramel will keep in the refrigerator, well wrapped in plastic wrap, for a couple of days.

Variation: This recipe produces a soft and delicate crème caramel, but it can be difficult to bake. If you use 5 large egg yolks and 8 large whole eggs, you will have something less delicate but easier to bake because the egg whites are what hold everything together.

> **To clean the caramel-crusted frying pan or mold, fill it with water and let it sit overnight. By morning the caramel will have dissolved.**

Bread Pudding

Yield: 6 individual bread puddings

In France, pastry chefs use day-old croissants and brioche to make bread pudding. Bread is very serious business there. It is baked fresh twice each day. Every morning before coffee, everyone in the village walks to the bakery to pick up the bread for breakfast and lunch just as it comes out of the oven. When we wake from our afternoon naps, everyone returns to the bakery to get the bread for dinner. It is a wonderful part of the culture to meet your neighbors at the shops. There is always a lot of discussion about the crust of the bread, how the humidity is affecting that day's bread, and the loyalty to one bakery over another. No one would dream of using the morning bread for dinner, and there would be an absolute revolution if anyone ever tried to sell day-old bread! You can use any bread for this dessert, leftover or fresh.

Whole milk	5 cups	40 ounces	1,120 grams
1 vanilla bean			
Granulated sugar	Scant 1 cup	7 ounces	200 grams
6 large eggs			
4 large egg yolks			
Golden raisins, hydrated with dark rum (page 28)	1¼ cups	7 ounces	200 grams
1 large loaf Brioche (page 192)			

Preheat the oven to 300°F (148°C).

Pour the milk into a 2-quart heavy-bottomed saucepan and place over medium-high heat. Use a sharp paring knife to slice the vanilla bean in half lengthwise. Separate the seeds from the skin by scraping the blade of the knife along the inside of the bean. Add all of the seeds and the skin to the saucepan and bring to a boil.

Pour the sugar, whole eggs, and egg yolks into a medium-size mixing bowl and whisk until well combined. The mixture should be thick, smooth, and homogenous. When the milk comes to a boil, temper the egg mixture by carefully adding about one third of the hot milk. Whisk immediately to keep the eggs from scrambling. Pour the tempered egg mixture into the saucepan containing the hot milk and whisk to combine. Pour the mixture through a fine-mesh sieve to remove the vanilla bean pieces and any overcooked eggs. It

will be easier to fill the molds if you strain the mixture into a large measuring cup with a spout.

Place six 4×2-inch molds on a baking sheet with 2-inch-high sides. Evenly distribute the rum-soaked raisins over the bottom of each mold. Cut the brioche into ¾-inch-thick slices and remove the crusts. Dice each slice into ½-inch cubes. Fill each mold about three quarters full with the brioche cubes. Fill the molds half full with the custard. Press down on the brioche to keep them from floating to the top and set the baking sheet in the oven (it's much easier to transfer the sheet with the molds only half full). Fill the molds to the top with the custard. It is important to fill the molds completely, since the custard loses volume as it bakes. The custard is baked in a hot water bath to insulate it from the direct heat of the oven and to keep the eggs from cooking too fast, which would cause them to separate. Pour enough hot water from the tap into the baking sheet to reach about halfway up the sides of the molds. (If you are using a convection oven, heat the oven to 200°F [93°C] and omit the water bath. In a convection oven a water bath is not necessary because the even circulation of the air insulates the custard from the direct heat of the oven.) Bake for about 45 minutes. The custard should tremble slightly when gently shaken. If you detect any liquid under the skin, the custard is underbaked. Continue baking, checking for doneness every 5 minutes. If at any point you see bubbles form around the side of the mold, lower the oven temperature by 25°F (14°C).

Remove the molds from the water bath and place on a wire rack for about 1 hour. Then refrigerate for 2 hours (or for up to 3 days) before serving; the bread pudding will continue to set in the refrigerator. Let the water bath cool before removing it from the oven.

When ready to serve, run the blade of a sharp knife around the inside edge of the mold to loosen the bread pudding from the side. Invert the bread pudding over the center of a plate and lift off the mold. Sometimes I like to decorate the plate by alternating drops of crème anglaise (page 21) and raspberry sauce (page 24) around the bread pudding. Then I swirl the sauces together with the tip of a paring knife.

Variation: If you want to make this in a single large mold or baking dish, follow the exact same directions using an 8-cup mold or baking dish. A large bread pudding will need to bake for about 60 minutes. Use the same test for doneness.

French Rice Pudding

Yield: 3-quart kugelhopf mold or baking dish; 10 servings

This is the French version of rice pudding. It calls for cream and gelatin. I think it is great served with fresh fruit.

Water, as needed			
Jasmine rice	2¼ cups	9 ounces	250 grams
Whole milk, heated	Generous 3½ cups	28 ounces	800 grams
I vanilla bean			
Pinch of salt			
Grated zest of I orange			
Grated zest of I lemon			
Granulated sugar	¾ cup	5.5 ounces	150 grams
Fresh ginger, peeled and chopped	I to 2 tablespoons	0.3 to 0.75 ounce	10 to 20 grams
3 gelatin sheets or I envelope powdered gelatin			
Golden raisins, hydrated with dark rum (page 28)	I ⅓ cups	7 ounces	200 grams
⅓ recipe Crème Anglaise, cold (page 21)			
Heavy cream	Scant 2 cups	14 ounces	400 grams

Preheat the oven to 350°F (176°C).

Pour the water into a 2-quart heavy-bottomed saucepan and place over medium-high heat. Allow the water to come to a boil and add the rice. When the mixture comes back to a boil, strain through a fine-mesh sieve and discard the water. The rice is first boiled in water to remove some of its starch; this will make the rice pudding creamier and more delicate.

Pour the milk into a 3-quart heavy-bottomed ovensafe saucepan and place over medium-high heat. Use a sharp knife to slice the vanilla bean in half lengthwise. Separate the seeds from the skin by scraping the blade of the knife along the inside of the bean. Add the seeds and skin to the heating milk. Add the salt, zests, sugar, and ginger. Cook, stirring occasionally, until bubbles form around the edge of the pan. Remove from the heat and mix in the drained rice. Cover the saucepan and place in the oven. Bake for 40 minutes.

continued

If you are using gelatin sheets, place them in a medium-size mixing bowl with enough cold water (about 2 cups) to cover. Let stand for about 5 minutes to allow the gelatin to soften and hydrate. Cold water hydrates the gelatin without letting it absorb too much liquid. Remove the gelatin from the bowl and squeeze out the excess water with your hands. If you are using powdered gelatin, sprinkle it over ¼ cup (2 ounces; 60 grams) of cold water. Let the gelatin bloom until it has absorbed all the water, about 1 minute.

Remove the rice mixture from the oven. Add the hydrated gelatin and use a rubber spatula to stir well until incorporated. Be careful when you stir the cooked rice; you don't want to break the grains and turn it into paste. Fold in the hydrated raisins. Fold a large scoop of the hot rice mixture into the cold crème anglaise to temper it. Then fold the tempered crème anglaise into the remaining rice mixture until combined.

Pour the heavy cream into a medium-size mixing bowl and whip to soft peaks with an electric mixer set on medium-high speed. Fold the whipped cream into the rice mixture. If the rice is still hot, allow it to cool before adding the whipped cream, or the cream will melt.

Spray the kugelhopf mold lightly with vegetable cooking spray. Fill the mold with the rice pudding. Use a rubber spatula to make the top smooth. Place the mold in the refrigerator for 2 to 3 hours to set.

To unmold the rice pudding, dip the mold into hot water for about 5 seconds. Do not allow the mold to heat too much, or the rice pudding will melt. Place a large flat plate facedown over the mold. Flip over the plate and mold at the same time so the mold is on top of the plate. Gently lift off the mold. I think it looks nice when garnished with fresh fruit.

Sabayon

Yield: About 6 servings

Sabayon can be served as a dessert or as a predessert. I like to serve it with ladyfingers. The traditional way is to make it with Marsala wine. You can also make it with any kind of fruit juice or with champagne. At the restaurant we make it and serve it in a big copper bowl. It is like being at a family meal where one person passes the ladyfingers while the other follows up with the sabayon. The hardest part about making sabayon is whipping it because your arm gets so tired (if you whip it by hand)!

5 large egg yolks			
Muscato d'Asti	⅓ cup	2.6 ounces	75 grams
Marsala wine	Scant ⅓ cup	2.3 ounces	65 grams
Granulated sugar	⅓ cup	3.2 ounces	90 grams
Corn starch	½ teaspoon	0.175 ounce	5 grams

Place a 2-quart saucepan half filled with water over high heat and bring it to a simmer. Make a double boiler by setting a large mixing bowl or copper pot over the simmering water. Place the egg yolks, Muscato, Marsala, sugar, and cornstarch in the bowl or pot and whisk until it is thick, fluffy, and tripled in volume, about 5 minutes. You can do this by hand or with an electric mixer set on medium-high. If the sabayon begins to separate, remove the mixing bowl from above the simmering water and continue to whisk the mixture until it is once again smooth and homogenous. To serve, you can pour the sabayon into small bowls. Use any dish you like, but serve it immediately.

Variation: Substitute ¾ cup (6.3 ounces; 180 grams) strained fresh grapefruit juice for the wines.

Kris's Apple Crisp

Yield: One 8-inch casserole; about 8 servings

This is a good dessert for any beginner to make. On our team, we decide the difficulty of a dessert based on whether we think Kris can do it. If she can, the rating is *Easy*. She doesn't cook or bake very often, but when she does, this is what she makes. I create fancy desserts all day at work, but when it is my turn to choose, this one is always on my list. Kris likes to use McIntosh apples for this recipe, but you can use any kind you like. If you like ice cream even a little bit, serve it with this dessert—apple crisp without ice cream is like cookies without milk!

10 McIntosh apples			
Unbleached all-purpose flour	¾ cup	4 ounces	120 grams
Granulated sugar	½ cup	3.8 ounces	110 grams
Light brown sugar	Firmly packed ½ cup	2.5 ounces	70 grams
Cold unsalted butter, cubed	½ cup	4 ounces	120 grams
Pinch of ground cinnamon			
Pinch of salt			
Pinch of freshly grated nutmeg			
Pecans or walnuts, chopped	½ cup	2.3 ounces	65 grams
Apple cider (optional)	¼ cup	2 ounces	60 grams
Vanilla ice cream			

Preheat the oven to 350°F (176°C). Use a sharp paring knife or apple peeler to peel the apples. Slice them in half and remove the cores, then slice the apple halves into thick segments. Kris likes to use thinner slices and I prefer chunks. Set aside.

Combine the flour, sugars, butter, cinnamon, salt, and nutmeg in a large mixing bowl. Use a pastry blender to cut the butter into the blended ingredients. The finished mixture should be crumbly, and you will be able to see small chunks of butter in it. Mix in the chopped nuts. Do this after you work in the butter so you won't have to crunch through the nuts.

Lightly spray an 8-inch casserole or soufflé dish with vegetable cooking spray. Fill the dish about half full with the apples. Add about half of the apple cider and cover with a generous portion of the flour mixture. Top with the remaining apples and cider. The apples should mound over the top of the dish because they will shrink as they bake. Cover with the remaining flour mixture. Place in the oven and bake, covered, for about 30 minutes. Then uncover and bake until the topping is a dark golden brown and appears dry, about an additional 30 minutes. Remove from the oven and spoon into small bowls. I always serve it warm with vanilla ice cream so the ice cream melts into the apple crisp.

We usually make a double batch. You can freeze the baked apple crisp well wrapped in plastic wrap. When ready, allow it to thaw. If I am going to reheat the whole dish, I do it in the oven at 350°F (176°C) for 20 to 30 minutes. Otherwise, spoon it into small bowls and reheat each bowl in the microwave on high power for 60 to 90 seconds.

Fruit Tempura

Yield: 8 servings

Ken Goto is the sous-chef who has worked with me for the last seven years. He is extraordinarily talented and I am grateful for all of his hard work and dedication. When I wanted to make tempura, he called his grandmother in Japan to get the recipe. Ken says the secret to good tempura is making sure all of the ingredients are very cold. A few hours before I begin, I put the water in the refrigerator, the eggs in a bowl of ice water, and the flour in a bowl in the freezer. The contrast in temperature between the cold batter and the hot oil is what gives the tempura its characteristic bubbly texture.

You can use any fruit you like. I have included a list of my favorites. I recommend that you use whatever fruit is in season and that you peel, pit, core, or cut it as necessary.

⅓ recipe Tea Ganache (page 209)

Crème Anglaise (page 21)

1 star fruit

1 Asian pear

1 banana

1 pineapple

5 kumquats

Vegetable or canola oil for deep-frying

For the tempura batter

2 large eggs, cooled in ice water

Very cold water, as needed

Cake flour, chilled in the freezer	2 cups	10.5 ounces	300 grams

To serve the tempura

Powdered sugar for dusting	1 cup	4 ounces	120 grams

Prepare the tea ganache as directed in the recipe and pour it into a small bowl. This is one of the sauces for the fried tempura. Allow it to cool slightly, but not so much that it thickens. It should be liquid enough to be able to easily dip the tempura.

Prepare the crème anglaise as directed in the recipe and let cool. Since crème anglaise is liquid, I like to serve it as a cold sauce. Pour it into a small bowl for dipping.

Prepare the fruit: Use a sharp paring knife to cut the star fruit into ¼-inch-thick slices. Peel, halve, and core the Asian pear, then cut it into ½-inch-thick slices. Peel the banana and cut it into ½-inch-thick slices. Peel and core the pineapple and cut it into ½-inch-thick slices. Here's an easy way to cut a pineapple: Use a serrated knife and cut off ¾ inch from the top and bottom of the pineapple. Stand it upright on a cutting board and place the blade of the knife at the top of the pineapple about ¼ inch in from the skin. Use the blade of the knife at a 45-degree angle to cut along the natural curve of the pineapple from top to bottom, slicing off the skin. Repeat this procedure, moving around the pineapple, until all of the skin is removed. Remove as many of the eyes as possible. The kumquats can be used whole.

Use an electric deep fryer or a 4-quart heavy-bottomed saucepan placed over medium-high heat to heat the oil to 330°F (165°C). If using a saucepan, check the temperature with a candy thermometer. It is important to maintain the right temperature, so you may need to adjust the heat or remove the pan from the burner to keep it where you want it. If the oil is too hot, the tempura will burn before it is evenly fried; if the oil is too cool, the tempura will absorb too much oil before it finishes frying.

Prepare the tempura batter: Break the eggs into a clear, cold 2-cup liquid measuring cup. Add enough of the cold water to equal a total of 2 cups of liquid. Use a chopstick to break the eggs apart and combine them with the water. Place the flour in a medium-size mixing bowl. Add the liquid, incorporating it into the flour using two chopsticks. The way this batter is mixed is very important. I mix with chopsticks; it is a very delicate way of mixing the flour. Do not overmix, or too much gluten (page 10) will develop, which would make the dough too chewy. It is okay if there are still a few lumps once all of the liquid has been incorporated.

Fry the tempura: Dip the fruit in the batter piece by piece, and immediately and carefully place each piece in the hot oil. Do not overcrowd the saucepan, or it will be difficult to turn over the fruit and it will not fry evenly. I use chopsticks to turn over the fruit, but you can also use a slotted spoon if you are careful. Fry the tempura until evenly golden brown on each side. Remove from the hot oil and drain on paper towels. Sprinkle with powdered sugar and serve with the dipping sauces.

Apple Strudel

Yield: One strudel; about 20 servings

The first time I saw someone make strudel was at the Hotel Negresco in Nice. An Austrian pastry chef had come to the hotel to do a demonstration. He tossed the dough over his head like it was pizza dough. The spinning caused the dough to stretch. That is a great technique if you can manage it, but I always end up with dough in places I don't want it. It is fun to work with strudel dough. It is amazing how thin you can make it. You know it is ready when you can practically read through it. If you don't want to make the dough, use store-bought phyllo dough.

For the filling

3½ apples, peeled, cored, and diced			
Cinnamon sugar	2 tablespoons	I ounce	25 grams
Grated zest of I lemon			
Golden raisins, hydrated with dark rum (page 28)	I cup	5.5 ounces	150 grams
Juice of ½ lemon, strained			
Walnuts, chopped	I cup	4.7 ounces	130 grams

For the dough

Unbleached all-purpose flour	1½ cups	7 ounces	200 grams
Bread flour	¾ cup	3.5 ounces	100 grams
Pinch of salt			
Corn oil	¼ cup	1.6 ounces	40 grams
Lukewarm water	¾ cup	5.5 ounces	150 grams
Extra virgin olive oil	I to 2 tablespoons	0.75 to 1.5 ounces	20 to 40 grams
Dry bread or cake crumbs, finely chopped	1½ cups	4 ounces	120 grams

Preheat the oven to 360°F (182°C).

Prepare the filling: Combine all the ingredients for the filling in a medium-size mixing bowl and toss to combine. I usually do this with my hands. Make sure everything is well combined. Set aside.

Prepare the dough: I think the best way to make this dough is by hand. Place the flours and salt in a medium-size mixing bowl and mix to combine. Add the corn oil and water slowly. You may not need all the water, depending on the humidity in the air and on how much moisture the flour will absorb. The dough should be soft and sticky. When the ingredients are combined, turn the dough onto the table and knead it until smooth. The dough will be ropy and dry in the beginning and become smooth and elastic as you knead it. Give the dough some strength by slapping it onto the work surface, folding it in on itself a few times, and then kneading it; this will develop the gluten (page 10). Pat the dough into a disk and rub it with a little olive oil. This will prevent a skin from forming on the dough. Let the dough rest at room temperature for a few hours.

continued

Homemade and Heavenly

It is best to work on a small rectangular table that you can move around on all sides. This will make it easier to stretch the dough. Cover the table with a clean large cloth. Use a smooth cloth that does not have any nap. Flour the cloth lightly and place the dough in the center. Use a rolling pin to roll the dough into a large thin rectangle. Roll it as big as you can. When the dough becomes too difficult to roll, pick it up in your hands and stretch it apart. To do this, use the backs of your hands to stretch the dough from the center toward the corners. Keep your fingers tucked into your palm, as if you were making a loose fist. Do not use your fingers, or the dough will tear. The dough should rest on the backs of your hands. Work slowly and rotate the dough as you stretch it. This is another recipe that is easier to do with a friend; when the dough becomes too big to hold, a friend can take one side. If you pull the dough too fast or too hard, it will break. If you make a hole, just fold it closed. This dough is incredibly elastic. The first time you try it, you will be amazed at how large it can stretch! When the dough becomes too large and awkward to stretch, place it on the table and continue to pull it gently. Stretch the dough until it is almost transparent. If the center becomes too thin, pull only the sides.

Assemble the strudel: When you have finished stretching the dough, sprinkle it evenly with the bread or cake crumbs. These will absorb the liquid in the filling, which helps keep the strudel dry as it bakes. Spread the filling over the dough, leaving a 1- to 2-inch border around the sides. Use a sharp paring knife to trim all of the edges clean and even. Roll the strudel from a long side toward you. To do this, grasp the cloth under the strudel and use it to begin to roll the edge of the strudel onto itself, forming a cylinder. Continue to roll the dough into a tight, even cylinder, using the cloth as a guide without rolling the cloth in the dough. When you have rolled the dough all the way, wet a pastry brush with water and brush the remaining edge of the cylinder and seal it closed. If necessary, seal each end of the cylinder and remove any excess dough.

Spray a baking sheet with vegetable cooking spray. Use the cloth to transfer the strudel to the baking sheet. This is easier than trying to move the strudel with your hands. Roll the strudel onto the baking sheet so that it rests on its seam and fold it in half to fit on the baking sheet. Place in the oven and bake until evenly golden brown, about 40 minutes. Remove the strudel from the oven and slice it with a sharp chef's knife. Serve the strudel warm. I like to eat it with vanilla ice cream.

> I like to sprinkle 2 to 3 tablespoons of melted butter on the stretched dough before adding the cake crumbs. This enhances the flavor and texture.

Chocolate Coconut Napoleon

Yield: 10 desserts

My best friend, Glenn Dopf, enjoys food more than anyone I know. He is always exploring different combinations of flavors. This is one of his favorite desserts.

Chocolate plays a predominant role in this recipe, so be sure to use a chocolate you like. I like to use Dove dark chocolate to give this dessert a nice flavor.

For the chocolate cream

Granulated sugar	Generous ⅓ cup	2.6 ounces	75 grams
6 large egg yolks			
Heavy cream	2 cups	16 ounces	450 grams
Whole milk	2 cups	16 ounces	450 grams
DOVE® PROMISES® Dark Chocolate, finely chopped		13 ounces	370 grams
Grand Marnier	¼ cup	1.8 ounces	50 grams

For the coconut tuiles

Shredded sweetened coconut	3¼ cups	9 ounces	250 grams
Granulated sugar	1 cup + 2 tablespoons	9 ounces	250 grams
4 large eggs			
Unsalted butter, melted	2 tablespoons	1 ounce	28 grams

To finish the dessert

Chocolate Sauce (page 25)	
Crème Anglaise (page 21)	

Prepare the chocolate cream: The base of the chocolate cream is a crème anglaise, which is poured over chocolate to make a ganache.

Pour half of the sugar into a small mixing bowl and set the remaining sugar aside. Add the egg yolks and whisk until well combined. The mixture should be thick, smooth, and homogenous.

Pour the heavy cream, milk, and remaining sugar into a nonreactive 3-quart heavy-bottomed saucepan, place it over medium-high heat, and bring to a boil. Temper the egg

mixture with the hot mixture by carefully pouring about one third of the hot mixture into the egg mixture. Whisk immediately to keep the eggs from scrambling. Pour the tempered egg mixture into the saucepan and place over medium heat, stirring constantly with a rubber spatula. The liquid will begin to thicken. When it reaches 182°F (83°C) on a candy thermometer and is thick enough to coat the back of a spoon, it is finished and should be removed from the heat. If you do not have a thermometer, you can tell that it is finished by using the following method: In one quick motion, dip the spatula into the crème anglaise and hold it horizontally in front of you. With the tip of your finger, wipe a clean line down the center of the spatula. If the trail keeps its shape, the crème anglaise is ready to be removed from the heat. If the trail fills with liquid, cook it for another minute and repeat the test. The objective is to remove the crème anglaise from the heat just *before* it boils. If the crème anglaise boils, the egg yolks will scramble. If this happens, you can still use it if you mix it with a hand-held immersion blender, food processor, or a blender. You will need a blade to liquefy the scrambled egg pieces. Remove from the heat, add the hydrated gelatin, and stir until dissolved.

Place the chopped chocolate in a medium-size mixing bowl and make a ganache by pouring the crème anglaise over the chocolate in two or three additions. Use a hand whisk to incorporate fully after each addition. The ganache should be thick, shiny, and smooth. Whisk in the Grand Marnier. Place in the refrigerator to cool and set. As the cream cools, the cocoa butter in the chocolate will harden and hold everything together. The cream will also become more flavorful as it cools. I like to make this a day in advance to give the chocolate flavor time to develop. (At this stage, the chocolate cream can be stored in the refrigerator, tightly covered with plastic wrap, for up to 3 days.)

Prepare the tuiles: Preheat the oven to 375°F (190°C). Combine the coconut, sugar, eggs, and butter in a medium-size mixing bowl and mix with a hand whisk until well combined. Place a silicon mat (page 6) on a baking sheet. (If you do not have a silicon mat, you can use a nonstick baking sheet.) Use a small offset spatula dipped in water to spread 4-inch circles of the tuile batter on the mat or baking sheet. Place in the oven and bake until evenly light golden brown, 8 to 10 minutes. Allow the tuiles to cool on a wire rack.

Assemble the Napoleon: Place one tuile in the center of each plate. Dip a large spoon in hot water and roll it through the chocolate cream to form a quenelle, or egg-shaped scoop, of chocolate cream. Place the chocolate cream in the center of the tuile and repeat for the remaining plates. Top with a second tuile and another quenelle of chocolate cream. Top each with a third tuile. Garnish the plate with chocolate sauce and crème anglaise. You could also use fresh berries in season or chocolate shavings (page 288). Serve immediately.

Banana Trifle

Yield: 6 to 8 servings

I discovered this classic English dessert when I first moved to this country. It is easy to make. You don't need any special equipment, and the end result is a yummy dessert that can be quite pretty. I use pound cake to make it, but you could use any cake. Trifle is usually made in a footed glass bowl so the layers are visible, but you can make it in anything you like. You could even make it in individual portions.

For the pound cake

½ recipe Basic Pound Cake (page 87) flavored with dark rum or Grand Marnier

For the caramelized banana sauté

5 large ripe bananas

Dark rum or Grand Marnier	**½ cup**	**3.5 ounces**	**100 grams**
Granulated sugar	**I cup**	**7 ounces**	**200 grams**
Unsalted butter (optional), cubed	**I tablespoon**	**0.6 ounce**	**15 grams**

For the flavored whipped cream

Heavy cream	**4 cups**	**32 ounces**	**900 grams**
Granulated sugar	**⅓ cup**	**2.6 ounces**	**75 grams**
Dark rum	**¼ cup**	**1.8 ounces**	**50 grams**
I vanilla bean			

To finish the trifle

Simple Syrup flavored with dark rum or Grand Marnier (page 86)

Prepare the pound cake: Make the pound cake batter as directed in the recipe, but flavor it with the rum or Grand Marnier when you add the eggs. This will intensify the flavor of the cake. Bake the cake in a cake pan instead of a baking sheet or loaf pan. Let the cake cool on a wire rack until ready to use. Unmold and remove the parchment paper from the back of the cake. You will need to slice the cake horizontally into ½-inch-thick layers. To do this easily, use a knife to mark the layers into the side of the cake. Place the cake on a revolving cake stand. Use a long, serrated knife to begin to slice the cake as you turn the stand. This will help keep the layer even as you cut it. Do not try to cut all the way through on

the first rotation. When you finish the first turn, keep turning while gradually cutting deeper into the layer until you are all the way through it. Separate the layers by sliding each one onto a flat plate or cake circle. Trim the layers as needed to fit inside your serving bowl.

Prepare the caramelized banana sauté: Peel and dice the bananas into ¼-inch cubes. Place them in a small mixing bowl with the rum or Grand Marnier and about one third of the sugar and let macerate for 10 minutes.

Heat a medium-size heavy-bottomed frying pan over medium-high heat. If it starts to smoke, the pan is too hot and you need to run it under cool water, dry it, and start again. When warm, sprinkle the remaining sugar into the pan. Try to keep the sugar in an even layer to allow it to caramelize at the same time. As soon as you see the sugar begin to melt, start moving the pan over the burner to keep the sugar from burning. Tilt the pan from side to side so that the melted sugar runs over the unmelted sugar. Cook until all of the sugar is light golden brown. I usually add a tablespoon of butter at this stage because it makes the caramel smoother. Add the banana mixture and spread it evenly in the pan. Cook over medium-high heat until most of the liquid has evaporated and the bananas are soft but not mushy. If the bananas are still firm when most of the liquid has evaporated, add a few tablespoons of water and continue cooking until they are ready. Remove from the heat and pour the caramelized bananas onto a plate. Cover with plastic wrap and set aside. Covering the hot bananas with plastic wrap keeps the caramel from drying as it cools.

Prepare the flavored whipped cream: Pour the heavy cream into a large mixing bowl. Add the sugar and rum. Use a sharp knife to slice the vanilla bean in half lengthwise. Separate the seeds from the skin by scraping the blade of the knife along the inside of the bean. Add the seeds to the heavy cream. Use an electric mixer set on medium-high speed to whip the cream to soft peaks. This is when the cream has the most volume.

Assemble the trifle: Place a large scoop of the flavored whipped cream on the bottom of the bowl and spread it to the edge. Top with a layer of pound cake. If you want to see the layers of the dessert, be sure the pound cake reaches the edge of the glass. Soak the cake with the flavored simple syrup. Top with a thick layer of sautéed bananas. Repeat all of the layers at least one more time; don't forget to soak the cake. Add as many layers as will fit, but remember to finish the trifle with a layer of the whipped cream. Serve immediately or refrigerate for a few hours. It is best to eat this dessert within a few hours of making it.

Variation: If you prefer, you can substitute peaches or apricots (peeled and pitted) or apples (peeled and cored) for the bananas. If you are really adventurous, vary the layers with all kinds of caramelized fruit.

Tiny Temptations

The recipes in this chapter are all one- or two-bite items. Make these when you are having a party, serving coffee, filling a buffet table, or need to make something to take with you to someone else's house. These recipes are also great as gifts. Most are very easy to make.

Chocolate Truffles

Yield: About 180 truffles

This is a candy everyone likes. Truffles are quite simple to make, and the process will be more fun if you have a friend to help you. Time is the biggest element in this recipe. It will be easier if you have the tempered chocolate ready and all the desired toppings spread out on parchment paper–covered baking sheets. Be sure to use a good bittersweet chocolate.

Once I was giving a class on truffles. Most places have the big professional immersion blenders available for me to use. I started making the ganache, and while it was mixing I pulled the mixer up a little too far, which caused the chocolate to be sprayed everywhere by the blade. I quickly dropped the blade back into the chocolate and looked down at my clothes. I was in my white chef's coat, but when I saw my clean coat, I started to smile. I like to be clean when I'm working. Then I looked at the audience in the front row. They were all licking themselves! Be careful when working with chocolate!

For the ganache

Heavy cream	Generous 2 cups	18 ounces	500 grams
Bittersweet chocolate, finely chopped		21 ounces	600 grams
Grand Marnier or Stoli Razberi vodka (optional)	Generous ¼ cup	2 ounces	60 grams

To enrobe the truffles

Bittersweet chocolate, tempered (page 8)	18 ounces	500 grams
White chocolate, tempered (page 8)	18 ounces	500 grams

To garnish the truffles

Dutch-processed unsweetened cocoa powder, sifted	2 cups	8 ounces	230 grams
Shredded sweetened coconut, toasted (page 245)	2½ cups	9 ounces	250 grams
Toasted nuts (page 127), finely chopped	About 2 cups	8 ounces	230 grams

Heat the heavy cream in a 2-quart heavy-bottomed saucepan until bubbles begin to form around the edge of the pan. Make sure that you have chopped the chocolate as finely as possible to allow it to melt quickly and easily. Place the chopped chocolate in a medium-size mixing bowl. Make a ganache by pouring about half of the hot cream over the chocolate and letting it sit for 30 seconds to melt the chocolate. Then slowly whisk until smooth

and homogenous. Do not add all of the hot cream to the cold chocolate at once; the shock of the temperature extremes would cause the fat in the chocolate to separate. As the chocolate melts, you will see some elasticity if there is no fat separation. This means the chocolate still has an emulsion; the fat molecules are still holding together. If the ganache separates, it loses its elasticity, collapses, and becomes very liquid. I use a hand-held immersion blender to ensure a smooth ganache and to keep the emulsion of the chocolate. Add the remaining cream gradually and mix until all of the hot cream is incorporated and the ganache is smooth and homogenous.

If the ganache separates, it is very easy to fix. Simply add a small amount of cold cream and whisk well. This will bring the ganache back together. The ganache should be thick, shiny, and smooth. Add the desired flavoring and mix until fully incorporated. Pour the ganache onto a plastic wrap–covered baking sheet and spread evenly with a rubber spatula. Cover the ganache with plastic wrap and allow it to cool for at least 4 hours at room temperature. I usually make the ganache at the end of the day and let it cool overnight. As it cools, it will thicken and set. *continued*

When the ganache has cooled to the consistency of toothpaste, scrape it into a pastry bag fitted with a ½-inch plain tip. Do not stir the ganache when you do this. Incorporating air by stirring will cause the ganache to harden. Pipe 1-inch-diameter mounds spaced 1 inch apart on a parchment paper–covered baking sheet. To pipe the mounds, hold the pastry bag at a slight angle and allow the tip to touch the parchment as you begin to pipe. Once you have formed the mound, stop squeezing and lift the tip straight up, leaving a small tail on the top of each mound. You can also use a spoon and drop small mounds of ganache onto the baking sheet. Let the truffles harden at room temperature for a couple of hours (or in the refrigerator for 15 minutes), until they are hard enough to roll with your hands.

When I roll the truffles, I usually wear surgical gloves. The gloves are not mandatory, but if you do not use them, be sure your hands are very clean. To roll the mound into a ball, place a truffle between both palms, squeeze slightly, and roll between your hands. The truffles will look nicer if they are as round as possible. When all the truffles are rolled into balls, they are ready to be coated. If they have become too soft, place them in the refrigerator for 1 to 2 hours until they are firm enough to dip.

You can use either a dipping fork or your hands to dip the truffles in chocolate. To use the fork, drop the truffle into the bowl of tempered chocolate and then retrieve it with the dipping fork. Hold the fork over the bowl for several seconds to allow the excess chocolate to drip back into the bowl. Gently scrape the bottom of the fork against the side of the bowl to remove any excess chocolate and roll the dipped truffle in the desired garnish. Place on a parchment paper–covered baking sheet. If you use your hands, dab some chocolate in the palm of one hand. Roll the truffle in that palm to completely coat it with chocolate. Place the enrobed truffle on the baking sheet. Repeat for the remaining truffles. This method is very quick, but it can also be extremely messy.

When all of the truffles have been coated once, repeat the enrobing procedure. This is necessary only when you enrobe the truffles by hand rather than with a fork. The truffles are usually more evenly coated when dipped with a fork. As soon as each truffle gets a second coating, immediately roll it in the desired garnish. You need to do this before the chocolate sets or the topping will not adhere. At this stage it is good to have a friend help because it is hard to dip and roll at the same time. Place the truffles on a clean parchment paper–covered baking sheet and allow them to set, about 5 minutes.

The truffles will keep for up to 2 weeks at room temperature when stored in an airtight container.

If you decide to roll the truffles by hand, it is important to make sure your hands are cold. A good trick is to dip your hands in ice water for a few seconds and then dry them. Do this immediately before rolling the truffles. If your hands are too warm and the truffles begin to melt while you are rolling them, redip your hands in the ice water, dry them, and proceed.

To toast coconut: Preheat the oven to 400°F (204°C). Spread the coconut on a baking sheet and place in the oven for about 3 minutes. Remove from the oven and stir to keep the sugar in the coconut from burning. Return to the oven and toast until golden brown, about 3 more minutes. Remove the baking sheet from the oven and cool on a wire rack.

Chocolate Ladyfingers

Yield: About 50 ladyfingers

Every time I make ladyfingers, I think about the time I made them for the graduation from my apprenticeship. The traditional recipe for ladyfingers is very difficult to make. It involves complicated steps and the end result is not always a stable mixture. Sometimes the ladyfingers collapse. It was very stressful. I have revised the original recipe to incorporate new techniques and to make it easier. I use more egg yolks than egg whites, which increases the fat but makes the ladyfingers softer. Cake flour has less protein, which keeps the ladyfingers from being tough.

If you do not own a pastry bag, use a large resealable plastic bag. Fill the bag and seal it. Cut off one of the bottom corners and you are ready to pipe from your homemade bag.

Cake flour	¾ cup + 2 tablespoons	4 ounces	120 grams
Dutch-processed unsweetened cocoa powder	¼ cup	1.2 ounces	30 grams
6 large egg whites			
Granulated sugar	¾ cup	5.5 ounces	150 grams
8 large egg yolks, slightly beaten			
Powdered sugar	¼ cup	1.2 ounces	30 grams

Preheat the oven to 400°F (204°C).

Sift the flour and cocoa powder together in a small mixing bowl and set aside.

Place the egg whites in a large mixing bowl and whip with an electric mixer set on medium speed until foamy. Make a French meringue by adding the granulated sugar 1 tablespoon at a time. When you whip egg whites, add the sugar slowly to allow the whites to gain some volume. When you have volume, add the rest of the granulated sugar. Increase the mixer speed to medium-high and whip to stiff but not dry peaks, about 5 minutes. When the whites are slightly stiff, reduce the mixer speed to low to allow even more air to be incorporated without overwhipping the egg whites. Let the egg whites continue to whip for about another 2 minutes. Stop whipping them if they begin to look dry or separated.

Very gently fold the egg yolks into the whipped egg whites with a rubber spatula until they are partially incorporated. Carefully fold the sifted mixture into the egg mixture. It is important to fold as gently as possible to avoid deflating the batter. Remember to fold all the way to the bottom of the bowl to fully incorporate both mixtures.

Place the batter in a pastry bag fitted with a ¾-inch plain tip. Pipe evenly shaped ladyfingers about ¾ inch wide on a parchment paper–covered baking sheet. Space them about ½ inch apart to allow them room to spread as they bake. To pipe the ladyfingers, hold the pastry bag at a slight angle and allow the tip to touch the parchment paper as you start to pipe. Squeeze gently, applying even pressure as you pipe the desired length. Then stop squeezing and lift the tip straight up, leaving a small tail on the end of each ladyfinger. Remember to dust the tops of the ladyfingers with powdered sugar to give them a nice crust.

Bake the ladyfingers until lightly and evenly browned, about 5 minutes. (The browning may be difficult to discern with the chocolate ladyfingers.) Remove from the oven and immediately remove them to a wire rack to prevent the heat of the pan from continuing to bake the ladyfingers. Set aside until ready to use. When cooled, the ladyfingers can be stored in an airtight container at room temperature for up to 2 days or in the freezer, well wrapped in plastic wrap, for up to 2 weeks.

Classic Tuiles

Yield: About 3 dozen

This is an easy treat to make to decorate any dessert. Pastry chefs make tuiles to accompany ice cream or as petits fours.

Granulated sugar	Scant I cup	7 ounces	200 grams
2 large egg whites			
I large egg			
Grated zest of ½ orange			
Cake flour	Generous ⅓ cup	2 ounces	60 grams
Granulated blanched almonds	2 cups	7 ounces	200 grams
Whole milk	Scant ½ cup	3.5 ounces	100 grams

Place the sugar, egg whites, and whole egg in a medium-size mixing bowl. Use an electric mixer set on medium speed or a hand whisk to mix until combined. Add the orange zest and flour and combine with the mixer still set on medium speed. Use a rubber spatula to fold in the almonds until fully incorporated. Fold gently so you do not break the almonds. Place the tuile batter in the refrigerator for 1 hour to allow the gluten (page 10) to relax. (At this stage the tuile batter can be stored in the refrigerator, in an airtight container, for up to 1 week.) Allowing the tuile batter to rest in the refrigerator overnight will give the orange and nut flavors time to develop, enhancing the flavor of the tuiles.

Preheat the oven to 375°F (190°C). Place a silicon mat (page 6) on a baking sheet. (If you do not have a silicon mat, you can use a nonstick baking sheet.) Use a small offset spatula or the back of a fork to spread the batter into 2-inch circles about ⅛ inch thick onto the mat or baking sheet. Dip your fingers in the milk and pat the tops of the tuiles. This will make them shinier and crunchier. Place the tuiles in the oven and bake until browned around the edges, about 10 minutes.

Remove the tuiles from the oven and let cool for about 30 seconds. Use an offset spatula to peel them off the silicon mat or baking sheet and lay them upright over a rolling pin or wine bottle. If you have a tuile pan, place them almond side down. Work quickly while the tuiles are still very warm and flexible. If they cool too much before you remove them

from the mat or sheet, return the cooled tuiles to the oven and let them warm until once again flexible, about 1 minute.

Allow the tuiles to cool completely and remove from the rolling pin, wine bottle, or tuile pan. The baked tuiles can be stored at room temperature in an airtight container for up to 5 days.

Variation: Use 1¾ cups (5.5 ounces; 150 grams) sliced almonds instead of ground almonds.

Chocolate Tuiles

Yield: About 6 dozen

The word *tuiles* in French refers to roof tiles. These cookies are curved to resemble the shape of the clay roofing materials found on almost every house.

Powdered sugar	3¾ cups	14 ounces	400 grams
Dutch-processed unsweetened cocoa powder	½ cup	2 ounces	60 grams
Water	½ cup	4 ounces	120 grams
Unsalted butter, melted	¾ cup	5.6 ounces	160 grams
Cake flour	Generous ¾ cup	4 ounces	120 grams
Blanched hazelnuts or any type of nuts, ground	¾ cup	3.5 ounces	100 grams

Preheat the oven to 400°F (204°C).

Place the sugar, cocoa powder, and water in a medium-size mixing bowl. Use a hand whisk to mix the ingredients until combined. Add the melted butter and mix until combined. Use a rubber spatula to fold in the flour just until incorporated. Do not overmix the batter, or it will become too elastic and the tuiles will shrink when baked. Break down any lumps with the spatula and mix them in gently. (At this stage, the batter can be stored in the refrigerator, in an airtight container, for up to 1 week. The batter will be easier to spread if you allow it to return to room temperature.) *continued*

Place a silicon mat (page 6) on a baking sheet. (If you do not have a silicon mat, you can use a nonstick baking sheet.) Use a small offset spatula to spread the batter into 2-inch circles about ⅛ inch thick onto the mat or baking sheet. Sprinkle the center of each circle with ground hazelnuts. Place in the oven and bake about 10 minutes.

Remove the tuiles from the oven and let cool for about 30 seconds. Use an offset spatula to peel them off the silicon mat or baking sheet and place them, hazelnut side up, over a rolling pin or bottle of wine. If you have a tuile pan, place them hazelnut side down. Work quickly while the tuiles are still very warm and flexible. If they cool too much before you remove them from the mat, return the cooled tuiles to the oven and let them warm until once again flexible, about 1 minute.

Allow the tuiles to cool completely and remove from the rolling pin, wine bottle, or tuile pan. The baked tuiles can be stored at room temperature, in an airtight container, for up to 5 days.

Bow Ties

Yield: About 30 Bow Ties

This recipe is called *Bugnes de Lyon* in France. Although the name implies this recipe is from Lyon, it is made all over France, especially in Provence. When I met Mrs. Santini from Pescatore Ristoranti in Tuscany, Italy, she showed me her recipe and technique for making this. I adopted her technique and married it with my recipe.

Sometimes my mom makes these when I am home in the summer. They are a favorite with the whole family, and I am especially happy to have someone else do the cooking!

Bread flour	**2 cups**	**9 ounces**	**250 grams**
Granulated sugar	**1½ tablespoons**	**1 ounce**	**25 grams**
Pinch of salt			
Grated zest of ½ lemon			
1 large egg			
Unsalted butter, melted and warm	**Scant 3 tablespoons**	**1.6 ounces**	**40 grams**
Extra virgin olive oil	**Generous 1 tablespoon**	**0.75 ounce**	**20 grams**
Dark rum	**2 tablespoons**	**1 ounce**	**25 grams**

Grand Marnier	3 tablespoons	1.6 ounces	40 grams
Unsalted butter, softened, as needed			
Vegetable or canola oil for deep-frying			

For dusting the bow ties

| Granulated sugar | Scant ½ cup | 3.5 ounces | 100 grams |
| Powdered sugar | Scant 1 cup | 3.5 ounces | 100 grams |

Place the flour, granulated sugar, salt, lemon zest, egg, melted butter, olive oil, rum, and Grand Marnier in a large mixing bowl. Use an electric mixer set on medium speed to beat the mixture until it forms a dough. When the dough holds together and no longer sticks to the side of the bowl, it is ready. Do not overmix, or the gluten will overdevelop (page 10), which will make the dough tough and elastic.

Turn the dough onto a lightly floured work surface and knead gently until smooth. Use a rolling pin to roll the dough into a 6 × 15-inch strip. Place the strip on a lightly floured parchment paper–covered baking sheet. The dough strip will be longer than the baking sheet, so fold the overlapping edges back onto the dough. Let the dough rest in the refrigerator for at least 1 hour. This will give the gluten a chance to relax. During this time, the fat in the dough will cool and the flavor of the dough will develop.

Remove the dough from the refrigerator and place on a lightly floured work surface. Place the dough horizontally in front of you so it will be easier to fold. Use a pastry brush to brush a light layer of softened butter from left to right over the left two thirds of the dough. Do not use too much butter, or it will ooze out when the dough is rolled and folded. Fold the dough in thirds by first folding the unbuttered end over the middle and then folding the buttered third over it. Make sure the seam of the dough is on your right.

When the butter has been added, the rolling technique becomes very important. The dough should be rolled in the opposite direction of the way the butter is spread. This helps to develop the layers of the dough. Keep the seam of the dough on your right and use the rolling pin to roll the dough from top to bottom. Roll it into a 6 × 15-inch rectangle. Rotate the dough so it is horizontally in front of you. Repeat, spreading two thirds of it with softened butter and folding it. Place the dough on a parchment paper–covered baking sheet and let rest in the refrigerator for 1 hour. Use two fingers to indent the dough with two marks. This will remind you that you have given the dough two folds.

Remove the dough from the refrigerator and repeat the rolling, buttering, and folding process two more times. Remember to roll the dough in the opposite direction of the butter each time. After the fourth and final fold, let the dough rest in the refrigerator for at least 1 hour to allow the gluten in it to relax.

Use an electric deep fryer or a 4-quart heavy-bottomed saucepan over medium-high heat to heat the oil to 330°F (165°C). If using a saucepan, check the temperature with a candy thermometer. It is important to maintain the temperature, so you may need to adjust the heat or remove the pan from the burner to keep it where you want it. If the oil is too hot, the bow ties will burn before they are evenly fried. If the oil is too cool, the bow ties will absorb too much oil before they finish frying.

Remove the ready dough from the refrigerator and place on a lightly floured work surface. Use a rolling pin to roll the dough into a very thin, about 1/16-inch-thick, rectangle. Rotate the dough (if necessary) so it is horizontally in front of you. Use a sharp paring knife to cut the dough in half from left to right. Next, cut the dough from top to bottom every 2 inches, creating small rectangles. Cut a small slit about 1 inch long in the center of each of the rectangles. Pick up the rectangles one at a time and pull the bottom (short end) of each rectangle up and through the slit, pulling it down in the back.

Carefully place about a half-dozen bow ties in the hot oil and fry until golden brown, 3 to 5 minutes. Turn them to evenly fry each side. As they cook, they will increase in size. Remove the bow ties from the hot oil with a large slotted spoon and set on paper towels or a clean dish towel to drain. Continue to cook more bow ties until you have used all of the dough.

While the bow ties are still warm, roll them in a bowl filled with the granulated sugar until evenly coated. Then dust them with the powdered sugar just before serving. They are best eaten on the same day they are made, but they will keep at room temperature in an airtight container for up to 2 days. Place them on top of paper towels to catch any excess oil.

> I like to use my electric pasta machine to roll out the dough because it rolls it evenly without overworking the dough.

Cut a small slit, about 1 inch long, in the center of each of the rectangles.

Pull the bottom (short end) of each rectangle up through the slit, pulling it down in the back.

Cloud Puffs

Yield: About 13 dozen

One summer I went to visit my best friend, Christian Cottard. He is a pastry chef and has the loveliest pastry shop in Antibes. Most of the time I go to the shop and stay with him until we go out for lunch. One particular day, he made our meal and served these Cloud Puffs with coffee. I was eating them like popcorn. This is an old French recipe using cream puff batter.

Vegetable or canola oil for deep-frying

For the pâte à choux

Water	**Generous ½ cup**	**4.5 ounces**	**125 grams**
Pinch of salt			
Pinch of granulated sugar			
Grated zest of ½ orange			
Grated zest of ½ lemon			
Unsalted butter, cubed	**3.5 tablespoons**	**1.8 ounces**	**50 grams**
Bread flour	**½ cup**	**2.6 ounces**	**75 grams**
2 to 3 large eggs			

For dusting the cloud puffs

Granulated sugar	**1 cup**	**7.7 ounces**	**220 grams**
Powdered sugar	**Generous 1 cup**	**4.7 ounces**	**130 grams**

Use an electric deep fryer or a 4-quart heavy-bottomed saucepan placed over medium-high heat to heat the oil to 330°F (165°C). If using a saucepan, check the temperature with a candy thermometer. It is important to maintain the temperature, so you may need to adjust the heat or remove the pan from the burner to keep it where you want it. If the oil is too hot, the puffs will burn before they are evenly fried. If the oil is too cool, the puffs will absorb too much oil before they finish frying.

Prepare the pâte à choux: Place the water, salt, granulated sugar, zests, and butter in a 4-quart heavy-bottomed saucepan, set it over medium-high heat, and bring to a boil. The paste is easier to mix in a large pan. The butter should be completely melted by the time

the mixture boils. Remove the saucepan from the heat. Add the bread flour all at once and incorporate it thoroughly with a wooden spoon.

Return the saucepan to the stove and cook over medium heat for about 3 minutes to dry out the paste. As it cooks, push the paste from side to side with the wooden spoon. Turn it onto itself to allow every side to touch the bottom of the saucepan, which helps it dry. Keep the paste moving, or it will burn. You will know the paste is dry when it begins to leave a thin film on the bottom of the saucepan.

Remove the saucepan from the heat and transfer the paste to a large mixing bowl. Mix with an electric mixer set on low speed or by hand for about 2 minutes to release some of the steam. This will prevent the eggs from cooking and scrambling when mixed together with the paste. Continue to mix and slowly add the eggs one at a time, incorporating well after each addition. (Adding the eggs in this manner ensures they will be evenly distributed throughout the batter.) After each egg is added, the paste will become loose and look separated. Don't worry. Once each egg is well incorporated, the paste will become smooth and homogenous again. The number of eggs used will vary depending on the size of the eggs and how well the *pâte à choux* is dried. The drier it is, the more eggs you will need. After you have added 2 eggs, check the consistency by scooping a large amount of the paste onto a wooden spoon. Hold the spoon horizontally about one foot above the bowl and watch as the batter falls from the spoon back into the bowl. If it is pale yellow, smooth, moist, slightly elastic, sticky, and takes 5 to 7 seconds to fall into the bowl, it is ready. If it appears rough, dry, and falls into the bowl in one big ball, it needs more eggs. Add another egg and check the consistency again after it is well incorporated. If the *pâte à choux* is too dry, it will not pipe well. If it is too wet, it will be loose, runny, and won't hold its shape.

Hold the pastry bag over the oil and pipe about ½-inch dollops of batter out of the tip onto the chopstick. Use the chopstick to cut the batter from the tip so the batter drops into the hot oil.

Prepare the cloud puffs: Place the *pâte à choux* batter into a pastry bag fitted with a ½-inch opening, no pastry tip. Dip a wooden skewer or chopstick into the hot oil. This will keep the dough from sticking to it. Hold the skewer or chopstick horizontally over the hot oil. Hold the pastry bag over the oil and pipe about ½-inch dollops of batter (about the size of a dime) out of the tip. Use the skewer or chopstick to cut the batter from the tip so the batter drops into the hot oil. Be careful not to splatter the hot oil onto your arms or face. You can also do this with a spoon if you do not have a pastry bag. Simply drop small scoops of the batter into the hot oil. Repeat until the saucepan is full of frying dough without crowding them. Fry the puffs until they are golden brown, 3 to 5 minutes. Turn them over to evenly fry each side. They will increase in size as they cook. Use a large slotted spoon to remove the puffs from the hot oil and set them on a paper towel or a clean towel to drain.

While the puffs are still warm, roll them in a bowl filled with the granulated sugar until evenly coated. Then dust them with the powdered sugar just before serving. They are best served immediately, since they tend to get soggy after a few hours.

If your oil is too hot, add a small amount of cold oil to lower the temperature.

Caramel-Dipped Fruit

Yield: 1 pound dipped fruit

This is a very easy treat to make. You can use any kind of fruit. I like to make my fruit skewers with fruit combinations that are colorful and tasty. Be creative!

If you use refrigerated fruit, allow it to come to room temperature a few hours before dipping it in the hot caramel. If you use cold fruit, condensation will form, creating moisture that will cause the sugar to melt. It is best to make these within three hours of the time you plan to serve them. Since fruit is mostly water, its moisture will cause the sugar to melt, which makes the treats sticky and gooey. When working with caramel, be sure to have a bowl of cold water on hand. If you get hot sugar on your fingers, immediately dip them in cold water to remove it and avoid a burn.

Water	Scant ½ cup	3.5 ounces	100 grams
Granulated sugar	Generous 2¼ cups	18 ounces	500 grams
Light corn syrup	Scant ⅔ cup	7 ounces	200 grams
Fresh fruit		16 ounces	454 grams

Place the water, sugar, and corn syrup in a 2-quart heavy-bottomed saucepan over medium-high heat. The corn syrup will make the cooked sugar harder and crunchier; it will also help prevent the cooked sugar from melting as quickly when it reacts to the humidity in the air. Insert a candy thermometer and cook the sugar mixture to 311°F

(155°C), what is know as the hard crack stage (page 14). Stir the sugar slowly as it cooks to ensure that it cooks evenly. If you do not stir it, the mixture will develop hot spots and the sugar will cook faster in those spots. Use a pastry brush to keep the inside of the saucepan clean as the sugar cooks, or the sugar may recrystallize. To do this, dip a clean brush in cold water and brush the inside of the pan clean.

Remove the cooked sugar from the heat and pour it into a medium-size heatproof glass bowl. The glass bowl will hold the temperature and stop the cooking process. It will also allow you to reheat the sugar in the microwave if necessary. If you leave the sugar in the saucepan, the sugar will continue to cook and turn dark brown. Occasionally stir the hot sugar to keep it from darkening due to the residual heat. Stirring also helps to keep its temperature even. I put a towel under the bowl to keep it from tipping and to protect my hands from the heat of the glass.

Peel, core or pit, and halve the fruit as necessary. Use a sharp knife to slice the fruit into small pieces. (This is not necessary for berries or grapes.) Arrange the fruit on toothpicks or small skewers in any combination you like. Leave enough room at one end of the tooth-pick or skewer so you will be able to hold it as you dip it in the hot sugar. Dip each tooth-pick in the hot sugar, coating the fruits completely. Wipe the toothpick against the rim of the bowl to remove any excess sugar and place on a sheet of parchment paper. Repeat until all of the fruit has been dipped. The fruit skewers should release easily from the parch-ment paper as soon as they cool. You can arrange them on a plate or use your imagina-tion to make a fruit skewer centerpiece.

To cool a hot thermometer, stand it upright in a tall container. Do not put in cold water, or it will break. Keeping it upright ensures the mercury will not separate as it cools. I usually buy the thermome-ters that come in a metal casing or cage. Always hang your ther-mometer when it is time to store it.

Home for the Holidays

Holidays are the special occasions we celebrate. They represent a time to look forward and a time to look back. We all remember our cherished traditions, the people with whom we share them, and, if you are like me, the things we ate.

The recipes that stand for Mother's Day in this chapter are more a celebration of all the great stuff my mom makes than they are a symbol for the holiday. Our memories of our moms are certainly as varied as the designs of a kaleidoscope. My mom's Ratatouille Turnovers are just one of the reasons I can't wait to go home.

I am grateful to have the opportunity to celebrate the Independence Day of two countries. In France, it is called Bastille Day and, in America, it is the Fourth of July. Both holidays include fireworks, so I created the Firecracker to honor both occasions.

Christmas is the holiday for children of all ages. Kris says I have a side of me that is perpetually eight years old. The Christmas desserts in this chapter include the traditional representation of the Yule log and the Christmas tree. The Reindeer and Sleigh is for the child in all of us.

All the recipes in this chapter are fun to make with family and friends. Spend time together and start your own traditions.

Mother's Day

Savory Snacks

Yield: 18 ratatouille turnovers or 20 cheese twists, 30 almond twists, 20 anchovy puffs, 20 olive puffs, and 24 mini ham croissants

My mom makes the best ratatouille and that is a fact. Sometimes she makes a dough and fills it with her ratatouille. Then she fries it on the stovetop in sunflower oil. The result is heavenly. Now her arthritis keeps her from making these treats as often as we would like, and my diet encouraged us to bake them.

People are always surprised when I make "regular" food, but in France pastry chefs make the dough that the cooks use for savory items like quiche or cheese twists. When I invited my mom on my television show for our Mother's Day special, even she asked me where I learned to make the dough for her ratatouille pockets.

If you buy the puff pastry instead of making it, you can put together hors d'oeuvres for a party in no time. In this recipe, you will learn how to make Mom's Ratatouille Turnovers, Cheese Twists, Almond Twists, Anchovy Puffs, Olive Puffs, and Mini Ham Croissants.

Classic Puff Pastry (page 33)

For Mom's ratatouille

Extra virgin olive oil	2 tablespoons	1.2 ounces	30 grams
1 large onion, peeled and chopped			
1 red bell pepper, seeded and chopped			

White part of 2 large leeks, washed and chopped

4 ripe beefsteak tomatoes, peeled, seeded, and chopped

Pinch of salt

Pinch of freshly ground black pepper

Pinch of dried herbes de Provence

For the egg wash

2 large egg yolks

1 large egg

Whole milk	¼ cup	1.8 ounces	50 grams

For the cheese twists

Freshly grated Parmesan cheese	⅓ cup	1.6 ounces	40 grams
Freshly ground black pepper	1 tablespoon	0.18 ounce	6 grams

For the almond twists

Ground blanched almonds	½ cup	2.3 ounces	65 grams

Pinch of salt

Pinch of freshly ground black pepper

For the puffs

10 4-inch anchovy fillets, drained

20 pitted olives

For the mini ham croissants

Ham, diced	½ cup	5.5 ounces	150 grams

Prepare the puff pastry: Make the dough as directed in the recipe and let rest in the refrigerator until ready to use.

Prepare the ratatouille: Heat the oil in a nonreactive 2-quart heavy-bottomed saucepan over medium heat. Add the onion and cook, stirring occasionally, until it softens slightly and begins to take on color. Add the pepper and cook, stirring, until it begins to soften. Add the leeks and cook, stirring, until slightly softened and colored. Add the tomatoes and let the mixture cook until the tomatoes release their juice. Lower the temperature and

Cheese Twists, Almond Twists,
Anchovy Puffs, and Olive Puffs

cook until soft and most of the liquid is gone, stirring, about 1 hour. Season to taste with the salt, pepper, and herbs. Stir the ratatouille often as it cooks to make sure the vegetables do not stick to the bottom and burn. When all of the vegetables are well cooked, pour the mixture into a bowl and let cool. Store in the refrigerator covered tightly with plastic wrap until ready to use.

Prepare the egg wash: Combine the yolks, whole egg, and milk in a small mixing bowl and whip with a hand whisk until well combined.

For the twists, puffs, and croissants: Preheat the oven to 400°F (204°C). Remove the puff pastry from the refrigerator and cut into thirds. Set one third aside and return the rest to the refrigerator.

Prepare the cheese twists: Place the piece of puff pastry on a lightly floured work surface and pat it into a rectangle. Use a rolling pin to roll the puff pastry into a 12 × 20-inch rectangle about ⅛ inch thick. Roll the dough thinly because it will rise in the oven. Flour the dough and table as needed to keep the dough from sticking to the table or the rolling pin. Place the dough on your work surface with a long side facing you. Use a pastry brush to coat the surface of the rectangle with some egg wash. Liberally sprinkle the Parmesan cheese over the rectangle, followed by the pepper. Use a sharp paring knife to cut the rectangle into twenty 1-inch-wide strips from top to bottom. Flip each strip so that the cheese is on the bottom. Twist each strip by rolling each end in opposite directions. Always remember to twist so that the topping faces out—that way you can see how they are flavored. Place the strips on a parchment paper–covered baking sheet and bake until well risen and golden brown, about 20 minutes. Cool completely on a wire rack before serving.

Prepare the almond twists: Remove another third of the dough from the refrigerator and cut it in half. Set one half

Liberally sprinkle the Parmesan cheese over the rectangle.

Use a sharp knife to cut the rectangle into strips from top to bottom.

Twist each strip by rolling the ends in opposite directions.

Cheese twist ready to be baked.

aside. Place the first half on the lightly floured work surface and pat into a rectangle. Use a rolling pin to roll the puff pastry into a 10 × 12-inch rectangle. Repeat the same process used to make cheese twists, using the ground almonds instead of the cheese. Cut the rectangle into ten 1-inch-wide strips. Next, cut each of these strips into three 4-inch-long pieces. Follow the same procedure for twisting, baking, and cooling.

Prepare the anchovy puffs: Pat the second half into a rectangle on the lightly floured work surface. Roll the dough into a 10 × 12-inch rectangle with a long side facing you and cut it in half from top to bottom. Use a pastry brush to coat one piece of the dough with egg wash. Lay the anchovy fillets spaced about 1 inch apart from top to bottom on the egg-washed dough. Place the other rolled-out dough half on top of the anchovies and mark each anchovy by pressing the dough on either side of each fillet. Use a sharp paring knife to cut between the puff pastry–covered fillets. Next, cut the filled strips in half from top to bottom to make small anchovy packets. Place on a parchment paper–covered baking sheet and brush with more egg wash. Bake until well risen and golden brown, about 20 minutes. Cool completely on a wire rack before serving.

Prepare the olive puffs: Remove the remaining third of dough from the refrigerator and cut in half. Set one half aside and set the other on the lightly floured work surface. Roll the dough into a 10 × 12-inch rectangle and repeat the procedure of making anchovy strips using olives instead. There is no need to cut these in half. Just cut between the olives to make small packages. Baking and cooling are the same.

Prepare the mini ham croissants: Roll the remaining piece of dough into a 10 × 12-inch rectangle on a lightly floured work surface. Place the rectangle with the short side in front of you and cut it into four 3-inch-wide strips from left to right. Next cut each strip into 6 triangles. Arrange the triangles on the work surface with the tips facing you. Gently pull each tip toward you; this light stretch adds layers to the finished croissant without adding density. Place a small amount of diced ham on the wide side of each triangle, about ½ inch from the edge. Use the tips of your fingers to roll the triangle from the base to the tip. Place the croissants, seam side down, on a parchment paper–covered baking sheet and brush the tops with egg wash. Bake until well risen and golden brown, about 20 minutes. Cool on a wire rack before serving.

Prepare the ratatouille turnovers: Remove the puff pastry from the refrigerator and cut it into thirds. Set one third aside and return the rest to the refrigerator. Place the dough on the lightly floured work surface. Use a rolling pin to roll the dough into a 12×20-inch rectangle. Use a 4½-inch fluted cutter to cut 6 circles from the dough. Make the cuts close together so you can get as many as possible from the rectangle. Discard the scraps. Dust each circle with flour and use the rolling pin to roll each into an 8-inch-long oval. Use a pastry brush to apply egg wash to half of each oval. Place a large tablespoon of ratatouille in the center of the egg-washed half. Fold the other half over the ratatouille center and seal the edges closed by pressing down firmly with your fingers. Place on a parchment paper–covered baking sheet. Repeat with the remaining two thirds of dough. Brush the tops with egg wash. Bake until well risen and golden brown, about 25 minutes. Cool on a wire rack before serving.

All of these puff pastry items are best eaten the day they are made.

Sweet Snacks

Yield: 24 raspberry or peach squares or 18 apple turnovers

The sweets in this recipe are completely different from regular tarts. Puff pastry dough is rich in butter and very light and flaky; by weight, it is a lot lighter than the dough used in other tarts. It doesn't contain any sugar, so you can use it to make savory or sweet things. The sweet taste in these goodies comes from the filling.

Classic Puff Pastry (page 33)

½ recipe Pastry Cream flavored with Grand Marnier (page 20)

For the egg wash

2 large egg yolks			
1 large egg			
Whole milk	¼ cup	1.8 ounces	50 grams

For the raspberry and peach squares

Fresh raspberries	About 5 cups	24.5 ounces	700 grams
2 recipes Apricot Glaze (page 27)			
24 canned peeled peach halves, drained, or fresh			

For the apple turnovers

Chunky applesauce	Scant 1¼ cups	13 ounces	365 grams
4 Granny Smith apples			
2 recipes Apricot Glaze (page 27)			

Prepare the puff pastry: Make the dough as directed in the recipe and let rest in the refrigerator until ready to use.

Prepare the pastry cream: Make, cool, and flavor the pastry cream as directed in the recipe. Store in the refrigerator until ready to use.

Prepare the egg wash: Combine the egg yolks, whole egg, and milk in a small mixing bowl and whip with a hand whisk until well combined.

Prepare the squares: Preheat the oven to 400°F (204°C). When the puff pastry is ready to roll, cut it into three equal pieces. Place one piece on a lightly floured work surface and

Peach Squares and Raspberry Squares

return the other two pieces to the refrigerator. Use a rolling pin to roll the puff pastry into a 12 × 24-inch rectangle. Place the rectangle on the work surface with a long side facing you. Cut the rectangle in half from left to right and in four from top to bottom, leaving you with eight 6-inch squares. Use a sharp paring knife to cut 90-degree angles into two opposite corners of each square. Begin each cut about ½ inch from the edge of the square. The leg of each angle should stop about ¼ inch from the leg of the opposing angle. Use a pastry brush to brush egg wash in the center of each square. Grasp one of the cut corners and lift it over the center of the square. Allow the cut corner to rest

Use a sharp knife to cut 90-degree angles into two opposite corners of each square.

Grasp one of the cut corners and lift it over the center of the square.

Allow the cut corner to rest just inside the opposite cut corner.

Repeat the fold with the other cut corner.

just inside the opposite cut corner. Repeat the fold with the other cut corner.

Place the squares on a parchment paper–covered baking sheet. Repeat the procedure with the remaining dough.

For the raspberry squares: Brush the tops with egg wash. Bake until well risen and evenly golden brown, about 15 minutes. Cool on a wire rack. Use a small offset spatula to spread a ¼-inch-thick layer of the pastry cream in the center of each square. Top with the raspberries. Use a pastry brush to coat the raspberry squares with apricot glaze.

For the peach squares: Before baking the squares, spread a ¼-inch-thick layer of the pastry cream in the center of each square. Use a sharp paring knife to slice each peach half into thick slices. Place one sliced peach half on top of the pastry cream. Place in the oven and bake until well risen and evenly golden brown, about 25 minutes. Cool on a wire rack. Use a pastry brush to coat the peach squares with apricot glaze.

Prepare the apple turnovers: Remove the puff pastry from the refrigerator and divide into three equal pieces. Place one piece on the lightly floured work surface and return the others to the refrigerator. Use a rolling pin to roll the dough into a 12 × 20-inch rectangle. Use a 4½-inch fluted cutter to cut 6 circles from the dough. Cut the circles as close together as possible to avoid waste. Discard the scraps. Dust each circle with flour and use the rolling pin to roll each into an 8-inch-long oval. Use a pastry brush to coat half of the oval with egg wash. Place about a tablespoon of apple-sauce in the center of the egg-washed half. Peel, halve, core, and slice the apples into 1-inch-long pieces. Divide the pieces among the ovals. Fold the other half over the filling and press the edges together to seal. Place the turnovers on a parchment paper–covered baking sheet. Repeat the entire procedure with the remaining two thirds of dough. Use a pastry brush to coat the turnovers with egg wash. Place in the oven and bake until well risen and evenly golden brown,

Apple Turnovers and Mom's Ratatouille Turnovers (page 262)

about 25 minutes. Cool on a wire rack. Use a pastry brush to glaze the tops with the apricot glaze.

All of the puff pastry items should be eaten the day they are made.

Raspberry Tart

Yield: One tart; 8 servings

One of the exercises during my pastry graduation was to make something from start to finish in front of the judges. The names of various desserts were written on small pieces of paper and placed in a basket. When it was my turn to choose, this is the dessert I was required to make. In French, it is called *Bande Jalousie*. I had seen it in several pastry shops, but I had never made it before that day.

For the filling

Linda's Red Raspberry Jam (page 26) or store-bought	⅔ cup	7 ounces	200 grams

For the tart shell

¼ recipe Classic Puff Pastry (page 33)

For the egg wash

2 large egg yolks

1 large egg

Whole milk	¼ cup	1.8 ounces	50 grams

To finish the tart

Apricot Glaze (page 27)

Use a sharp knife to cut 1-inch-long slits from the center to the folded edge of the dough, but do not cut through the seam.

Prepare the jam: Make the jam as directed in the recipe. You can set aside the amount needed for this recipe and let cool. Can the rest.

Prepare the puff pastry: Make the dough as directed in the recipe and let rest in the refrigerator until ready to use. Preheat the oven to 375°F (190°C). When the dough is ready to roll, place on a lightly floured work surface and use a rolling pin to roll it into a 12 × 14-inch rectangle. Place the rectangle on the work surface with a long side facing you. Use a sharp paring knife to cut it in half from left to right. Place one piece on a parchment paper–covered baking sheet.

Prepare the egg wash: Combine the egg yolks, whole egg, and milk in a small mixing bowl and whip with a hand whisk until well combined. Use a pastry brush to brush a 1-inch border of egg wash along each long side of the rectangle on the baking sheet. This will be the bottom of the tart.

Assemble the tart: Use an offset spatula to spread the jam down the center of the tart shell. To make the lattice top, place the second rectangle of dough with a long side facing you on a lightly floured work surface and lightly flour the top. Gently fold the rectangle in half from the bottom to the top but do not crease it. Use a sharp paring knife to cut 1-inch-long slits from

The center of the rectangle should be filled with two rows of 1-inch-long slits.

the center to the folded edge of the dough but do not cut through the seam. Carefully unfold the dough. The center of the rectangle should be filled with 2 rows of 1-inch-long slits. Gently and carefully pick up the rectangle and place it over the jam-filled tart shell, with the lattice centered directly over the jam. Press down the edges to adhere the top to the bottom. The egg wash on the bottom layer will help form a seal between the two layers of dough. I like to make a decoration along the edge of the dough on the long sides of the tart. To do this, I gently press the tips of my first and second fingers into the dough, right at the edge. Then I use the back of a paring knife to mark the spot between my two fingers by pushing the dough in ¼ inch. I repeat this all along the long sides of the tart to give the tart a scalloped edge.

Use a pastry brush to coat the top of the tart with egg wash, then place it in the oven. Bake until slightly risen and evenly golden brown, about 25 minutes. Check the bottom of the tart by lifting it slightly off the parchment paper using an offset spatula. You want to be sure the bottom is fully baked, or the tart will be soggy. Remove from the oven and cool on a wire rack. Use a pastry brush to glaze the top of the tart with the apricot glaze. I like to serve this tart the day it is made.

Apple Tart Runway

Yield: One tart; 8 servings

Here is a fun presentation for apple tart, typical of what's found in a lot of bakeries in France. The bakers like it because it is so easy to make (especially if you buy the puff pastry)—it does not require a mold, and it can be created in any length.

¼ recipe Classic Puff Pastry (page 33)

For the egg wash

2 large egg yolks

1 large egg

| **Whole milk** | ¼ cup | 1.8 ounces | 50 grams |

For the filling

| **Chunky applesauce** | ⅓ cup | 3.5 ounces | 100 grams |

4 to 5 Granny Smith apples

To finish the tart

Apricot Glaze (page 27)

Dessert Circus at Home

Prepare the puff pastry: Make the dough as directed in the recipe and let rest in the refrigerator until ready to use. Preheat the oven to 400°F (204°C). When the dough is ready to roll, place it on a lightly floured work surface and use a rolling pin to roll it into an 8 × 18-inch rectangle. Place the rectangle on the work surface with a long side facing you. Use a sharp paring knife to cut two 1 × 18-inch strips from the top of the dough. Place the remaining rectangle on a parchment paper–covered baking sheet.

Prepare the egg wash: Combine the egg yolks, whole egg, and milk in a small mixing bowl and whip with a hand whisk until well combined. Use a pastry brush to brush a 1-inch border of egg wash along each long side of the rectangle on the baking sheet. Place one of the thin strips on each side of the rectangle, over the egg wash. Try to keep the strips straight and even. These edges will keep the filling inside the tart shell, as they rise slightly higher than the rest of the tart. Brush the tops of the two strips with egg wash.

Prepare the filling: Use an offset spatula to spread the applesauce down the center of the tart shell. Peel, core, and halve the apples. Slice each half into ¼-inch-thick slices and lay them lengthwise on the tart, overlapping the slices slightly. Use a pastry brush to brush egg wash over the tops of the apple slices. Sometimes I make a decoration along the edge of the dough on the long sides of the tart. To do this, I gently press the tips of my first and second fingers into the dough, right at the edge. Then I use the back of a paring knife to mark the spot between my two fingers by pushing the dough in ¼ inch. I repeat this all along the long sides to give the tart a scalloped edge.

Place the tart in the oven and bake until the sides have risen slightly and the tart is golden brown, about 25 minutes. Check the bottom of the tart by lifting it slightly off the parchment paper using an offset spatula. You want to be sure the bottom is fully baked, or the tart will be soggy. Remove from the oven and cool on a wire rack. Use a pastry brush to glaze the tart with the apricot glaze. This will add shine and sweetness to the baked tart. It is best to serve this tart within a few hours of removing it from the oven.

Banana Cream Pie

Yield: One 10-inch pie; 8 servings

I understand that the only dessert as American as apple pie is banana cream pie. Here is my version of this American classic.

Pâte Brisée (page 30) or ½ recipe Pâte Sablée (page 32)			
½ recipe Pastry Cream flavored with Stoli Limonaya vodka (page 20)			
Heavy cream	¾ cup + 2 tablespoons	7 ounces	200 grams
2 large ripe bananas			
Juice of ½ lemon, strained			
Bittersweet chocolate, tempered (page 8)		7 ounces	200 grams
To finish the tart			
Heavy cream	¾ cup + 2 tablespoons	7 ounces	200 grams

Prepare the tart dough: Make the dough as directed in the recipe and let it rest in the refrigerator until ready to use.

Prepare the pastry cream: Make, cool, and flavor as directed in the recipe. Store in the refrigerator until ready to use.

Preheat the oven to 375°F (190°C).

Remove the dough from the refrigerator. Lightly give the dough a few quick raps with the rolling pin to slightly soften it. This will make it easier to roll. Lightly flour the work surface and each side of the dough. Roll the dough into a 12-inch circle about ¼ inch thick. Transfer the dough to a 10-inch tart pan by rolling it around the rolling pin. Unroll the dough over the tart pan. Gently press the dough into the pan, especially where the bottom and side of the pan meet. Don't forget to press the dough up the side of the pan; this will help the dough hold its shape as it bakes. Remove any excess dough by rolling the rolling

pin over the top of the pan to make a nice clean cut. Dock the bottom of the tart shell with a fork. Place the tart shell in the oven and bake until evenly golden brown, about 25 minutes. If the dough begins to rise unevenly as it bakes, release the air by gently piercing the dough with the tip of a paring knife. Cool the tart shell on a wire rack until ready to use. Just before using, remove the tart pan. If using a tart pan with a removable bottom, simply push up on the bottom of the pan and release the side. Use an offset spatula to slide the tart shell off the bottom of the pan onto a flat plate. If using a regular tart pan, place a flat plate upside down over the cooled tart shell. Place one hand on either side, grasping both plate and tart pan, and flip them both over so that the tart pan is now on top. Gently lift off the tart pan. Place a second flat plate upside down over the bottom of the tart shell. Once again, flip both plates so that the tart shell is now right side up. Remove the first plate.

Prepare the filling: Pour the heavy cream into a medium-size mixing bowl and whip to soft peaks with an electric mixer set on medium-high speed. Use a rubber spatula to fold the whipped cream into the pastry cream. Set aside.

Peel the bananas and use a sharp paring knife to cut them into ¼-inch-thick slices. Sprinkle the banana slices with the lemon juice. This will keep them from browning. Use a rubber spatula to fold the banana slices into the pastry cream mixture.

Use a pastry brush to coat the bottom of the tart shell with a thin layer of the tempered chocolate. This will keep the tart from becoming soggy. The chocolate should set almost immediately. If not, place in the refrigerator for 10 minutes. Fill the tart shell with about half of the pastry cream filling.

Use an offset spatula to spread a very thin 9-inch circle, barely ⅛ inch thick, of tempered chocolate onto a sheet of parchment paper. By the time you finish spreading the chocolate, it should be almost set. Don't worry if the circle is not perfectly round; it only needs to fit inside the tart shell. Flip over the sheet of parchment and peel it away from the chocolate circle. Place the chocolate circle in the tart shell. Spread the remaining pastry cream filling very gently over the chocolate.

To finish the pie: Pour the heavy cream into a medium-size mixing bowl and whip to stiff peaks with an electric mixer set on medium-high speed. Place the whipped cream in a pastry bag fitted with a ½-inch star tip. Decorate the top of the tart as desired. If you don't have a pastry bag, use a rubber spatula to spread the whipped cream over the top of the tart. Slice and serve. I recommend that you eat this tart within 1 to 2 days of making it. Refrigerate any leftovers.

The Firecracker

Yield: 6 desserts

Americans celebrate the Fourth of July and the French celebrate Bastille Day. Both holidays include fireworks. When I am home in France, we drive to the top of a big hill behind our house to watch the fireworks. The South of France is very dry, so they light the fireworks over the water. The sailboats in the port make a beautiful backdrop for the evening. I think this dessert will cause quite a stir when you serve it. You could add real sparklers to the top in place of the chocolate sparklers that I made.

Linda's Red Raspberry Jam (page 26) or store-bought	**⅔ cup**	**7 ounces**	**200 grams**
White chocolate, tempered (page 8)		**16 ounces**	**454 grams**
Powdered red food coloring (page 11), as needed			
For the filling			
Heavy cream	**2 cups**	**16 ounces**	**454 grams**
Grand Marnier	**2½ tablespoons**	**1.2 ounces**	**30 grams**
Fresh blueberries, cleaned	**About ½ U.S. dry pint**	**9 ounces**	**250 grams**
Fresh raspberries	**About 1 cup**	**4.5 ounces**	**125 grams**

Prepare the jam as directed in the recipe. Set aside the amount needed for this recipe and allow it to cool. Can the rest.

Prepare the firecrackers: To make the shooting stars, refer to the template (page 282) and copy this shape on a piece of cardboard. Use a pair of scissors to cut the template from the cardboard.

Divide the tempered white chocolate between two bowls, one bowl containing two thirds of the chocolate. Use a rubber spatula to mix the powdered food coloring into the smaller bowl of white chocolate. I use powdered coloring because liquid food color would cause the chocolate to seize. Be sure it is well incorporated to avoid streaks. The food coloring is very concentrated, so add it slowly and carefully. The chocolate will not turn dark red because white chocolate is actually cream colored. It will only get as dark as a pastel shade of red.

continued

Place a transfer sheet (page 6) in front of you with a long side facing you. The sheet I use has stars on it but you can use any design you like. When you spread chocolate over the design, the food coloring attaches to the wet chocolate and transfers the design to the chocolate. Use an offset spatula to spread about an ⅛-inch-thick layer of red chocolate onto the transfer sheet, completely covering the design. Allow the chocolate to set slightly, until it is no longer wet to the touch but the sheet is still flexible. Place a sheet of parchment paper over the chocolate, leaving a ½-inch border on one of the longest sides uncovered. Gently and carefully roll the parchment paper side against a rolling pin, rolling from one long side to the other. Cut off any excess parchment paper and seal the firecracker closed with the uncovered chocolate edge. Gently slide the rolling pin from the firecracker. You should be left with a hollow chocolate tube. Place the tube in the refrigerator to set completely. Repeat the entire process with a second transfer sheet.

Spread about a ⅛-inch-thick layer of chocolate onto the transfer sheet.

When the chocolate has set, remove the firecrackers from the refrigerator. Remove the parchment paper from inside the firecrackers by gently turning and pulling it from the inside of the tube. Carefully peel away the back of the transfer sheet. It should release from the chocolate quite easily. Use a hot sharp chef's knife to cut each firecracker into three equal pieces. To do this, heat the knife under very hot water and wipe it dry. Hold the knife blade against the side of the firecracker where you want to make the cut. Do not press on the knife, or the firecracker will break. Allow the heat of the knife to "cut" through the chocolate by melting it. Repeat until all of the firecrackers are cut and set aside until ready to use.

Place a piece of parchment over the chocolate.

Use an offset spatula to spread an ⅛-inch-thick layer of tempered white chocolate onto a sheet of parchment paper. Let the chocolate harden slightly, 4 to 5 minutes. The chocolate should

Roll the sheet, parchment paper side up, against a rolling pin.

be firm enough to cut but it should not be hard. Use the tip of a sharp paring knife to trace the shooting star template into the chocolate, being sure to cut all the way through the chocolate. Cut as many as you would like. I use two or three for each dessert. Work quickly, or the chocolate will become too hard to cut. If you do this on top of a wooden cutting board, the chocolate will stay pliable longer.

Cover the chocolate sheet with a sheet of parchment paper and flip over both. Peel the parchment from what is now the top. Separate all of the chocolate cutouts and set aside.

Make a cornet (page 16) and fill it half full with tempered white chocolate. Use a sharp paring knife to cut a small opening at the tip. You will use the cornet to draw long streaks of white chocolate that begin with a width of about ¼ inch and narrow to a point. Draw them onto a sheet of parchment paper, then let the chocolate set completely. When it is set, you will be able to lift the streaks from the paper. These will add drama to the dessert.

Prepare the filling: Pour the heavy cream into a medium-size mixing bowl and whip to soft peaks with an electric mixer set on medium-high speed. Use a rubber spatula to fold in the cooled jam. When fully incorporated, fold in the Grand Marnier.

Assemble the firecracker: Gently heat the bottom of each firecracker with the blade of a hot knife to melt the chocolate slightly and use the melted chocolate to adhere the firecracker to the center of a serving plate. Use a large spoon to fill each firecracker three quarters full with the filling. Use the tempered chocolate to "glue" two or three shooting stars to the back of the firecracker. I like to vary the height of each shooting star; I think this adds lightness and movement to the dessert. Insert the chocolate streaks into the filled firecracker so they too stick out at various heights. Fill the firecracker with the blueberries. Garnish the plate with blueberries and raspberries and serve.

Christmas
Bûche de Noël

Yield: One 14-inch bûche; about 12 servings

This is a traditional French Christmas cake, its name translating as Yule log. Every year I make them for family and friends of the restaurant. I try to have fun with the small decorations and vary them, just to keep things interesting. Here is the version I made for Christmas this year. Don't be intimidated by the size of the ingredients list. There are a lot of components but you can take some shortcuts.

continued

For the biscuit

2 large eggs			
2 large egg yolks			
Granulated sugar	Scant ½ cup	3.5 ounces	100 grams
Whole milk	½ tablespoon	0.2 ounce	7 grams
2 large egg whites			
Cake flour	⅓ cup	1.8 ounces	50 grams
Powdered sugar for dusting			

For the chocolate pastry cream

½ recipe Pastry Cream (page 20)			
DOVE® PROMISES® Dark Chocolate, finely chopped		3.5 ounces	100 grams

For the soaking syrup

Simple Syrup flavored with Grand Marnier
    (page 86)

For the mushrooms

3 large egg whites			
Granulated sugar	Scant ½ cup	3.5 ounces	100 grams
Powdered sugar, sifted	Scant 1 cup	3.5 ounces	100 grams
Dutch-processed unsweetened cocoa powder for dusting	½ cup	1.9 ounces	55 grams

For the chocolate trees and fences

Bittersweet chocolate, tempered (page 8)		16 ounces	454 grams

For the coffee buttercream

3 large egg yolks			
1 large egg			
Water	⅓ cup	2.6 ounces	75 grams
Granulated sugar	Scant 1 cup	7 ounces	200 grams
Cold unsalted butter, cubed	1½ cups + 1 tablespoon	12.5 ounces	350 grams
Coffee extract to taste			

Red, green, and yellow liquid food coloring, as needed

To finish the bûche

Powdered sugar for dusting	Scant ½ cup	2 ounces	60 grams
Chocolate shavings (page 288)			

Prepare the biscuit: Preheat the oven to 420°F (215°C). Place the whole eggs and yolks in a medium-size mixing bowl. Add ⅓ cup (2.3 ounces; 65 grams) of the granulated sugar and the milk. Use an electric mixer set on medium-high speed to whip the mixture until it lightens in color and triples in volume, about 6 minutes.

Place the egg whites in a large mixing bowl and whip with an electric mixer set on medium speed until foamy. Make a French meringue by adding the remaining 2 tablespoons (1.2 ounces; 35 grams) granulated sugar, 1 tablespoon at a time. Once all of the sugar has been added, increase the mixer speed to medium-high and whip to stiff but not dry peaks, about 5 minutes.

Use a rubber spatula to fold part of the egg mixture into the meringue. By adding the yolk mixture in two additions, you bring the consistency of each closer to that of the other, reducing the risk of deflating the meringue. When most of the yolk mixture has been incorporated, add the remaining yolk mixture to the meringue. Place the flour in a fine-mesh sieve and sift over the meringue mixture. Gently fold this in with a rubber spatula, remembering to fold all the way to the bottom of the bowl. Use an offset spatula to spread the batter in an even layer on a parchment paper–covered baking sheet by lightly resting the edge of the spatula on the batter and pushing the excess toward the edges. If you press too hard, you will deflate the batter. Liberally dust the top of the biscuit with powdered sugar and place in the oven. Bake the biscuit just until it begins to brown on top, about 5 minutes. The biscuit is baked at a high temperature for a short amount of time to lock in the moisture. The moisture is especially important here because that is what will allow you to roll the cake without cracking it. Immediately upon removal from the oven, run the blade of a knife around the inside of the baking sheet to loosen the cake from the sides. Unmold the cake by inverting the baking sheet onto a sheet of parchment paper and allowing the biscuit to drop out of the baking sheet. Peel off the parchment paper from the back of the biscuit and allow it to cool.

Prepare the chocolate pastry cream: Make the pastry cream as directed in the recipe and let cool. Place a 1-quart saucepan half filled with water over medium heat and bring it to a simmer. Make a double boiler by setting a large mixing bowl over the simmering water. Place the chocolate in the mixing bowl and allow it to melt completely, stirring occasionally. When all of the chocolate has melted and is smooth and warm, remove the mixing bowl from above the simmering water. Add the cold pastry cream to the warm chocolate and mix them together using a rubber spatula.

Prepare the roulade: Place the biscuit on your work surface with a long side facing you. Soak the cake with the flavored simple syrup. Use a large offset spatula to spread the chocolate pastry cream evenly over the cake, spreading it all the way to the edges. Start at one long end and, rolling toward you, roll it into a tight cylinder. Place the roulade on a parchment paper–covered baking sheet and place in the refrigerator for a few hours to set.

Prepare the mushrooms: Preheat the oven to 250°F (121°C). Place the egg whites in a large mixing bowl and whip with an electric mixer set on medium speed until foamy. Make a French meringue by adding the granulated sugar 1 tablespoon at a time. When you have volume, add the rest of the granulated sugar. Increase the mixer speed to medium-high and whip to stiff but not dry peaks, about 5 minutes. Once the whites are slightly stiff, I like to reduce the mixer speed to low to incorporate even more air without overwhipping the egg whites. Let the egg whites continue to whip for another 2 minutes. Stop whipping if they begin to look dry or separated. Remove the meringue from the mixer and gently fold in the powdered sugar using a rubber spatula. Remember to fold all the way to the bottom of the bowl. Place the meringue in a large pastry bag fitted with a ¼-inch plain tip. You will pipe the mushroom pieces onto a parchment paper–covered baking sheet.

To make the stems, hold the pastry bag at a 90-degree angle and gently squeeze out a dime-size mound of meringue. Stop squeezing and pull straight up, leaving a small tail. Repeat until you have as many mushroom stems as you need. To make the caps, pipe ½-inch mounds onto the baking sheet. It will be easier if you hold the pastry bag at a slight angle and allow the tip to touch the parchment as you start to pipe. Once you have formed the mound, stop squeezing and lift up the tip. Sprinkle the caps of the mushrooms with some of the cocoa powder and place all in the oven. Bake until the meringue feels firm and dry, about 60 minutes. Leave the oven door cracked open so moisture can escape. If the meringue begins to take on color, the oven is too hot; reduce the oven temperature by 50°F (10°C) and continue to bake. Remove the meringues from the oven and cool on a wire rack. If you have time, turn off the oven and leave the meringues on the baking sheet in the oven until the oven cools. This will take about 1 hour and will allow the meringue to dry completely.

Prepare the chocolate trees: Make a cornet (page 16) and fill it half full with the tempered chocolate. Pipe a long, thick chocolate raindrop on a sheet of parchment paper. Draw a cake comb (page 120) through the chocolate, starting at the center of the raindrop and moving from left to right. Repeat, starting at the center and moving from right to left. You should be left with a chocolate pine tree. Repeat for as many trees as you would like. Allow the chocolate to set before peeling the parchment paper from the trees.

Prepare the chocolate fence: Fill a cornet half full with the tempered chocolate. Pipe a 3- to 4-inch-long railroad track with the outside rails spaced about 2 inches apart and the inside rails spaced about ½ inch apart onto a sheet of parchment paper. Pipe as many fences as you would like. Allow the chocolate to set before peeling the parchment paper from the fences.

Prepare the coffee buttercream: Place the egg yolks and whole egg in a large mixing bowl and whip with an electric mixer set on medium-high speed until thick, light, and tripled in volume, 5 to 7 minutes.

Pour the water and granulated sugar into a 1-quart heavy-bottomed saucepan and place over medium heat. Insert a candy thermometer into the mixture. The sugar is ready when it reaches 250°F (121°C), what is known as the soft ball stage (page 14). Make a *pâte à bombe* by pouring the cooked sugar down the side of the bowl into the whipping eggs. Do not pour the hot sugar onto the beaters, or it will splatter. Continue whipping the *pâte à bombe* until the outside of the bowl is warm but not hot, 2 to 3 minutes. Add the butter all at once and beat on medium speed until incorporated. Increase the mixer speed to medium-high and whip until thick, smooth, and shiny, about 10 minutes. Remove about ⅓ cup and set aside. Add the coffee extract to the remaining buttercream and whip until well combined.

Assemble the bûche: Place the roulade on a presentation platter. It is better to decorate the bûche directly on the platter so you don't have to move it. Once decorated, it is very fragile and hard to move. Use a sharp knife to slice a 1½-inch-thick slice from each end of the roulade. These will become the gnarls on the log. Use a small offset spatula to spread a thick layer of buttercream over the bûche. Spread the buttercream from left to right along the length of the bûche in long streaks. Place the trimmed ends or gnarls on top of the bûche, one at each end. Cover these with the buttercream and spread smooth. Run a cake comb through the buttercream along the length of the bûche to give it texture. It should now resemble a tree branch or log. Place the bûche in the refrigerator for about 15 minutes to allow the buttercream to set.

Make the ivy and flowers: Divide the unflavored buttercream evenly among three bowls and color each with one of the food colorings. Add as much food coloring as needed, but be careful, since they are very concentrated. Mix with a whisk or spoon. Make three cornets and fill one half full with pink buttercream, one with green, and one with yellow. Cut the tips to create small openings in the cornets containing the pink and yellow buttercreams.

Decorate the bûche: Remove the bûche from the refrigerator. To make the ivy, use the green icing cornet. Pipe long curved lines down the length of the bûche. This is the ivy that grows wild on a log. Place small yellow dots along the ivy to form the center of each flower. Surround the yellow dots with pink dots to form the flower petals. To make the leaves, cut the tip of the cornet to a point using a pair of scissors (see below). Place the cornet on the ivy in the spot where you want to pipe a leaf. Squeeze gently until a small dab of buttercream comes out of the tip. Stop squeezing and pull the cornet away from the bûche in one quick motion, leaving a tail on the dab. It should look like a leaf. Repeat until you have as many leaves as you like. Stick together the caps and stems of the mushrooms using a dab of buttercream and place on the bûche. Add the trees and fences. Dust the bûche with powdered sugar and sprinkle with chocolate shavings. Refrigerate for 1 hour, then serve and enjoy!

> To make chocolate shavings you will need a very large, smooth block of chocolate and a very sharp knife. *Use extreme caution.* It will be easier if you hold the knife at a 45-degree angle and push the blade away from your body across the top of the chocolate block. You can also use a vegetable peeler to make smaller shavings.

Cornet

The Christmas Tree

Yield: 10 to 12 desserts

This is one of my seasonal signature desserts at Le Cirque. I first made the dessert to celebrate a tradition Kris and I started with our friends. We have a farm high in the mountains of France. Every year when our friends come to visit us, we ask them each to transplant a tree somewhere on our property. Armed with shovels, we walk until each person finds the tree he or she would like to transplant. We ask them to place the trees where they would like, and then we name each tree after the friend who planted it. When we visit our farm, we feel as if our friends are with us.

I use the cone-shaped paper cups usually found at water dispensers to form the trees. A clean paint sprayer is what gives the trees the appearance that they are covered with snow. I think this step is worth the extra effort.

½ recipe Basic Pound Cake (page 87)

For the white chocolate mousse

1½ gelatin sheets or ½ envelope powdered gelatin

White chocolate, finely chopped		9 ounces	250 grams
Heavy cream	2 cups	16 ounces	450 grams
Pistachio paste (page 13)	2 tablespoons	1.2 ounces	30 grams

To assemble the trees

Golden raisins, hydrated with dark rum (page 28)	Scant ⅔ cup	3.5 ounces	100 grams
Simple Syrup flavored with Grand Marnier (page 86)			

To decorate the trees

White chocolate, finely chopped		5.5 ounces	150 grams
Cocoa butter (page 9), finely chopped		5.5 ounces	150 grams

For the royal icing

1 large egg white

Powdered sugar	1½ cups	6 ounces	175 grams
Juice of ½ lemon, strained			

To finish the dessert

"M&M's"® Milk Chocolate Mini Baking Bits	1 cup	7 ounces	200 grams
Pâte de Fruit squares rolled in granulated sugar (page 76)			
Raspberry Sauce (page 24)			
Mango Sauce (page 24)			
Crème Anglaise (page 21)			

Place 10 to 12 paper cones tip side down in wineglasses and place the glasses on a baking sheet. The wineglasses will hold the cones steady as you fill them. The baking sheet will make it easier to move the glasses in and out of the freezer.

Prepare the cake: Make the pound cake batter as directed in the recipe and bake it on a parchment paper–covered baking sheet instead of in cake or loaf pans. Place on a wire rack to cool. When cooled, invert onto your work surface and peel off the parchment paper. Use a 2-inch plain cutter to cut 10 to 12 disks from the cake. Set aside until ready to use. Store the remaining cake in the freezer for up to 3 weeks.

Prepare the trees: The trees are made of white chocolate mousse. Place the gelatin sheets in a medium-size mixing bowl with enough cold water (about 2 cups) to cover. Let stand for about 5 minutes to allow the gelatin to soften and hydrate. Cold water hydrates the gelatin without letting it absorb too much liquid. Remove the gelatin from the bowl and squeeze out the excess water with your hands. If you use powdered gelatin, sprinkle the gelatin over ¼ cup (2 ounces; 60 grams) of cold water. Let the gelatin bloom until it has absorbed all the water, about 1 minute.

Place the chopped white chocolate in a medium-size mixing bowl. Pour ⅔ cup (5.5 ounces; 150 grams) of the heavy cream into a 1-quart heavy-bottomed saucepan, place over medium-high heat, and heat until bubbles begin to form around the edge of the pan. Remove the pan from the heat and make a ganache by pouring the hot cream over the chocolate. Let stand for about 30 seconds to allow the heat to distribute throughout the bowl. Add the hydrated gelatin and gently stir the mixture with a rubber spatula. The hot cream will cause the chocolate to melt and the gelatin to dissolve. By slowly mixing the heavy cream and chocolate together, the fats in them will combine to form an emulsion (page 17). Stir the ganache until it is smooth and homogeneous. Add the pistachio paste and stir until fully combined. Prepare an ice bath (page 3) and place the mixing bowl over it. Stir the ganache occasionally to evenly distribute the temperature. The ganache is ready when it has thickened. Test this by coating a rubber spatula and drawing a line through it. If the line holds for 5 to 10 seconds, it is ready. If the line fills in immediately, the ganache is too warm. Keep cooling and retest every 30 seconds. The ganache should not cool so much that it begins to harden and set. If this happens, warm it up over a saucepan of simmering water, removing it every 10 seconds and whisking gently until it is smooth and viscous.

While the ganache is cooling, pour the remaining 1⅓ cups (11 ounces; 300 grams) heavy cream into another medium-size mixing bowl and whip to soft peaks with an electric mixer set on medium speed. When the ganache is cool but not cold, fold in the whipped cream in two additions until combined. The ganache should not be so cold that it has begun to set and is grainy, yet it should be cool enough that it doesn't melt the whipped cream. If the mousse begins to seize while you are folding in the whipped cream, warm it by placing it over a saucepan of simmering water 5 seconds at a time until it is smooth again, but do not warm it so much that the whipped cream begins to melt. Fold in any remaining whipped cream. When all of the whipped cream has been incorporated, the mousse will be loose and pourable. Don't worry; it will set in the freezer.

continued

Fill a pastry bag fitted with a ½-inch plain tip with the white chocolate mousse. Tuck just enough of the pastry bag into the tip to create a seal before you begin to fill the bag, or you will end up with mousse all over your shoes! Fill each paper cone half full with the white chocolate mousse. Divide the raisins evenly among the cones and fill almost to the top with more mousse. Leave enough room for a pound cake circle.

Soak the cake circles with the flavored simple syrup and place them soaked side down over the mousse. Press gently. Place the filled cones in the glasses in the freezer until set, about 3 hours or overnight.

Unmold the trees by simply peeling off the paper cones, starting at the seam. Set the mousse cones on the parchment paper–covered baking sheet and return them to the freezer.

Decorate the trees: Place a 1-quart saucepan half filled with water over medium heat and bring it to a simmer. Make a double boiler by setting a large mixing bowl over the simmering water. Place the white chocolate and cocoa butter in the bowl and allow them to melt, stirring occasionally. (This step can also be done in a microwave at medium-high power. Heat the mixture in 45-second increments until fully melted, smooth, and very warm.) Heat the mixture over the simmering water until it is completely smooth and very warm.

The difference in temperature between the warm mixture and the frozen cones will cause the mixture to harden on contact. This will give the trees the appearance of being covered with a fine layer of snow. Pour the heated mixture through a fine-mesh sieve into the spray gun container. Remove the trees from the freezer and spray them with the mixture. Cleanup will be much easier if you use a plastic-lined cardboard box as a backdrop to the baking sheet when you spray the desserts. Return the sprayed desserts to the freezer.

Make the royal icing: Combine the egg white and powdered sugar in a medium-size mixing bowl and whip with an electric mixer set on medium speed until opaque and shiny, about 5 minutes. Add the lemon juice and continue whipping until completely incorporated, about 3 minutes. The royal icing should be light, fluffy, and slightly stiff. You may need to adjust the consistency by adding more egg whites if the icing is too dry or more powdered sugar if it is too wet. Fill a cornet (page 16) half full with the royal icing and cut a small opening at the tip. Remove the trees from the freezer. Starting at the top of each tree and spiraling downward to the base, pipe a continuous line of royal icing. Adhere the "M&M's"® Mini Baking Bits to the royal icing, spacing them apart at random. This will represent the string of lights traditionally found on Christmas trees. Use the royal icing to draw strings and bows on the *pâte de fruit* squares. Place one tree in the center of each plate. Surround each with four or five *pâte de fruit* "presents." Dot the plate with raspberry, mango, and crème anglaise sauces. Merry Christmas!

The Reindeer and Sleigh

Yield: 8 reindeer and sleighs

This is another holiday signature dessert. Everyone loves the story of Rudolph and Santa's sleigh. You will use the technique of cutting around templates to make this dessert. You can alter the templates to suit your own style. I think it is amazing to start with a flat disk of chocolate and end with a three-dimensional dessert.

½ recipe Brownies (page 134)		
Bittersweet chocolate, tempered (page 8)	16 ounces	454 grams
Royal Icing (page 290)		
8 red "M&M's"® Milk Chocolate Mini Baking Bits		
Raspberry Sauce (page 24)		
Crème Anglaise (page 21)		
Mango Sauce (page 24)		

Prepare the brownies as directed in the recipe and let cool. Cut into 1-inch squares and set aside. These will be the presents on the back of the sleigh.

Make the reindeer and sleigh. Refer to the reindeer and sleigh templates (page 295) and copy these shapes onto cardboard. Use a pair of scissors to cut the shapes from the cardboard. Place an 18 × 24-inch sheet of parchment paper on your work surface. Use an off-set spatula to spread an ⅛-inch-thick layer of tempered chocolate on the paper, being sure to spread it all the way to the edges. Lift the chocolate-covered paper by its corners and move it to a clean space on your work surface. Let the chocolate harden slightly, 4 to 5 minutes. The chocolate will be firm enough to cut, but it will not be hard. Use the tip of a sharp paring knife or an X-Acto knife to trace around the cardboard templates, being sure to cut all the way through the chocolate. Cut out 8 reindeer, stands, and sleighs and 16 sleigh skis. Work quickly, or the chocolate will become too hard to cut. When all of the pieces have been cut, allow the chocolate to finish setting

Use the tip of a knife to trace around the template, being sure to cut all the way through the chocolate.

before removing the scraps. Use the tempered chocolate to "glue" the reindeer to the stands and two skis to the bottom of each sleigh.

Prepare the royal icing as directed in the recipe. Fill a cornet (page 16) half full with the royal icing and cut a small opening at the tip. Use the cornet to pipe the spots on the back of each reindeer and to pipe the eyes. I like to use a red "M&M's"® Milk Chocolate Mini Baking Bit for the nose, adhering it with a small dot of royal icing. You can make a royal icing nose if you prefer. Use royal icing to draw strings and bows on the brownie squares.

Place one reindeer and sleigh on each plate. Pile two or three brownies on each sleigh. Decorate the plate with raspberry sauce, crème anglaise, and mango sauce and serve.

Sources

Annieglass
310 Harvest Drive
Watsonville, CA 95076
800-347-6133
Handmade sculptural glass dinnerware

Bernardaud NA
41 Madison Avenue
New York, NY 10010
800-600-1744
Porcelain, tableware

Broadway Panhandler
477 Broome Street
New York, NY 10013
212-966-3434
Cooking and baking equipment and supplies,
other specialty items

Carnavale, Inc.
900 Pennsylvania Street
Memphis, TN 38106
800-548-9979
901-775-2333(fax)
Tabletop and fine decorative accessories

Dairyland USA
1300 Viele Avenue
Bronx, NY 10474
718-842-8700
Specialty ingredients

Dean & DeLuca
Catalogue information: 800-221-7714
Store locations: 212-431-1691
Specialty ingredients

The Foreside Company
33 Hutcherson Drive
Gorham, ME 04038
207-854-4000
Decorative accessories for the home

Fossilglass
430 Greenwich Street
New York, NY 10013
212-966-2798
212-274-1069(fax)
fossilglass@aol.com
Handmade glassware

Gilmore Glassworks
P.O. Box 961
Millerton, NY 12546
518-789-6700
518-789-6161(fax)
Pressed glass bowls, hand-blown tumblers and
stemware

Hermès
800-238-5522
Circus pattern China

Hobart Corporation
701 South Ridge Avenue
Troy, OH 45374
937-332-3000
937-332-2142(fax)
www.hobartcorp.com
Commercial bakery and food preparation
equipment

King Arthur Flour Company
The Baker's Catalogue
P.O. Box 876
Norwich, VT 05055
800-827-6836
Flour, baking supplies, equipment

Nan Swid Design
55 West 13th Street
New York, NY 10011
212-633-6699
212-633-0030(fax)

NY Cake and Baking Distributors
56 West 22nd Street
New York, NY 10010
800-942-2539; 212-675-CAKE
Baking supplies, gum paste flowers,
equipment, cake-making supplies

Paris Gourmet Patisfrance
(for the trade only)
161 East Union Avenue
East Rutherford, NJ 07073
800-PASTRY-1

Pavillon Christofle
680 Madison Avenue
at 62nd Street
New York, NY 10021
212-308-9390
www.christofle.com
Flatware, china, holloware, table linens

Rosenthal U.S.A., Ltd.
355 Michele Place
Carlstadt, NJ 07072
201-804-8000
China

Studio K Glassware
2311 K Thornton Road
Austin, TX 78704
512-443-1611
chrismayes@worldnet.att.net
Fused glass

Team Torres, LLC.
P.O. Box 303
New York, NY 10101-0303
212-489-4847
www.jacquestorres.com
Specialty equipment and ingredients

Villeroy & Boch
800-Villeroy (845-5376) U.S.
800-387-5732 Canada
Flatware, china

Index